The Springtime That Never Came

The Springtime
That Never Came

Bishop Athanasius Schneider
in conversation with Paweł Lisicki

SOPHIA INSTITUTE PRESS
Manchester, New Hampshire

Contents

Introduction 3

1. When Misfortune Looms 11

2. What About Celibacy? 19

3. The Gnostic Threat 35

4. The Illusion of Progress 49

5. Protestant Sources 73

6. The Leftist Face of the Church 117

7. How Many Religions Are True? 167

8. Between Heaven and Hell 191

9. Automatism and Anthropocentrism .209

10. The Rupture of Continuity 237

11. In an Orderly Formation 281

The Springtime That Never Came

Abbreviations

CCC = *Catechism of the Catholic Church*

GS = Pastoral Constitution on the Church *Gaudium et Spes*

Introduction

White, empty spaces covered with snow. When I woke up, I couldn't tell at first if I was still dreaming, or already awake. I stretched my neck, felt a cramp in my shoulders, and the mild pain brought me back to consciousness. The voice of the captain from the loudspeakers announced that we were about to land.

The flight was not too long — just over four hours. This is what a train trip from Warsaw to Rzeszów takes. Once it took me almost that long to get home from work. It was during the holidays, and the traffic caused by all the holiday shoppers made my Warsaw commute from Włochy to Mokotów a real nightmare.

It was a four-hour flight plus a five-hour time difference. When I opened my eyes after a short nap in the middle of the night, I saw the rising dawn. The vast territory covered in white was Kazakhstan. Of course, before leaving I checked the weather forecast. I knew that I should expect the thaw followed by a sudden drop in temperatures: minus 20°F at night, and minus 4°F during the day. It is not particularly pleasant to take a walk in such temperatures, as my older readers may remember. So I was prepared, but expecting it is one thing, and seeing it is another. Recent winters in Poland have been mild and rainy, with occasional snow that would last merely a few days or would just melt immediately. Kazakh snowdrifts reminded me of my childhood, with Poland submerged in snow and immersed in the fluffy silence that only true winter can bring. That was my view of Kazakhstan from the plane windows — but infinitely more empty.

Bishop Athanasius Schneider was waiting for me at the exit. I noticed him right away. With his slight, somewhat ascetic physique and a black coat, he stood out

3

in the crowd, distinctively set apart from the locals. I went up to him, shook his hand, and bowed down to kiss his ring. Usually, this is no longer done. Generally, when greeting Church officials, ring kissing, bowing, and genuflecting are avoided. Episcopal rings have a somewhat unclear status. They are seemingly still a mark of episcopal dignity, but increasingly often those who wear them don't know what to do with them. Bishops who are born democrats demonstrate it by avoiding any signs of superiority. The rings on their fingers resemble somewhat the signets worn by the nouveau riche: they are easy to see, but it's not clear how they should be used. With Bishop Schneider, it is different: kissing the ring is natural and proper, perfectly becoming his slight, unassuming, humble posture.

In the parking lot, I almost fell to the ground. It was as slippery as an ice rink. I carefully followed the bishop, who pointed the key toward one of the cars. Unfortunately, the small, gray Volkswagen did not respond. We were standing in front of it, and the bishop tried pressing the black key fob in different ways, to no avail. I tried to help, and didn't succeed. Finally, the bishop decided to take more immediate action and tried inserting the key in the keyhole. Still nothing. After a few minutes, doubts came over me. It looked as if my stay in Nur-Sultan was starting in a very unlucky way. And suddenly the bishop remembered that the car we had been trying to unlock was not the car in which he came. By mistake, we kept trying to unlock a different car. "My apologies," he said quietly, "but this is not my car. I borrowed it from a priest and it is very similar to the one we've been trying to unlock." Fortunately, nobody noticed anything. It would have been amusing to have been arrested with Bishop Schneider at the Nur-Sultan airport for attempted car break-in.

Soon we were heading for downtown. The bishop drove slowly, carefully, and cautiously. As soon as we started driving, he asked if I wanted to pray, and began reciting the Hail Mary.

We were passing by newly-built skyscrapers and the grand thoroughfare of the city. A year earlier, in March 2019, the capital of Kazakhstan changed its name from Astana to Nur-Sultan, to commemorate the first Kazakh president who served the country from December 1991 to March 2019. Until recently, the capital had no more than two or three hundred thousand inhabitants. Today, it is a rapidly developing metropolis with over a million people. Before my arrival I read that the Kazakhs' ambition is to make their capital a second Dubai. Everything in the city seemed new: the dome of the mosque glistening with gold, the minarets around it, new apartment buildings with light oriental ornaments, skyscrapers in the financial district, two golden high-rises, public buildings with roofs shaped like nomad yurts. The city of the twenty-first century built on the steppe.

Ave Maria, gratia plena, Dominus tecum ... The bishop, unperturbed, was saying the words of the prayer calmly and slowly, heeding neither my presence nor this modern, dynamic city. Without further problems, we reached the parking lot of the Catholic cathedral, a simple red-brick structure, somewhat similar to such churches in the Warsaw district of Ursynów.

Why Kazakhstan? Why Nur-Sultan? How did this bishop, probably the best-known traditionalist bishop of the Catholic Church, end up living and working — mostly online — from here? Divine Providence is unfathomable. How is it possible that out of over five thousand bishops in the Church today it should be he, the auxiliary of Nur-Sultan, and his voice, that elicit such interest? Why is it his comments that are immediately posted on leading conservative websites in the USA, Italy, and Germany?[1] There is no other Church leader whose words command such attention.

Bishop Schneider is not concerned about being politically correct. You will not hear from any other Church leader the things he says. He doesn't seek applause or sensationalism. He weighs his words, he is cautious and restrained, yet firm and clear. In a world full of slogans and clichés, his voice is different. He is not afraid of being blunt, even when discussing Vatican II documents, the positions of other bishops, or the current pontificate. During our conversation, he said several times that he has resolved not to perform any "mental gymnastics." When I first listened to his answers, I could not believe my ears. In conversations with other Church leaders, I would encounter a wall when touching upon delicate topics, such as the legacy of Vatican II or actions of recent popes. I expected an unwillingness to confront the mistakes, and a dialectical line of reasoning. Psychologically, it is understandable. We don't criticize the Council because the Church has invested too much in defending it. Even the smallest deviation from such a strategy would open the doors to criticism. The conversation with this bishop was different. At some point I asked how he came to be so open in his criticisms and assessments of the actions of the Church in the last half-century. He replied: "When I became

[1] Bishop Schneider's articles and opinions can be found at lifesitenews.com, remnantnewspaper.com, onepeterfive.com, katholisches.info, and corrispondenzaromana.it, among others.

a bishop, I realized that I cannot escape responsibility. Being a bishop entails an obligation." After all, bishops are successors of the apostles.

Bishop Schneider was not evasive when asked about the state of the world today, about the civilization so heavily influenced by LGBT ideology, feminism, and ecologism. What he had to say really stood out from the barrage of words in the media. Not only is it thoughtful, it is also prayerful, with each word rooted in a different, greater, more important word, uttered by Christ.

The bishop spoke about his ancestors and the faith that was passed down to him in his book *Christus Vincit*.[2] He comes from a family of so-called Germans of Russia. His ancestors moved to the tsars' empire in 1809 from the southwestern part of Germany, Alsace-Lorraine. How important remembrance was in family transmission is best illustrated by the fact that the bishop can list the names of all his ancestors from previous generations, starting with those who first migrated to Russia.

In an interview with American journalist Diane Montagna, he spoke about the heroism of the German priests persecuted under communism: out of over two hundred priests working in southern Ukraine and on the Volga, not a single one apostatized. Almost all were martyred or imprisoned. The last bishop, Josef Aloysius Kessler, died in Germany, expelled from his diocese by the Communists in 1922. The bishop also spoke about the death of his grandfather Sebastian Schneider, who was shot by the Communists when his son, the bishop's father, was seven years old.

The bishop's ancestors, on both his father's and his mother's sides, were very religious people. Their life followed the rhythm of Church holidays, solemnities in honor of the Mother of God, memorials of saints, Advent, and Lent. Secular time was empty and arid; holy and sacred time was relevant. The profane was subordinate to the sacred. Faith was passed down like a treasure, an intact inheritance from generation to generation. The first shock came with Bolshevik rule and mass persecutions; the second came with the outbreak of the Second World War. Initially, the Wehrmacht dealt a crushing blow to a Soviet army retreating in panic. As a result, the bishop's family was briefly deported from Russia to Germany. However, the German victories didn't last. After the defeat at Stalingrad, the balance tipped in favor of the Soviets, who regained the lost lands, occupied new ones, and captured Berlin. After Hitler's defeat, the Schneider family was once again transported

---

2   Athanasius Schneider and Diane Montagna, *Christus Vincit: Christ's Triumph Over the Darkness of the Age* (New York: Angelico Press, 2019).

to the Soviet empire. The bishop's father and mother were then sent to the Ural Mountains for forced labor.

Great historical upheavals don't destroy the Faith. The Church and her hierarchy were gone, bishops and priests disappeared. All that remained was the Catholic faithful. For ten years, the deportees passed on the Catholic faith despite the lack of priests, sacraments, the Mass, or the Eucharist. Like Catholics in Japan between the sixteenth and nineteenth centuries, lay Catholics in the Soviet empire saved the Faith. "Families transmitted the Faith, and every day they prayed. For example, in Lent, on Fridays in the evening after this hard work, neighboring families came together and prayed the Stations of the Cross."[3] Only years later did priests begin to appear, such as Bl. Fr. Oleksiy Zarytskyj, who lived in exile in Karaganda.

From his early years, Bishop Schneider was surrounded by people of strong, unwavering faith. It formed him and gave him strength of character. I think that those experiences he described are the origin of his current stance. The bishop learned firsthand what it means to be faithful. In order to survive a confrontation with a lethally hostile, hateful regime, religion must maintain a steadfast foundation. People can die and suffer; a malicious persecutor can take their lives and freedoms, can force them into slave labor and lock them up in concentration camps, but cannot destroy their faith as long as it is rooted in an immutable rule.

A real change in their family life occurred in 1969, at a time of a certain thaw. Mass persecutions stopped. The State did everything it could to ridicule religion and limit its reach. Rather than kill or imprison, it would obstruct and discourage the believers. The Schneider family — the parents and the future bishop along with his brother and sister — left Kyrgyzstan for Estonia. The future bishop was eight at the time. "You are German and Catholics. I do not want you to grow up to become Communists"[4] — this is how the father explained the reasons for the move. The family settled in southern Estonia, near the Latvian border, around sixty miles from the city of Tartu, which had a Catholic church. They went there every Sunday, leaving at six in the morning, when it was still dark, and returning at night. Mass was celebrated by a Capuchin, Fr. Janis Pavlovskis, a Latvian who spent seven years in the Karaganda Gulag under Stalin. Years later, in 2016, Bishop

[3] Ibid., 9.
[4] Ibid., 16.

Schneider celebrated Mass in the traditional Roman rite in the same Tartu church where he received his first Communion. The Schneiders returned to Germany in 1973. The future bishop was twelve. The family odyssey that began when Russia was ruled by Alexander I ended in 1973, under early Brezhnev, when Willy Brandt was chancellor of West Germany.

Bishop Athanasius Schneider arrived in Kazakhstan in 2001 and became in 2006 auxiliary bishop of Karaganda. He received his episcopal consecration from Cardinal Angelo Sodano in St. Peter's Basilica in Rome. Bishop Schneider has been residing permanently in the capital of Kazakhstan since 2011. He is still distinguished by the piety that he discusses in the book.

In Nur-Sultan, I lived in a small guest room in the rectory by the cathedral. We started our conversations after breakfast, and every time the bishop asked that we pray for the guidance of the Holy Spirit. Later in the day, in the evening, I was the only participant in the traditional Mass that he celebrated in a tiny chapel. When the bishop took me to the airport, at noon he prayed the Angelus.

The Diocese of Nur-Sultan is administered by Polish Archbishop Thomas Peta, who also received me with great hospitality. The conversations at the table took place in Polish (apart from the archbishop, there are four more Polish priests there), in German, or in Russian, when other guests joined.

Together with Archbishop Peta and Archbishop Emeritus Jan Paweł Lenga, Bishop Schneider wrote a confession of faith, which included truths rejected or questioned in the Church today.

It was a strange feeling to be in this corner of the world forsaken by God and man — where years earlier the Communists created a gigantic network of gulags — with mere tens of thousands of Catholics (out of eighteen million Kazakhs who are either religiously indifferent or profess Islam) and to discuss the most important challenges for the Church, the sources of the crisis, the wounds she has suffered, and ways to overcome the disease. It was a strange feeling — here, in this place where Stalin decided to strip people of their identities, memories, and attachments — to listen to Latin prayers, silent, persistent, Roman, and immutable.

The sound of these prayers has an extraordinary power. It's as if they became a shield. These prayers have been passed down by generations of Catholics from time immemorial. They originated in Rome when it was still ruled by pagan emperors; they were brought to Germany by St. Boniface, and to Poland by St. Adalbert. Essentially they are immutable. *Te igitur, clementissime Pater* — the beginning of the Canon; even in a small chapel only a murmur reaches me. Silence as a sign of reverence, prayer as contemplation. Prayer as continuity and unity with past generations; communion across the ages for the whole earth. The ritual, sanctified by its very repeatability, purified of the subjective, opens the gate to eternal beauty for all sinners.

Earlier, *Dignum et iustum est* — those words, uttered in the same form by those whose bodies are buried in the oldest Roman catacombs, now resound every day in a place that has never played a significant role (or any role) in the history of the Church. On the map of the history of Christianity, Kazakhstan is a big *terra incognita*. It brings to mind only the fate of the hundreds of thousands of those who were deported here. Those who are more erudite and interested in the life of the Church may connect this place with Bl. Fr. Władysław Bukowiński, a great figure of indomitable character, a true missionary to Kazakhstan, who spent many years as a prisoner of labor camps and in exile and died in 1974. To this day you can meet people who knew him — several of them were mentioned by Archbishop Peta.

But what is the significance of this peripherality of Kazakhstan? Centuries ago, Ireland was such a remote province, and then it was from there that the Church was reborn. It was the Irish and Scottish monks who kept the treasure and later shared it again with those who had lost it. If this is the will of God, Kazakhstan may be the place from which a spark could come that will reignite the Faith. Or at least one of the sparks. Perhaps this could be the reward of Providence for the merits of all Catholics — Germans, Poles, Lithuanians, people of other nations — who were persecuted by the Bolsheviks for decades? Who did not yield, did not surrender, who persevered?

We can't preclude that Catholics should be awakened by the words of the German bishop of Nur-Sultan. After all, what does it matter where the Truth can be heard and from where it reaches a person? The important thing is to describe clearly and without prevarications the same rule of faith always and everywhere. The same rule as in the first centuries of Christianity and in the times of Communist persecutions. It must be the same measure by which we can and should judge everything.

The reader will be the judge of how well the most important thoughts of Bishop Schneider, the result of many years of reflection on the condition of the Catholic Faith, have been captured in this book. I was edified by his words. Yes, he often expresses strong and undiluted opinions. Many may call them "controversial," but

I would avoid that, because today we often label as controversial that which is right, which the world doesn't want to hear.

The bishop doesn't beat around the bush. He attempts to address the roots of the disease and is not afraid to touch festering wounds. When you have walked with him all the way, when you have reached the end, you will be encouraged — as was I. It's obvious that here is someone who takes the Faith seriously, someone who is guided by regard for God rather than regard for man. And that is why what he is saying can be the springboard of hope.

My conversation with Bishop Schneider took place over several days in early February of 2020. The coronavirus pandemic had not begun, nor did we know the exact text of the papal exhortation *Querida Amazonia*. I received the bishop's answers to these questions in April and incorporated them into the text of chapters 1 and 2.

— Paweł Lisicki

1

When Misfortune Looms

Many people are wondering about the effects of the coronavirus pandemic, which started in China, then attacked different countries in Europe, and finally the USA. For a Catholic, of course, the fundamental question is about the spiritual effects that will be caused by waves of the disease. What do you think about the behavior of those Church leaders who suspended the celebrations of the Eucharist in their dioceses? Could one say that the pandemic-related panic has affected the bishops?

> Yes, that has been my general impression, that the majority of the bishops responded hastily and in panic when they banned all public celebrations of the Eucharist, or, in an even more puzzling move, when they closed the churches. Such bishops acted more like secular bureaucrats than shepherds. By focusing exclusively on various hygienic safeguards, they lost sight of the supernatural view of reality and abandoned the primacy of the eternal good of the souls.

Many European countries closed their churches completely. Some bishops didn't even allow Mass celebrations for Easter. In Poland also, at the time when several dozen people were allowed in stores, the number of the faithful in churches was limited to five.

> As long as supermarkets are open and accessible, and as long as people have access to transportation, there is no compelling reason to ban assembling in churches. Churches are able to provide hygienic safeguards that are just as good, or even better. For example, before each Mass

the pews and doors could be disinfected, and each person entering the church could sanitize his hands. Other similar measures could also be undertaken.

An inspiring example of a supernatural perspective during the pandemic can be found in the President of Tanzania, John Magufuli. President Magufuli, who is a practicing Catholic, said the following on Sunday, March 22, 2020 (*Laetare* Sunday): "I urge you, fellow Christians, and even Muslims, do not cease to gather to praise and worship God. That is why we as the government have not closed the churches or mosques. On the contrary, they should always be open, so that people can have recourse to God. Churches are places where people can seek true healing, because it is there that the true God lives. Do not be afraid to praise God and seek His face in the church."

Priests are probably in a particularly difficult situation. On one hand, they wish to console the faithful, on the other hand, they need to conform to regulations issued by bishops. The question is, what should they do, for example, when the faithful are asking them to hear their confessions? What would your advice be?

Priests must remember that they are first and foremost shepherds of immortal souls. They are to imitate Christ, who said:

> I am the good shepherd. The good shepherd giveth his life for his sheep. But the hireling, and he that is not the shepherd, whose own the sheep are not, seeth the wolf coming, and leaveth the sheep, and flieth: and the wolf catcheth, and scattereth the sheep: And the hireling flieth, because he is a hireling: and he hath no care for the sheep. I am the good shepherd; and I know mine, and mine know me. (John 10:11–14)

If a priest takes all necessary precautions in a reasonable way and uses discretion, he does not have to follow regulations from his bishop or the government to suspend celebrations with the faithful. Such regulations are merely human law; in the Church, however, the supreme law is the salvation of souls. In such situations, priests have to be especially creative to make it possible for the faithful, at least a small group, to participate in Mass and receive the sacraments. This was the pastoral attitude of all priests — martyrs and confessors — during times of persecution.

Can the disobedience of priests toward authorities, and in particular Church authorities, be considered legitimate in certain cases (for example, if the priest is banned from visiting the sick and the dying)?

If Church authorities prohibit a priest from doing that, he must not comply. Such a prohibition is an abuse of power. Christ did not give to the bishop the power to forbid visiting the sick and the dying. A true priest will do everything in his power to visit a dying man. Many priests did that, even when it meant risking their lives, during persecutions and pandemics alike. There are many examples of such priests in the history of the Church. For example, St. Charles Borromeo distributed Holy Communion on the tongue to people who were dying from the plague. In our times, we have the moving and edifying example of priests, particularly in the Bergamo region in northern Italy, who contracted the disease and died because they took care of dying coronavirus patients.

Liturgical Easter celebrations at the Vatican took place practically without any lay faithful.

Considering the strict ban on mass gatherings issued by the Italian government, it is understandable that the pope could not have celebrated the liturgies of Holy Week with a large number of the faithful. For example, I think that the Holy Week liturgies could have been celebrated by the pope with due reverence and without restrictions in the Sistine Chapel (which was the custom of the popes before Vatican II), with the clergy (cardinals and priests) and a select group of the faithful who would have followed hygienic precautions. There is no logic in the ban on the lighting of the fire, the blessing of the water, or baptisms during the Easter Vigil, as if all these were spreading the virus. Pathological fear prevailed over common sense and a supernatural view [of reality].

When I said on a TV program that supernatural life is the most important thing for a
Catholic, many viewers were outraged. In your opinion, how is the Church managing
the coronavirus pandemic?

> The attitude of the Church reveals a loss of the supernatural perspec-
> tive. In recent decades, many Church leaders have been involved
> mostly with secular, worldly, and temporal matters, and as a result
> they have become blind to supernatural and eternal reality. Their
> eyes have been filled with the dust of earthly matters, as St. Gregory
> the Great once said.[5] Their reaction to the Covid-19 pandemic has
> revealed that they care more about the mortal body than they do
> about the immortal soul, forgetting the words of our Lord, "For what
> shall it profit a man, if he gain the whole world, and suffer the loss of
> his soul?" (Mark 8:36). The bishops who are now trying to protect
> (sometimes through disproportionately great means) the bodies of
> the faithful from infection are too often bishops who gave a tacit per-
> mission for the poisonous virus of heretical teaching and practice to
> spread among their sheep.

It's been said that the pandemic could have a sobering effect, that it could remind
Catholics about the proper hierarchy of values. Cardinal Vincent Nichols said recently
that when the Covid-19 pandemic is over, we will start to feel a new hunger for the
Eucharist. Do you agree with that?

> My hope is that these words can prove true for many Catholics. It is a
> common human experience that a prolonged scarcity of an essential
> reality ignites a longing for it in human hearts. That applies, of course,
> to those who truly believe and who love the Eucharist. Such an expe-
> rience is also helpful for a deeper reflection on the meaning and the
> importance of the Blessed Sacrament. Perhaps those Catholics who
> have gotten so used to the *Sanctissimum* that they started perceiving it
> as ordinary and common will experience a spiritual conversion, will
> see their mistake, and henceforth will start approaching the Blessed
> Sacrament as something extraordinary and noble.

---

[5] *Liber Regulae Pastoralis* II, 7.

Many think that the current pandemic is God's punishment for the sins of the Church or, speaking more broadly, of the world. Others say that perceiving misfortunes befalling humanity as divine punishment is a mark of an immature faith and a pagan mentality. There are also those (including the Primate of Poland) who claim that the pandemic is definitely not God's punishment. Do you think that any of those opinions is right?

In my opinion, the coronavirus pandemic is undoubtedly a divine intervention for the purpose of punishing and cleansing a sinful world and the Church. We must not forget that our Lord Jesus Christ perceived physical calamities as divine punishment. For example, we read:

And there were present, at that very time, some that told him of the Galileans, whose blood Pilate had mingled with their sacrifices. And he answering, said to them: Think you that these Galileans were sinners above all the men of Galilee, because they suffered such things? No, I say to you: but unless you shall do penance, you shall all likewise perish. Or those eighteen upon whom the tower fell in Siloe, and slew them: think you, that they also were debtors above all the men that dwelt in Jerusalem? No, I say to you; but except you do penance, you shall all likewise perish. (Luke 13:1–5)

Any reader of the Old Testament will see that the calamities that befell mankind at the time — drought, deluge, plague, or wars — were regarded as a fulfillment of God's designs. Can the way in which God handled His chosen people in the Old Testament be of help in understanding the current situation?

The Covid-19 pandemic, to the best of my knowledge, has created an unprecedented situation in the Church. I am thinking about the almost worldwide ban on all public celebrations of the Holy Mass. One can see a partial analogy to the ban on Christian worship in almost all of the Roman Empire in the first three centuries after Christ. The current situation, however, is unprecedented, because in our case the ban on public worship was issued by Catholic bishops, and [in some cases] it happened even before relevant government regulations were published.

In a way, our situation can be compared to the suppression of sacrificial offerings in the Temple of Jerusalem during the Babylonian captivity of God's chosen people. In the Bible, divine punishment was perceived as grace: "Blessed is the man whom God correcteth: refuse not therefore the chastising of the Lord: For he woundeth, and cureth: he striketh, and his hands shall heal" (Job 5:17–18) and "Such as I love, I rebuke and chastise. Be zealous therefore, and do penance" (Rev. 3:19). The only adequate responses to afflictions, catastrophes, pandemics, and other such situations — all of which are tools in God's hand to awaken people from the slumber of sin and indifference toward divine commandments and eternal life — are penance and a sincere conversion to God. In the following prayer, the prophet Daniel gives an example of a truly trusting attitude that should be adopted by the faithful of all times along with a model of how to behave and pray at a time of an affliction:

> And all Israel have transgressed thy law, and have turned away from hearing thy voice.... Incline, O my God, thy ear, and hear: open thy eyes, and see our desolation, and the city upon which thy name is called: for it is not for our justifications that we present our prayers before thy face, but for the multitude of thy tender mercies. O Lord, hear: O Lord, be appeased: hearken and do: delay not for thy own sake, O my God: because thy name is invoked upon thy city, and upon thy people. (Dan. 9:11, 9:18–19)

Because of the pandemic, many bishops have started encouraging the faithful to receive Holy Communion in the hand instead of on the tongue, and some bishops have explicitly forbidden reception on the tongue. What do you think about that?

The situation in which the public celebration of the Holy Mass and the distribution of Holy Communion are suspended is so unusual and so grave that we can look for a much deeper meaning in it. Those events are happening almost exactly fifty years after Holy Communion in the hand was introduced (in 1969) and after a radical reform of the rite of the Holy Mass was implemented (1969–1970) along with its protestantizing elements (such as the Offertory prayers) and the horizontal and instructional style of celebration (moments of improvisation, celebration in a closed circle and toward the people). The practice of distributing Holy Communion in the hand has led in the last fifty years to unintentional and intentional sacrileges of the Eucharistic Body of Christ on an unprecedented scale. For over fifty years, the Body of Christ has been trampled (mostly unintentionally) by the feet of clergy and laity in Catholic churches all over the world. The phenomenon of theft of consecrated hosts has also been growing at an alarming rate.

The practice of receiving Holy Communion with our hand and fingers resembles the act of eating ordinary food. This way of receiving Christ in the Eucharist has weakened faith in His Real Presence, in transubstantiation, and in the divine and exalted nature of the consecrated Host among many Catholics. Subconsciously, in the understanding of those faithful, the Eucharistic presence of Christ has turned into a blessed bread or a mere symbol. Now the Lord has intervened and deprived almost all the faithful of the opportunity to participate in Holy Mass or receive Holy Communion sacramentally.

The innocent and the guilty undergo this affliction together, because in the mystery of the Church all are unified as her members: "And if one member suffer any thing, all the members suffer with it" (1 Cor. 12:26). The current[6] suspension of the public celebration of the Holy Mass and the distribution of Holy Communion could be seen by the pope and bishops as God's rebuke for the last fifty years of Eucharistic profanations and trivializations, but simultaneously also as a merciful appeal for a true Eucharistic conversion of the whole Church. May the Holy Spirit touch the hearts of the pope and the bishops, prompting them to issue specific liturgical norms, so that the Eucharistic worship of the whole Church may be purified and redirected anew toward the Lord.

When the current affliction ends, the pope should issue specific liturgical directives wherein he would invite the whole Church to turn toward the Lord in the manner of celebration (which means that both

---

[6] As of April 2020. — *Ed.*

the celebrant and the faithful should be facing the same way during the Eucharistic Prayer). The pope should also prohibit the practice of distributing Holy Communion on the hand because the Church cannot continue with impunity to treat the *Sanctissimum* in the small consecrated Host in such a minimalistic and risky manner.

The prayer of Azariah, a portion of which every priest recites at Mass during the Offertory rite, could inspire the pope and the bishops to undertake concrete acts of reparation and the restoration of glory to the Eucharistic sacrifice and the Eucharistic Body of Christ:

> In a contrite heart and humble spirit let us be accepted.... Let our sacrifice be made in thy sight this day, that it may please thee: for there is no confusion to them that trust in thee. And now we follow thee with all our heart, and we fear thee, and seek thy face. Put us not to confusion, but deal with us according to thy meekness, and according to the multitude of thy mercies. And deliver us according to thy wonderful works, and give glory to thy name, O Lord. (Dan. 3:39–43)

2

What About Celibacy?

Are we living in the era of the end of celibacy? An overwhelming majority of participants in the Amazon synod was in favor of ending it. Why is this such a controversial issue? To what degree does the future of the Church depend on celibacy? Although Pope Francis did not support any changes in this area in his document *Querida Amazonia*, still some bishops and cardinals are invoking article 111 of the synodal document, which contains a proposal to allow married men to be ordained to the priesthood. If such a change were to be introduced, it could have a universal character.

Definitely. That is the question, the honest and real question. If married men can be ordained in Amazonia, why not in other places with a similar shortage of priests? After all, such shortages plague many European countries and both Americas. What reason could the Vatican give for refusing to ordain married men in, let's say, Germany, if they could be ordained in Amazonia? It does not take great intelligence to realize that the decision to ordain married men in one part of the world would necessarily cause a domino effect. Ultimately, this would lead to the abolition of celibacy in the Latin Church, for the first time in two thousand years, as far as the rule is concerned. It is an extremely serious matter.

Of course, the example of the Greek Catholic priests, who are, after all, members of the Catholic Church and still have wives, is often brought up in this conversation. It is, however, a different situation.

First of all, we are talking about the Roman Church. Secondly, this issue should be approached from a historical perspective. It was the Greek Church, and later the Orthodox Church, that first abandoned the apostolic tradition. In the seventh century, during the so-called second synod of Trullo (an imperial hall in Constantinople), a decision was made that priests and deacons can have intercourse with their wives also after ordination. The only exception was the bishops, who were not allowed to do that. This was a case of loosening the original discipline, which was practiced since the earliest times, rooted in the apostolic tradition and mentioned already in the Bible. The apostles observed it from the very beginning.

If someone was ordained priest or bishop, from that moment on he had to observe complete sexual continence, regardless of whether he had a wife or not — such was the earliest teaching, such was the universal rule. It went back even to the Old Covenant, although there, of course, it was priesthood in the flesh, through blood descent. Priesthood was passed down from generation to generation through the begetting of offspring. This was the case since the times of Aaron. In the case of the New Covenant, priesthood was no longer transmitted through the begetting of offspring but through ordination. That is why we talk about priesthood in the order of Melchizedek, not the order of Aaron. However, even in the case of the carnal priesthood it was recognized that sexual abstinence had to be observed during the exercise of priestly duties in the temple. We see that also in the story of Zechariah, the father of John the Baptist, who, in order to offer sacrifices to God, had to remain completely continent during his week-long temple service. This was, therefore, a divine precept, which in principle was observed by the apostles.

Our Savior Jesus Christ, as the true great high priest of the New Covenant, set an example for us by preserving virginity. He Himself had no wife and was sexually continent throughout His life. It was in this state that He also offered the sacrifice on the Cross — and in this way made it a binding rule for His Church till the end of time. We could say that He followed in the footsteps of the Old Covenant: when a priest offers the sacrifice of the New Covenant, the Eucharist, he must remain in a state of sexual continence. Even the Orthodox Church keeps that rule. After all, it concerns the apostolic transmission coming from God. To this day, Orthodox priests who are married are obligated to abstain from sexual relations for at least the night preceding the celebration of Mass. During that time, they cannot have intercourse with their wives. I know many Orthodox priests who behave like priests of the Old Covenant in this situation. For two weeks, they celebrate the liturgy and say the Mass, and during that time they have no intercourse with their wives, resuming their marital life only after a break. This gives a strange impression, as if they had reverted to the rules of the Old Covenant.

However, a true priest of the New Covenant should, as a rule, offer the sacrifice of Christ daily, which means he must observe sexual continence daily. Thus, he cannot have a wife.

It follows from what you have said that celibacy belongs to the nature of the priesthood. That it is not an accidental, historical decision, introduced in a particular context, but a principle internal to the priesthood. However, many Church leaders, including bishops and archbishops, claim the opposite. According to them, celibacy is part of an ecclesiastical practice, part of the heritage of the Roman, Latin Church — something that could be abolished at any point: keeping it may have been justified in the past for political or disciplinary reasons, but it does not have any timeless, absolute, or religious value.

Bishops who express such opinions are simply displaying ignorance, both theological and historical. In fact, the book by Cardinal Robert Sarah and Pope Benedict XVI shows the opposite.[7] Celibacy understood as a duty of complete continence belongs to the nature of the priesthood. As I have said before, our Savior Himself understood it clearly and demonstrated it when He offered Himself as a sacrifice on the Cross, and this was also how the apostles understood it from the very beginning. When Jesus called them, some had wives, others did not. John was not married, Peter had a wife, and Paul did not. The

[7] Benedict XVI and Robert Cardinal Sarah, *From the Depths of Our Hearts: Priesthood, Celibacy and the Crisis of the Catholic Church* (San Francisco: Ignatius Press, 2020).

Gospel of Luke includes a dialogue between Peter and Jesus, where the apostle says:

> Behold, we have left all things, and have followed thee. Who said to them: Amen, I say to you, there is no man that hath left house, or parents, or brethren, or wife, or children, for the kingdom of God's sake, Who shall not receive much more in this present time, and in the world to come life everlasting. (18:28–30)

Jesus Himself is clearly talking about the apostles leaving their wives! It is important to be reminded of this, because today the following argument is used in favor of abolishing celibacy: "after all, Peter himself was married." Yes, he was married before being called, but after he was called, he himself said, "we left all things." This dialogue attests precisely to that: Peter, just like the other apostles who had wives, no longer engaged in sexual intercourse after he was called.

St. Paul says exactly the same thing in the First Epistle to the Corinthians, "Have we not power to carry about a woman, a sister, as well as the rest of the apostles, and the brethren of the Lord, and Cephas?" (9:5). So here is what is missed or deliberately overlooked by many: this is not about a woman-wife, but about a woman-sister! Paul clearly writes that Peter and the others were accompanied by a woman-sister. Women helped with apostolic work as sisters: this is logical and reasonable. These words contain no evidence that Peter had sexual relations with his wife after being summoned to become an apostle. Let me repeat, it was exactly the opposite, as evidenced conclusively by the term "woman-sister."

In the discussion of celibacy, another passage from Paul's epistles is referenced frequently: the part of the Epistle to Timothy in which the apostle describes the characteristics of a bishop. There, he writes, "It behoveth therefore a bishop to be blameless, the husband of one wife" (1 Tim. 3:2). Look, they say, Paul himself writes that a bishop can have a wife. It is supposed to be proof that the earliest Christians did not know celibacy. Putting aside the fact that even among the Orthodox, the bishop cannot be married, something else is more important: those who want to use this text against celibacy do not realize that among many virtues of the bishop, one in particular is especially relevant for this discussion. When a parallel fragment of the Epistle to Titus lists a set of qualities of a good bishop, the term "continence" is used. Paul writes:

> For a bishop must be without crime, as the steward of God: not proud, not subject to anger, not given to wine, no striker, not greedy of filthy lucre: but given to hospitality, gentle, sober, just, holy, continent: embracing that faithful word which is according to doctrine, that he may be able to exhort in sound doctrine, and to convince the gainsayers. (Titus 1:7–9)

In the Greek language, the term *enkrates* refers to man and *enkrateia* as a quality denotes continence. In the first and second centuries after the birth of Christ, this was a technical term referring exclusively to sexual continence. If, then, Paul writes that the bishop should be *enkrates*, he does not mean just continence or abstinence, but a complete sexual continence. There was even an extreme cult at the time called the "Encratites," who completely rejected sexual relations, even in marriage. The Church never held such views on marriage.

Another important question: the apostle writes that the bishop should be the husband of one wife. Why? Why could you not have ordained a man who had a second wife, because he had been widowed earlier? The first wife died, he became a widower, so he took another wife because he had small children. There must have been many examples of situations like that. It would not have been anything unusual. Life expectancies were much shorter, so cases in which a widower was left with small children and took another woman to be his wife were not infrequent. After all, you had to raise the children, and the Church never condemned second marriages for widowers. But Paul clearly writes about the husband of one wife. Why is that, given that the cases of widowers remarrying were in conformity with the law? Because a second marriage was a sign that such a man is unable to live in continence.

With all that in mind, it is clear that sexual continence (*enkrateia* in Greek) was a condition *sine qua non* for ordination. From the moment of ordination, deacons, priests, and bishops alike, regardless of whether they had wives or not, were all obliged to observe sexual continence. This has been the constant teaching of the Western Church, the Roman Church.

The authenticity of this teaching is also demonstrated by examples from the life of the Orthodox Church — which I can observe closely while living here, in Kazakhstan. Few people know that in the Orthodox Church, too, marriage after ordination is not allowed. If an unmarried man is ordained, he must remain unmarried for the rest of his life. Similarly, if an Orthodox priest loses his wife and becomes a widower, he is not allowed to remarry, regardless of how long his marriage lasted. I know a case of an Orthodox priest whose wife died merely a year after they got married. From now on, he must remain unmarried and live in celibacy. This is another indication, this time from the Orthodox tradition, that sexual continence belongs to the essence of priesthood. If that was not the case, if celibacy were not part of the essence of priesthood, why would the Orthodox Church prohibit sexual intercourse during the period of celebration of sacrifice? Why would it not allow priests who are widowers to remarry?

You have mentioned that those who advocate the abolition of celibacy don't have sufficient knowledge. However, you can find books by authors such as Alfons Stickler or Stefan Heid that describe the meaning and tradition of priestly celibacy in great detail. All you need to do is read them. So is it a problem of ignorance, or aversion, or even ill will? Why is the movement advocating the abolition of celibacy so strong today?

According to Johann Adam Möhler, a great German theologian and expert on Church history who lived in the nineteenth century, greatness of spirit has always manifested itself in one way in the history of the Church; it was the mark of those who advocated for celibacy, as was demonstrated perfectly by the reform led by Pope Gregory VII. The willingness to embrace celibacy has always been a sign of the vitality of Catholicism. Today it is difficult to see such a willingness — I mean a certain comprehensive phenomenon. What are the reasons for this?

Obviously, different people can have different motivations; each should be considered individually. But the main reason is a tendency toward a certain naturalism. In this context, we can also talk about Pelagianism. It's the conviction that salvation can be achieved without sacrifice, without the cross, by accepting a certain theory. Through word and instruction, but not through participation in Christ's sacrifice and taking up the cross. This, however, is a false approach. Jesus stated clearly that no one can be His disciple if he does not take up his cross and follow Him, "And whosoever doth not carry his cross and come after me, cannot be my disciple" (Luke 14:27). This applies to all the faithful, not just to priests. Christ desires to be followed. He took upon Himself suffering, poverty, and passion. This is the way of the Church, the way of each priest, and also the way of each believer. There is no salvation without sacrifice — this is the constant teaching of the Church. That is why God chose sacrifice, He took upon Himself the sacrifice of the Cross. This is the way of the Church. We can understand the meaning of suffering only if we offer ourselves. Only faith can open our eyes: priests can bear true spiritual fruits by participating in the sacrifice of Christ and being united to Him in His suffering. The history of the Church demonstrates that clearly. Both apostles and great saints were people who participated in the sufferings of Christ to the highest degree. They were also the ones who bore the most spiritual fruit. Priesthood without suffering and sacrifice would be meaningless. It would just be a form of a *petit bourgeois* ideology. A degeneration of the priests of the New Covenant would follow, as they, rejecting sacrifice and the cross, would become a caste of scribes.

You have already mentioned the book *From the Depths of Our Hearts* by Cardinal Sarah and Benedict XVI, which was published at the beginning of 2020. Excerpts from the book appeared in the press shortly before the publication of the papal exhortation *Querida Amazonia*. As soon as news of the book reached the public, the authors were flooded with criticism, and, in the official narrative, Benedict XVI demanded that his name be removed from the title page. What is your view of this controversy? Why did the book cause such a stir? Shortly after its publication, the Prefect of the Papal Household, Georg Gänswein, lost his job. What is this all about?

Any objective observer must have seen that Cardinal Sarah and Benedict XVI's defense of celibacy stirred up a storm in the media and the Church establishment. To some extent, this includes Vatican officials themselves. Their angry reactions prove that the majority expected a complete abolition of celibacy. And suddenly, just before what seemed like a breakthrough, one of the most important voices in the Church weighs in — Pope Emeritus Benedict XVI is a figure of great authority, unequalled by anyone other than Pope Francis, as a result of both his former function and esteem for his theological thought — and, to use a somewhat colloquial expression, ruins all the fun. Even more so since he was accompanied by Cardinal Sarah, a man who commands great respect in the Church. They ruined all the fun. Such people must be eliminated immediately.

They need to be called to order.

Yes, and forced to comply. That is what they tried to do through a shameless campaign of slander and lies. That was the point of the attack on both authors. Their opponents didn't present any arguments, but instead started a smear campaign. It was claimed that Benedict XVI knew nothing about the book, that he was being used, that he didn't realize what it was about. Thankfully, Cardinal Sarah was able to demonstrate through relevant documents that these were all lies. From the very start, Benedict XVI was involved in the process of creating the book and was aware of its form at every stage. The cardinal proved that the former pope was familiar not just with the contents of the book, but also the design of the cover page. On December 3, 2019, the cardinal showed the cover page to Benedict XVI, who approved it. How can anyone claim, then, that Benedict XVI did not know what he was signing? That is simply a lie.

Let me repeat: Cardinal Sarah proved this beyond any doubt. So I don't know why Archbishop Georg Gänswein tried to contradict it. After all, this is not a situation of word against word. All Archbishop Gänswein had was words, but Cardinal Sarah presented documents on which he based his words. Thus, I am sorry to say, but ultimately,

we can conclude that Archbishop Gänswein took part in the smear campaign against both authors. He joined the choir of those who were enraged by a simple theological and historical reflection presented by a pope emeritus and a cardinal — the choir of those who did not want to have a conversation and listen to sound arguments about the essence of priesthood and its connection to celibacy. There was no calm exchange of views, but instead an uproar.

> This shows, however, that the arguments of those advocating the aboli-
> tion of celibacy are very weak, and it was they themselves who revealed
> their weakness. In fact, they wanted to suppress, even stifle, the voice
> of truth. I find it very sad that those in charge at the Vatican, especially
> Pope Francis himself, didn't stand up for Benedict XVI and Cardinal
> Sarah.

What is your view of the papal document *Querida Amazonia*? The document has been controversial from the very beginning, and there are drastically different opinions about it.

> First of all, I am grateful to Pope Francis for resisting the pressure to
> relax the law of priestly celibacy or to approve the sacramental ordi-
> nation of women. Secondly, we should emphasize in all fairness that
> the text of *Querida Amazonia* as a whole is an improvement over the
> final document of the Amazon Synod. To quote just a few examples:
> *Querida Amazonia* talks about "interior conversion" (56), whereas the
> final synod document has whole chapters grouped under the titles of
> "integral conversion" and "ecological conversion" that even talk about
> "the ecological conversion of the Church and the planet" (61).
>
> The final document doesn't mention the limitations of culture
> or the way of life of the original peoples, whereas *Querida Amazonia*
> mentions those limitations twice in the moral sense (see 22 and 36).
> *Querida Amazonia* warns against closed "indigenism," whereas the final
> document is silent on the topic.
>
> The word "adoration" is missing in the final document, but it does
> get a mention in *Querida Amazonia*. Instead of talking about "incultur-
> ated theology" (final document), *Querida Amazonia* talks about "an
> inculturated spirituality." The final document uses the word "grace"

only twice, and in an anthropocentric way, whereas *Querida Amazonia* mentions grace ten times, in a more theological meaning, as can be seen in the following formulations: "Christ is the source of all grace" (87); in sacraments, "nature is elevated to become a locus and instrument of grace" (81); "God is in things … by grace" (footnote 105).

These are certainly positive changes in comparison to the final document. However, when we read through the text of the exhortation, don't we also find aspects that are alarming?

This is a legitimate question. While noting the improvements made to *Querida Amazonia*, we mustn't remain silent about the lamentable doctrinal ambiguities and errors it contains, as well as its dangerous ideological tendencies. One of the problematic things, for example, is an implicit approval of pantheistic and pagan spirituality, when *Querida Amazonia* speaks of the material land as a "sacred mystery" (5); about entering into communion with nature, "if we enter into communion with the forest" (56); about the Amazonian biome as a "theological locus" (57). The affirmation that "only poetry, with its humble voice, will be able to save this world" (46) borders on pantheism and paganism. A Christian cannot condone such ideas and expressions. The apostles would never have allowed the native symbols of the Greco-Roman society, such as the statue of Artemis, or Diana, in Ephesus, to be "assimilated in some way" (see Acts 19:23ff.). Certainly no apostle or holy missionary would have stood by and accepted the following statement from *Querida Amazonia:* "It is possible to take up an indigenous symbol in some way, without necessarily considering it as idolatry" (79).

The designation in *Querida Amazonia* of the Blessed Virgin Mary as "the Mother of all creatures" (111) is also very problematic theologically. The Blessed and Immaculate Mother of God is not the Mother of all creatures, but only of Jesus Christ, the Redeemer of mankind, and is therefore also the spiritual Mother of all people redeemed by her divine Son. The idea embodied in the phrase "Mother of all creatures" can be found in pagan religions, such as the Pachamama cult and the New Age movement, as seen in the following description:

Earth Mother, in ancient and modern nonliterate religions [is] an eternally fruitful source of everything.... She is simply the mother; there is nothing separate from her. All things come from her, return to her, and are her.... She simply produces everything, inexhaustibly, from herself.[8]

One of the major erroneous trends in *Querida Amazonia* is the promotion of naturalism and minor traces of pantheism and disguised Pelagianism. This change of direction in the Church does considerable damage to the well-being and salvation of souls.

Overall, is *Querida Amazonia* more a sign of hope, or another manifestation of a crisis?

It's hard to say. Although riddled with problematic, questionable, and theologically unclear expressions, *Querida Amazonia* also contains valuable statements, such as this one about priests (no. 88):

That is his [the priest's] great power, a power that can only be received in the sacrament of Holy Orders. For this reason, only the priest can say: "This is my body." There are other words, too, that he alone can speak: "I absolve you from your sins." Because sacramental forgiveness is at the service of a worthy celebration of the Eucharist. These two sacraments lie at the heart of the priest's exclusive identity.[9]

Pope Francis presents a supernatural and devoutly Catholic vision at the end of *Querida Amazonia*, praying: "Mother..., bring your Son to birth in their hearts" (111), "Mother..., reign in the Amazon, together with your Son" (111). Given the massive spiritual attack on the primacy of Peter, the publication of *Querida Amazonia* — along with Pope Francis's stance to uphold the apostolic norm of priestly celibacy and the divine truth about sacramental ordination being reserved for

---

[8] "Earth Mother," by the editors of *Encyclopædia Britannica*, www.britannica.com/topic/Earth-Mother.

[9] The penultimate sentence is grammatically incomplete in the Vatican text.

men — is, despite its theological limitations and errors, a sign of hope in the midst of an ongoing turmoil.

Why have the liberal media become so involved in abolishing celibacy? After all, it is the same media that normally talk about the freedom of choice, diversity, about everyone's right to choose and shape their lives, which is touted as a great achievement of the liberal world. Why is it that in this case they are so invested in abolishing celibacy?

Exactly, that is the question. Theoretically, any reasonable person should say: if everyone has the right to choose, if State and Church are separate, if, as the media claim, they should remain separate forever — which is the basic dogma today — then why such interest? Celibacy, strictly speaking, is an internal Church issue; why, then, does it attract such great interest among secular, non-Christian media? Why are they so outraged, and why do they demand that it be abolished at all costs? This stands in clear contradiction to their professed views.

In my opinion, this is just another proof that the modern world is unwilling and unable to come to terms with the existence of truth, holiness, and the supernatural. The world has a certain allergy, sometimes even hatred, toward everything that is sacred or supernatural. The work of the leftist media is the best example of that. Celibacy, on the other hand, is a clear, living demonstration of the supernatural. A man who renounces sexual intercourse for life is unbearable to them. For indeed, this cannot be understood in natural terms. We must appeal to the supernatural. In this sense, priestly celibacy is a living sign of the reality of the supernatural. It's proof of the existence of the supernatural. Of course, history has shown that priests have failed time and again to observe celibacy, that they have violated the rule in this regard. That is simply fallen human nature.

In our times we also have a great crisis caused by the sexual abuse of minors. However, it must be remembered that such abuse, which always deserves condemnation, is committed in a statistical sense by a small percentage of priests. Statistically speaking, there are far fewer cases of abuse among priests than among other social or professional groups. I am referring here not only to pedophilia, but also to other offenses against the moral law with regard to chastity. Most priests live out their faith through grace. They renounce sexual activity, making a joyful sacrifice of it. This is only possible by the grace of God. Those bishops and priests who ultimately want to abolish celibacy have gone over to the side of the enemy; they have joined the choir of the enemies of the Church and have taken their side. They want to throw away this precious pearl of celibacy, handed down to us by Tradition, left to us by Jesus and His apostles. For two thousand years, the Roman Church has stood by it and defended it against all possible attacks. Today, many of those who consider rejecting celibacy think that they are finally nearing their goal. They have already won many victories by infiltrating the Church, especially since the Second Vatican Council. They have succeeded in introducing elements of relativism into the Church's teachings and, above all, into her liturgy. In the same way, the naturalism they have been preaching has influenced the lives of priests. Now the last bastion before them is celibacy. This is why defending it is so crucial. This is why the pope should not give way even by a fraction of an inch. Should he succumb, we might say that it would be the fall of the remaining walls protecting the apostolic and divine tradition.

Isn't the current confusion additionally exacerbated by the new phenomenon of the co-existence of two popes in Rome? Never before in the history of the Church did we have a situation where the current pope and pope emeritus would be living side by side. Doesn't the responsibility for the chaos fall also on Benedict XVI, and was not the way in which he abdicated a contributing factor here? Why did he stay in Rome after the abdication? Why did he keep the title of "pope emeritus" and the white cassock? Why does he continue to give the apostolic blessing?

There is no denying that there has been a great deal of chaos as a result of the abdication. It's been getting worse with each day. The faithful and the priests say that this confusion is unbearable. This duality is contrary to the nature of the Church, contrary to her divine constitution. We have only one pope. There is only one hierarchy. We don't have two heads at the top of it, but one. With two heads there could only be a monstrosity. Unfortunately, the source of this confusion is the great mistake of Pope Benedict XVI. I am convinced that after his death the Church will have to clear this up. This will be an important task for the next pope: he will have to safeguard the Church emphatically so that such a situation can never happen again. The present state leads to disorientation and confusion among the faithful. Benedict XVI is not the pope, but he behaves like the pope, dresses like the pope, retains the title "His Holiness," and gives, as you mentioned, the apostolic blessing. There has never been a "pope emeritus" in the history of the Church. One thing should be kept in mind: papacy is not a sacrament.

Exactly. A major article on this topic was recently published by Roberto de Mattei. He pointed out what he called the fundamental error of Benedict XVI, who apparently regards the papacy as a higher degree of the sacrament of Holy Orders.

The fullness of the sacrament of Holy Orders is conferred by episcopal consecration. Episcopal consecration is a sacrament. That is why we say: bishop emeritus. However, someone elected to be the pope does not receive another degree of ordination. He is pope for a limited time, until his death, or his abdication. When either happens, he is no longer pope. A man who resigned as pope remains what he was in virtue of sacramental ordination. And in virtue of his ordination, this man is a bishop. The logical conclusion, then, is that after resigning from the papacy the former pope is a bishop; therefore, he should dress as a bishop and use the name he used as a bishop. This is a rational, logical consequence. I think it should be clearly codified in ecclesiastical law, in the code of canon law, so as to avoid such situations in the future.

Several days after the publication of Benedict XVI and Cardinal Sarah's book, the Italian newspaper *La Repubblica* published an extensive interview with Pope Francis conducted by a well-known Italian atheist and leftist Eugenio Scalfari. It was actually a lengthy article, in which some of the pope's words were featured as quotes. One of them said: "In an organization whose membership counts hundreds of millions, there will always be someone who opposes change," that is, opposes the abolition of celibacy. What do you think about the relationship between Pope Francis and Eugenio Scalfari? What is the significance of their conversations and the fact that they are being published, since

this is probably the sixth, maybe the seventh time? Nobody knows exactly how many conversations there have been, since Scalfari quotes the pope without specifying the conversation. How can we explain the fact that the pope's first response to Benedict XVI and Cardinal Sarah's book appeared in a newspaper notorious for its criticism of the Church and dislike of Catholicism?

> I find the pope's conversations with this left-wing radical atheist regrettable. To me, it is highly unclear. The pope must be transparent. Both the bishops and the faithful must understand what he means, what he is saying to them, what he wants to communicate. This is what I mean by transparency. There is no transparency in his relationship with Scalfari. We have repeated interviews with a well-known journalist, and we don't know exactly what the pope actually said and what was attributed to him. This is not fair play. Scalfari says that the pope said something to him, and quotes it, but later it turns out that it was not the pope who said it, but Scalfari. Afterward, the pope (or the Vatican press office) could say that what appeared as a papal statement was actually just an interpretation, Scalfari's personal feeling. So ultimately, nothing of what Scalfari publishes can be taken seriously. As a result, everyone is wondering what Francis really said. Perhaps he said that, or perhaps he didn't. That means that he is sowing doubt. Or, in other words, trying to muddy the waters.

Why? To what end?

> I don't know. That would be a question for the pope. However, this is never what an apostle should do. Neither Jesus nor the apostles created confusion in the minds of the faithful. They didn't want to lead them into a state of confusion, uncertainty, or restlessness. Please note: those conversations result in doubts and suspicions against the pope. Is it possible, people are asking, that the pope could say things contrary to the Faith? For example, in one interview Francis allegedly told Scalfari that Satan won't exist forever and similarly, neither will the damned, because in some way they will be destroyed and eliminated. This is a very dangerous claim. So far, however, the pope has not denied saying that, but neither has he confirmed it. As I said, the result is manifest:

doubts and suspicions are multiplying. Did he say it or not? In what context? What did he mean by it? It's as if important truths of faith have become cloudy. We are in a foggy situation. I think this is dangerous behavior, I would not even hesitate to call it irresponsible.

I am looking merely at objective facts: the confusion and cloudiness, and the growing suspicion among the faithful. This is how relativism in matters of faith and morals spreads. It creates the impression that clear formulations regarding matters of faith are no longer important. Everything becomes relative. It's possible to live, we are told, without clear teachings. If one statement has exactly the same value as another statement contrary to it, we have fallen into relativism. This is why I believe that as the result of actions such as conversations with Scalfari, a mentality of relativism spreads in the Church. This leads to a situation in which the demand for clarity, for unambiguity — the way Jesus taught — loses its meaning.

3

The Gnostic Threat

In the foreword to Taylor Marshall's *Infiltration*, you wrote that the modern world has been built on the principles of the French Revolution, "the absolute freedom of man from any divine revelation or commandment; the absolute equality that abolishes not only any social or religious hierarchy, but even differences between the sexes; and a brotherhood of man so uncritical that it even eliminates any distinction on the basis of religion."[10] If this diagnosis is correct, can Christians still survive in such a world?

Indeed, we have been witnessing an increasingly fierce attack on humanity as such. The French Revolution was a symbolic breakthrough. It was then that the ideas propagated by Freemasonry became known on a large scale. The first target of their attack was divine revelation itself, the supernatural. If you reject revelation, if you reject the existence of God as the Lawgiver, ultimately you reject the order of nature created by Him. The order of nature in itself is also dependent on divine revelation (we are talking about God's natural revelation) and on the laws that God instituted in nature. The order of nature can exist only when those laws are observed.

One such fundamental law of nature, a law that is most obvious and necessary, is the existence of two sexes, the existence of man and woman. This is the root of the existence of society. Creation must

[10] Athanasius Schneider, foreword to Taylor R. Marshall, *Infiltration: The Plot to Destroy the Church from Within* (Manchester, NH: Crisis Publications, 2019).

observe these limits set by God. Down to the smallest cell in our bodies, each of us is either a man or a woman. This is the way God has made us, and these boundaries must not be crossed. Freemasonry, which has rebelled against God, ultimately wants to destroy the order of nature that flows from Him. That is why we are now being told, "No — why should we remain within the limits of what man is or what woman is? It's not fair that God decreed it this way, and neither that which is male nor that which is female are binding. Let everyone create anew whatever they feel like. Man has to be god unto himself. What God has made cannot be good. It is we who must create man anew as we please. The existence of two sexes comes from God, but we reject this. We must make our own creation. Instead of two sexes we will introduce many 'genders.'" This is how gays, lesbians, bisexuals, and so on emerge. This is what gives rise to insanity and the term describing it: LGBT. What we have here is an unequivocal rebellion, ultimately a satanic rebellion, against the order of creation. It is the ultimate, perverse result of the idea of absolute equality and freedom. If "genders" are determined by arbitrary will, the order of creation is destroyed.

There is one thing the rebels cannot achieve. They cannot transcend the boundaries of the physical world. If you put your hand in fire, you will have to withdraw it, or else you will get burnt and hurt. This law can't be changed. Similarly, they can't get rid of the sun, the moon, or the stars. The universe will keep moving until God in His wisdom decides to say "enough." They are not able to change that. Similarly, they can't control the basic laws of biology. They do, however, try to change the rules of logic or mathematics. This is the case when someone says that two plus two equals five, although — I'm saying this jokingly — this tendency to bend the laws of mathematics strangely doesn't apply to situations where rebels are checking their own bank accounts. In this case, when it comes to their own profit or salary, two plus two always equals four.

Freemasonry imagined that God is the great architect of the world, the great builder. They wanted to take power and authority away from Him and put Man in His place. But behind Man, whom they supposedly elevated, Lucifer is lurking.

You mentioned the attack on revelation. However, when reading the writings of contemporary theologians, one may get the impression that revelation is very unclear also to them. In their opinion, revelation is constantly developing, and in their view the notion of revelation as a given, closed, immutable set of truths must be challenged. Revelation must keep developing in history, it should become deeper with each era, and it should grow and expand to include new content.

To some extent, such an understanding is typical of *gnosis*. This intellectual trend was born at the turn of the first and second centuries after Christ, so basically at the time when our Lord and the apostles lived. It was the first attack on the Church. Gnosis was particularly fashionable among the intellectuals at the time. Ultimately, it was about the idea that man can achieve salvation and deliverance through his own thinking, independent of divine historical revelation. The path to salvation was not through external revelation, but through one's own mental constructs. In the second century, this current of thought attempted to infiltrate the Church, but thank God one man was successful in preventing it. I am referring to St. Irenaeus of Lyon, who could be called the spiritual grandson of St. John. Through Polycarp, he had an almost direct connection to the apostle John. It was he who sounded the alarm in the Church and identified the danger of the poison that was beginning to enter the Church, at least in some communities, at the time. He wrote a five-volume work *Against Heresies* (*Adversus Haereses*), in which he exposed the Gnostics.

The Gnostic tendency was defeated then, but it has kept resurfacing in the history of the Church. It is all about replacing a truth given from above with one's own mental construct: it is man's task to create truth and salvation. This was ultimately what Martin Luther pursued when he said that *he* will interpret God's Word in *his* way. He himself, rather than the Tradition, would decide how to interpret Scripture. He would determine and create the interpretation. Therefore, in principle, the theories of Luther — the thought that he passed on — are a form of gnosis. Instead of revelation passed down through the immutable teaching of the Church, he introduced his own understanding. Private interpretation replaced Tradition.

Another incarnation of this Gnostic tendency, this drive toward self-salvation and the creation of "truth," is precisely Freemasonry. We can say that it is gnosis equipped with political power, with power over the world. As I've said, gnosis appeared already in the century after Christ, but first without political power, and therefore it was not so dangerous. In the eighteenth century it was different: the followers of gnosis gained power and political influence and began to take over key State positions. Their influence on public opinion and society grew.

Another mutation of gnosis was German idealism, in which reality actually turns out to be an idea, a thought. Reality is not something I accept from the outside, for example, by virtue of faith, but rather it is a construct of my own "I." This can be seen most clearly in Hegel's philosophy, in Hegelianism, which to a large degree permeated modern Catholic theology. It was from this fusion that modernism was born over a hundred years ago, and then, with the Second Vatican Council, neo-modernism. Certainly there were indications of it prior to the Council, but it really blossomed during that time. I believe that today many theologians and bishops are plagued by Hegelianism. Some succumb to it consciously, others unconsciously. Hegel said that there is nothing unchangeable, immovable. Everything is developing. After the thesis comes the antithesis, and from their combination is born the synthesis. This is exactly the reasoning of many Catholic Hegelians today: Catholicism before the Council was a thesis, the conciliar and post-conciliar Church was an antithesis, and now we are moving toward a synthesis. So when they are told that the popes taught exactly the opposite of what was found in certain passages of conciliar documents, they respond that this is normal. Earlier we had the thesis, now we have the antithesis, and eventually, in a few decades, the Catholic teaching will reach the synthesis. This is an extremely dangerous approach. Essentially, it's simply a new form of modernism, which is why it should be really important to study anew the analysis of this phenomenon presented by Pope Pius X in his encyclical *Pascendi*. When you read it today, you can see how relevant the text is.

In his book *Ecclesiastical Winter,* Fr. Alfonso Gálvez claims that we are currently living at the time of the deepest crisis in Church history. A crisis much deeper than the Arian crisis or Luther's rebellion. He is not alone in thinking that — there are many who think that the degree of chaos and uncertainty in the Church today can't be compared to anything we know from earlier times. What do you think about that?

> It definitely can't be denied. In earlier periods, the disagreements fo-cused around particular erroneous teachings that created chaos and division in the Church. During the Arian heresy, for example, its fol-lowers rejected the belief in the divinity of Christ the Son of God, which in turn meant rejecting the mystery of the Holy Trinity. But even Arians didn't reject the belief that Christianity is the only true religion. Neither did they reject the teaching that the Eucharist is the sacrifice of Christ. Luther, however, rejected certain essential elements of Christian teaching, among them, for example, five of the sacraments and the whole sacramental structure. Similarly, he rejected Church Tradition — it was a significant revolution. But even he recognized the existence of the Holy Trinity and didn't believe that there was salvation outside of Christianity. According to Luther, Christianity was still the only true religion, willed by God. However, because of the influence of modernism, the appearance of modernist elements in some conciliar documents, and above all because of the dangerous passages in the conciliar document on religious liberty, *Dignitatis Humanae,* the cur-rent crisis is much deeper than the earlier ones we know from history. I am thinking, for example, of the claim that man has a natural right to religious freedom.

> Here is the passage:

>> This Vatican Council declares that the human person has a right to religious freedom. This freedom means that all men are to be immune from coercion on the part of individuals or of social groups and of any human power, in such wise that no one is to be forced to act in a manner contrary to his own beliefs, whether privately or publicly, whether alone or in association with others, within due limits. The council further declares that

the right to religious freedom has its foundation in the very
dignity of the human person as this dignity is known through
the revealed Word of God and by reason itself.[11]

Similarly, it further reads:

the right to religious freedom has its foundation not in the
subjective disposition of the person, but in his very nature.
In consequence, the right to this immunity continues to exist
even in those who do not live up to their obligation of seeking
the truth and adhering to it and the exercise of this right is not
to be impeded.[12]

This is one of the most dangerous statements. This places Christianity
on par with all natural religions and thus implicitly challenges its position as the only true religion. If the human person by nature has the right
to freedom, that is, in not being impeded in choosing and practicing
different religions, this ultimately means that God positively willed
this right of freedom to choose also a false religion, and thus could not
have demanded man's obedience toward His one and only revelation.
I see in this a huge danger of relativism, according to which there is
no truth binding in itself. If we claim that all religions are positively
willed by God, which is supposed to follow from natural law, this will
ultimately lead to the collapse of Christianity. We are dealing here with
a direct attack on Christianity as such.

You just said that this statement according to which every person has the natural right
to religious freedom, rooted in the very dignity of the human person, is extremely
dangerous. But this particular teaching was recognized by all post-conciliar popes as
the greatest achievement of the Council. This view can be found in countless speeches,
addressed both to the faithful and to people outside the Church. How, then, should we
understand it? According to Paul VI, John Paul II, Benedict XVI, and Francis (two of
whom have been canonized), the teaching about the natural right to religious freedom

---

[11] Second Vatican Council, Declaration on Religious Freedom *Dignitatis Huma-*
nae, 2.
[12] Ibid.

rooted in the dignity of the human person is a major achievement of the Council, a true fruit of the Holy Spirit, but you claim the opposite, that this teaching is dangerous.

I think there is at least partial confusion here. I'm afraid that the statements of these popes on this issue lack clarity. If we take the charitable approach, a certain misunderstanding may have occurred. Perhaps they focused primarily on the first part of this sentence from the conciliar declaration, "This freedom means that all men are to be immune from coercion on the part of individuals or of social groups and of any human power, in such wise that no one is to be forced to act in a manner contrary to his own beliefs...." Regarding that, the popes may have rightly concluded that this is about opposing attempts at imposing religion by force, as often happens with Muslim or Hindu fundamentalists. In both of these cases, obedience to religion is imposed with force: the person will either accept (say) Islam and declare his obedience, or may have to face death or persecution. In this sense, saying that "men are to be immune from coercion" is correct.

This statement is nothing new. Rejecting coercion as a method of evangelization has always been present in the Church's teaching.

Yes, but I'm trying to clarify here how the popes who adopted this teaching may have been reasoning. To a certain extent, this is probably how John Paul II and Benedict XVI thought: in the last few decades there has been a sharp rise in religious extremism in the Islamic world, and Christians are being killed there if they don't want to accept the Muslim religion. That's why it's important to emphasize that according to natural law a person can't be forced to embrace a religion. You are right, this is nothing new, it has been a constant teaching of the Church.

But the problem is that the sentence of the conciliar declaration that nobody can be forced to embrace a religion doesn't end here. Here we see the comma, the famous comma. The second part of that sentence adds that with regard to religious freedom "no one is to be forced to act in a manner contrary to his own beliefs, whether privately or publicly, whether alone or in association with others." Further on it proclaims that such a right to religious freedom has its foundation in the very dignity of the human person, and as such it's positively willed by God. Thus, man can freely disseminate any religious doctrine and must not be prevented from doing so. This is precisely the danger and the novelty. God doesn't want the dissemination of error. There is no natural right to propagate error. There is no natural right to choose a false religion.

For example, there is no natural right to choose a satanic religion. In the USA, the so-called Church of Satan has been operating for a number of years. As far as their civil rights are concerned, they have exactly the same legal standing, the same tax privileges and civil protections as any other religious community. The Church of Satan has the same privileges and the same legal standing as the Catholic Church or Protestant communities. However, God cannot positively will that man should choose for himself the religion of Satan, cultivate it, and spread it (thus, there is no such natural law). And He can't will that no one should be able to prevent man from doing so.

The text of *Dignitatis Humanae* only stipulates that this freedom be exercised "within due limits." However, this is a very weak safeguard that applies only to cases of public disturbances. But when we talk about the right to religious freedom, it's not a question of a public disturbance, but of the root of truth, the nature of man. Let me repeat, we are dealing here with a huge mistake. Man by nature doesn't have the right to choose his own religion. God didn't want man to choose a religion arbitrarily. Quite the opposite. God clearly said, "Thou shalt not have strange gods before me" (Exod. 20:3). People worship other gods against God's will. God doesn't will that His Son be rejected — which is what happens in Islam or Judaism. If we have a natural right to choose, let's say, Islam, then by choosing this religion, which rejects Jesus as the Son of God, I am exercising my right, doing the right thing. In this way, rejecting faith in Jesus as the Son of God ultimately turns out to be something good, because it is natural and willed by God. God, however, wants everyone to accept His revelation in Christ. Naturally, He wants us to accept it freely, but it is about a right of free acceptance of the unique truth, rather than a right of free choice between truth and falsehood. In this way, a door has been opened to the spread of relativism.

In this discussion we must also take into account a third factor, which we could call social or civic. From the perspective of State law, all people are equal. This is theoretically the case in an atheistic State or in a State that adopts a form of State religion. In such a State one can appeal to the principle of religious freedom and say that Christians should have the same rights as all other citizens. This was the case with communism. During meetings with Communist leaders, arguments could be made by appealing to universal human rights, to the freedom of conscience. There was no other ground on which to base the argument, except having the right to freedom of religion as a citizen who had the right to choose his or her religious beliefs. However, this would only be a purely positive law of the State, allowing me as a citizen to do the same thing that every other citizen has the right to do.

Yes, but such a law is not rooted in human nature. Rather, it is a certain practical, historic situation that requires an appeal to such arguments as the equality of citizens before positive laws and statutes.

Exactly. That is precisely so. We can speak of certain historical circumstances, such as the establishment of a Communist or atheistic State, which force us to appeal to the positive law in effect in that State. In such a situation you can't appeal to divine law, which says that the true religion must be recognized. That would be ineffective. This situation, of a State that is atheistic or even hostile to religion, must be distinguished from the situation of a State where the majority of citizens, including the majority of those in power, are Catholics. In such a State, other religions should not enjoy the same privileges as the Catholic religion. Of course, all people have certain basic civil rights, which is also what the Church taught before the Council, defending the principle of tolerance. In this case, everything depends on the circumstances. This means that a Catholic State can grant its non-Catholic citizens the right to practice their religion freely and not prevent them from worshipping. Tolerance entails that the existence of such non-Catholic communities is not impeded, but they are not allowed to have an influence on the society similar to the Catholic Church's. If they were given the same influence over society, it could lead — as it does in practice — to Catholics beginning to leave the Faith. Cases of mass apostasy start occurring, a departure from the true religion in favor of a false one. The Catholic State should help to ensure that children and young people, those who are most vulnerable to such influences and fads, are protected from the propaganda of non-Catholic religions. If the majority of the society is Catholic, then parents want their children to remain Catholic. They certainly don't wish their growing children to be bombarded by the media, in online forums and in public spaces by Islamic or cult propaganda, or encouraged to join other false religions. It's well known that children and adolescents are the groups most easily influenced by social engineering and mass propaganda. Permitting such freedom when it comes to promoting other religions is therefore undemocratic — I am now arguing from a civic point of view. In a democracy, after all, the wishes of the majority should be respected. And the wish of the majority of Catholic parents is that their children remain faithful to the Faith of their ancestors. But if the State grants other religious communities exactly the same opportunities for spreading their doctrines as it does to the Catholic Church, then Catholicism may be in danger.

I saw that firsthand in Latin America, when I lived in Brazil for seven years. Until a hundred years ago, the country was almost one hundred percent Catholic. Now, Catholics are slightly over fifty percent — depending on the source. This is largely a result of opening the country to Protestant sects, which were given exactly the same privileges and freedom to spread their teaching as the Catholic Church. Those sects quickly reached the provinces, won over the simple people, and developed an effective propaganda campaign using resources from abroad. I believe that the parliament of a predominantly Catholic country had the right to veto this situation and protect the Catholic majority. Yes, we tolerate followers of other religions, they are allowed to build places of worship and educate their children, and we will not interfere, but, since we are talking about a predominantly Catholic State, justice demands that we defend the social influence of the only true religion, which is that of the Catholic Church. The same applies to governments.

A minister cannot be simultaneously an atheist in the government and a Catholic in church on Sunday. The government can't be atheistic in such a Catholic-majority State. That would violate divine law.

Both man and society as a whole were created to glorify God. God's first commandment to man and to human society is to worship Him. Of course, we must give glory to the true God both individually and in community, for man is a social being. This means that people are obligated not only as individuals but also as a community to publicly give glory to the true God, the Triune God. It's also a command directed to State authorities and to governments. It's not about the government meddling in Church affairs, such as the question of celibacy, but the government does have a duty to give honor to God. There should be a crucifix hanging in the parliament. Catholic politicians should participate in Catholic ceremonies and manifest their allegiance to the Faith during feast days — for example, when there are Catholic processions. They must publicly manifest that they acknowledge God.

Only when that is the case can we say that tolerance for other religions is possible. Those religions, however, should be given neither equal opportunities for spreading their beliefs nor equal recognition in the public square. We must always observe a basic rule: based on natural law as well as the truths of revelation, we must remember that error can never have equal rights with truth. That would be an extreme injustice.

Your analysis closely echoes what Archbishop Marcel Lefebvre said in his dispute with the supporters of the declaration on religious freedom. Am I to understand that in your opinion it was the French archbishop who was right about religious freedom, rather than his critics and opponents in Rome? Did the post-conciliar popes make a mistake in this dispute about the significance of religious freedom?

Yes, that is precisely what I think. They have contributed in practice to the expansion of religious relativism through this ambiguous, vague teaching about the idea of religious freedom. This perspective reached its peak at the interreligious meetings in Assisi organized by John Paul II, where all religions were put on the same level — at least that's how it looked from the outside. The next step crossing over the line was the document signed by Pope Francis in Abu Dhabi in 2019, where it was said explicitly that God in His wisdom wills the existence of different religions. This is obviously the wrong path. It cannot be reconciled with divine revelation and two thousand years of Church Tradition. In the case of the new teaching on religious freedom it is difficult to appeal to the so-called "hermeneutic of continuity." In this, Archbishop Lefebvre was right.

It's often the case in history that people are not understood until some time after their death. Occasionally, a certain distance is needed. Now, almost fifty years after the discussion on the meaning of religious freedom in which Archbishop Lefebvre participated, we can see and understand more clearly the errors he identified. We can see the consequences brought about by an ambiguous understanding of religious freedom — first Assisi, now Abu Dhabi. From this perspective, we can clearly see how Archbishop Lefebvre's arguments were correct, and we can see his deep solicitude and accurate diagnosis of the dangers as early as in the 1960s and '70s. Increasingly we can recognize his invaluable contribution to the defense of the correct understanding of religious freedom according to the constant tradition of the Church. His was a truly prophetic voice. It happens that prophets are not recognized, as was the case here: the prophetic voice of Archbishop Lefebvre was simply ignored. In fact, no in-depth dispute with him was undertaken. I read an extensive biography of Archbishop Lefebvre — and in it you can see clearly that the Vatican didn't take his doctrinal objections seriously. In essence, he was told: "we are right and you must listen, and the teaching of the council on religious freedom constitutes an organic development of doctrine." However, this goes against what is obvious. You can say such things, but they have no foundation in reality. There is no organic development here. It is an attempt at squaring a circle or simply a response appealing to authority and power. We have power, you have to conform.

In this dispute, Archbishop Lefebvre invoked the teaching of preconciliar popes, starting with Gregory XVI in the early nineteenth century. In this way, he was pointing to a teaching that had been constant for almost two hundred years. He was told in the Vatican, in reply, that this was merely an opinion of those popes. But how can this be? How is it possible that from the end of the eighteenth century until mid-twentieth century, till the death of Pope Pius XII, so many popes were wrong? It would have been rather an exotic period in Church history. Well, yes, but what came before them? When did the break with the previous teaching happen? At what moment did this exotic element appear? Well, there is no such moment. It's impossible to point to another moment in history when a break similar to the one that happened on the issue of religious freedom during the Second Vatican Council would have occurred. At that moment, this break was evident. Hence the desire to square the circle — there was never such a break before. The popes referenced by Archbishop Lefebvre accepted exactly the same teaching as their predecessors. It is a continuous line. Ultimately, there is no difference in this matter between the teaching of the popes from the nineteenth century up to Pius XII and that of Gregory the Great at the beginning of the seventh century or the earlier teaching of the Church Fathers such as St. Augustine or St. Ambrose. Throughout this period, there was no break. Anyone who can read can see this. Therefore, the argument invoked by the Vatican — that Archbishop Lefebvre relied only on the teachings of a few nineteenth-century popes — is false and unacceptable also from a historical perspective. No. There is a strict continuity of teaching on the question of religious freedom, beginning with the Church Fathers of the third and fourth centuries after Christ and ending with Pius XII. We can speak here of a continuous development in the proper sense of the word. Yes, in this question Archbishop Lefebvre was right.

4

The Illusion of Progress

Are we really in a crisis, after all? Many observers could claim the opposite. Our lives are increasingly longer, safer, and more enjoyable than before. According to popular belief, man is merely a higher species of animal — more specifically, a higher species of mammal. It's an accidental evolution of species, and human death is not about anything metaphysical, but is just a technical issue that can be resolved in the future. History is a constant progress of mankind, and in a hundred years our lives will be even more comfortable and longer than today. So we are not in a crisis, and only those unable to welcome change would say so. What do you think about such an approach?

This is pure illusion. This account has nothing to do with the facts. Never before have we lived in such a tense situation and in an atmosphere of such great fear. A simple fact: look at airport security. We are being checked more and more thoroughly every year. If, in fact, people's lives are getting safer and more comfortable, why the constant airport checks? As recently as forty, fifty years ago you would go to an airport just like you would go to a train station. Now, after the terrorist attacks of 2001, there is an atmosphere of fear everywhere. These airport checks are almost morbid; they are becoming more and more thorough and intimate. Never in modern history has the civilian population been exposed to the danger of constant terrorist attacks to the same extent as we are today.

In the same way, we could point to the threat posed, for example, by illness, by pandemics — let's look at how the world is responding to the Covid-19 sanitary crisis. If our lives are increasingly better and safer, how can we account for such a gigantic wave of panic? The conviction that humanity is in a constant state of progress, that the future always means better and more comfortable lives, is pure illusion.

So you don't believe in constant progress?

This is not a question of faith, but of reality. It's enough to open your eyes wide. Is it comfortable when before our very eyes a mass murder of unborn children is happening? In clinics, millions of innocent lives are being slaughtered — yes, I am using this strong word intentionally. They are all being murdered in their mothers' wombs. Never before has humanity experienced anything like this on such a scale. Such mass murder cannot mean progress. I am convinced that a horrible punishment will strike people for allowing this. Whoever fails to see that is building castles in the air, creating a deception, and separating himself from reality.

But this optimism and conviction about the constant progress of humanity is also increasingly penetrating the Church. At the opening of Vatican II, Pope John XXIII was warning against the "prophets of doom," as he called them. On October 11, 1962, he said, "These people see only ruin and calamity in the present conditions of human society. They keep repeating that our times, if compared to past centuries, have been getting worse. And they act as if they have nothing to learn from history.... We must quite disagree with these prophets of doom who are always forecasting disaster, as if the end of the world were at hand. In the present course of human events, by which human society seems to be entering a new order of things, we should see instead the mysterious plans of Divine Providence, which, through the passage of time and the efforts of men, and often beyond their expectation, are achieving their purpose and wisely disposing of all things."[13] Could it be that right now you are playing the part of the prophet of doom? In the same year, 1962, the archbishop of Milan, later Pope Paul VI, talked about the upcoming springtime of the Church. This optimistic tone is found

---

[13] John XXIII, Opening Address to the Council (October 11, 1962), https://jakomonchak.files.wordpress.com/2012/10/john-xxiii-opening-speech.pdf.

in many passages of the Council documents. It is also clearly visible in the previously mentioned declaration *Dignitatis Humanae*. In its preamble, we read: "A sense of the dignity of the human person has been impressing itself more and more deeply on the consciousness of contemporary man, and the demand is increasingly made that men should act on their own judgment, enjoying and making use of a responsible freedom, not driven by coercion but motivated by a sense of duty" (*Dignitatis Humanae* 1). That is, we live in a wonderful era, in which more and more people are realizing their dignity and there is widespread recognition of responsible freedom. But this is probably a description of some other reality.

> This is a total illusion. Something simply incredible. I am unable to comprehend it. Later, however, Paul VI viewed the world somewhat more realistically.

Yes, later, in the '70s. The times of the Council, however, were times of constant enthusiasm and hope.

> I don't know how to explain it. I cannot understand at all how someone like John XXIII, a man of his age, a man who lived through two world wars, could be saying such things. It's puzzling. A true enigma.
> For me, the famous phrase of John XXIII — "prophets of doom" — is ambiguous. I don't really understand it. After all, all the true prophets in the Bible were, in that sense, "prophets of doom." They were constantly warning of impending punishment, condemning sin, and calling to repentance. On the other hand, those who prophesied progress, safety, and comfort are referred to as false prophets in the Bible. The only prophets of salvation were those who foretold the coming of the Savior of the world, Jesus Christ. They did not promise deliverance from God's punishment, nor did they foretell only earthly prosperity or peace. No, all of that could be found in the teachings of the false prophets. The true prophets were, in this sense, prophets of doom. Doom — which in this case signified the gravity of the situation. God was the first one to prophesy doom, immediately after the first sin, after the expulsion from Paradise. In all seriousness, He told Adam that he will die. Eve, He said, you will bring forth children in pain. For you are dust, and to dust you shall return — these are the words

that man heard. So, the phrase "prophet of doom" has something ambiguous about it.

Furthermore, all those optimistic descriptions of progress can result only from an inaccurate perception of reality. We must remember that our current modern era, which goes back to the French Revolution, began with genocide. It was in this modern era that the guillotine was invented. The first mass persecution of the Church also happened during the French Revolution, at the same time when human rights were being proclaimed. The great apostasy from the Faith started in the nineteenth century. It was the society at the time that turned its back on revelation and on the supernatural toward naturalism and rationalism. And later, the twentieth century came with the Bolshevik Revolution and mass crimes. This is our time, our era. John XXIII must have known about it, just as he must have known about the millions killed during World War I. And later, we have World War II with Hitler's dictatorship and Stalin's. The modern era is precisely the time of the great apostasy from Christ. Even in Christian countries, the unbelief and the departure from the Church's moral rules have become increasingly evident. Even if abortion was not legalized before the Council, in practice it was already widespread. Artificial contraception was also very common, first in Protestant, and later in Catholic countries. It was during the pontificate of John XXIII that the contraceptive pill was invented and popularized. At the time it was touted as a great accomplishment for mankind. The pope was able to read and learn about all of that. Also about the catastrophic impact of this invention on the family. The invention of hormonal contraception led to the outbreak of a Sexual Revolution, to a new era of sexual liberation, to unrestrained permissiveness. Clear signs of a sexual permissiveness in the Western countries were already evident at the time.

How then could John XXIII have said that the world reached such a high point in our times? In the light of God's revelation, by the beginning of the Council we had no moral progress but an enormous regression. The only progress has been in the area of technology: the development of medicine, the fact that it is possible to help people more effectively when they are ill, means of transportation, planes, cars, telephones, and the Internet. Yes, this is also progress, I agree, why not? Only it was progress in the physical and temporal dimension, but not spiritual progress. What's more, the progress of civilization led to a cultural regression, to the decline and fall of art. It led to the corruption of music, which was stripped of beauty, and instead, through the avant-garde, the promotion of ugliness started. There was progress in technology and medicine, but definitely not in culture.

We must conclude, then, that both John XXIII and the Second Vatican Council greatly misjudged reality. Man was increasingly gravitating toward the physical, the temporal, and the worldly. True progress, the progress of the soul that needs supernatural faith, was no longer discussed. It was eliminated and overlooked. This tendency toward highlighting the import of that which is physical, temporal, limited, worldly, and finite became apparent with the pontificate of Pope John XXIII, and has now reached its peak during the pontificate of Pope Francis.

Exactly. Pope Francis has called on all states and governments to sign a global pact that will lead to a "new humanism."[14] What could this be about? What kind of strange language is this? It has nothing to do with Tradition.

It has nothing to do with the Gospel. It sounds like an implementation of Freemasonry's agenda, which always supported so-called humanism. In their view, human reality has been reduced to this short, earthly existence. Similarly, the pact is discussed in such a way as if man lived only here, on earth. Heaven, eternity, God's revelation have been effectively mostly excluded. We are dealing with a betrayal of the Gospel. Supporting humanism is not the task of the pope or the Church. They should be saving souls. Their fundamental task is concern for eternity and preaching Christ to the world and all the nations. They should be doing it with the greatest possible zeal, even to the point of sacrificing their own lives. The stakes are enormous: it's a question of saving souls

---

[14] See Pope Francis, Message of His Holiness Pope Francis for the Launch of the Global Compact on Education, www.vatican.va/content/francesco/en/messages/pont-messages/2019/documents/papa-francesco_20190912_messaggio-patto-educativo.html.

from eternal damnation, from Hell. The battle is raging to help these souls to go to Heaven — that is the greatest blessing for humanity. This is the great task ahead of the pope and the Church: bringing souls to salvation through preaching the truth. Saving the body and involvement in earthly interests are tantamount to turning our backs on Christ and eternity. The body, after a few years in the grave, will turn to dust anyway. For me, this turn toward humanism at the expense of the supernatural constitutes a betrayal of Christ. This is not the true mission of the Church. Instead, we should strive for a pact of all people professing the one true, Catholic, apostolic faith. This is the real Church: a true community for those who have been redeemed by the precious Blood of Christ, who became children of God through Baptism and faith. This is the true unity between people. But basing the unity on natural foundations is a departure from our first task: evangelization.

Many people have fallen away from the Faith because they concluded that the ancient biblical accounts are incompatible with the findings of modern science. The almost-universal acceptance of Darwin's theory of evolution, which seems to contradict the biblical account of the creation of man, is particularly important from this point of view. In the case of the first man and woman, Adam and Eve, did God create their souls only, or did He create souls together with bodies, the whole human person? Did Adam and Eve really exist, or did multiple individuals of the human species exist from the very beginning, as some claim? Is the emergence of the human species a matter of chance, natural evolution, or perhaps an accidental genetic mutation, as claimed by Darwin's theory and its modern new versions? How can we explain to people today that creation is not a matter of chance, but the work of rational, wise Providence?

First of all, by appealing only to the light of natural reason, we can discover the existence of God as Creator. He must, therefore, be a personal being. Since He is infinite, which we can discover by natural reason, He must have infinite intellect. God, then, must be infinitely wise. So if we examine man and we can see that he is a being endowed with finite wisdom, we discover that the source of his creation and life must have been infinite intelligence. The wisdom of Providence amazes anyone who looks at man, who examines him down to the last cell and tissue. How can we talk about chance here? How can anyone assume that man's existence is accidental and at the same time recognize that all the functions of his body are designed with such precise, accurate purpose? On top of that, we have the knowledge coming from divine revelation contained in the Holy Scriptures and Tradition. God has said of Himself that He is the Creator, the personal Creator. He created all things visible and invisible. God directly created man, Adam and Eve, bringing forth Eve from the man. It's a fact revealed to us by God. We must believe in it and accept it if we have faith. God, as revelation shows, spoke to Adam and Eve, that is, He entered into a personal relationship with them: it's impossible to speak to a collective. God forbade them to eat from the tree of the knowledge of good and evil, and when they sinned and disobeyed, He held them accountable. We can see here a dialogue between individuals.

But perhaps this is just a poetic metaphor, tailored to the mentality of people who had no scientific understanding?

Except that the whole Tradition of the Church, Jesus Himself, and the apostles, including the apostle Paul, treated this account as a factual report. They considered Adam to be a real person, an actual person. The Fathers of the Church thought the same. This is the most compelling reason why this account should not be interpreted metaphorically. Let's take the text by St. Paul, who wrote:

> But death reigned from Adam unto Moses.... For if by the offense of one, many died; much more the grace of God, and the gift, by the grace of one man, Jesus Christ, hath abounded unto many.... For if by one man's offense death reigned through one; much more they who receive abundance of grace, and of the gift, and of justice, shall reign in life through one, Jesus Christ. Therefore, as by the offense of one, unto all men to condemnation; so also by the justice of one, unto all men to justification of life. For as by the disobedience of one man, many were made sinners; so also by the obedience of one, many shall be made just. (Rom. 5:14–15, 5:17–19)

We can see clearly here that St. Paul is talking not about a group of people, but about one man, Adam. We can say that the offense of one brought death on all, but not that the offense of all brought sin on all. That would be absurd. Sin entered the world through one man, not through mankind. Just as sin came through one man, so did salvation come through one Jesus Christ. This strict logical parallel between Adam, the first man, and Jesus Christ is so strong that it cannot be maintained without assuming that Adam was one, actual man. Just as Christ cannot be a metaphor referring to a collective, neither can Adam. One Adam, one Jesus Christ. The dogma of original sin also rests on the recognition that Adam was one, actual person. This is the only way to understand the transmission of original sin to all humanity.

We must also remember that the early Church Fathers starting in the late first century and the second century after Christ, including St. Ignatius of Antioch, St. Justin, and St. Irenaeus, clearly recognized Mary as the new Eve. Just as sin came through one woman, Eve, when she obeyed the serpent, the voice of the Evil Spirit, so the other, new Eve, Mary, obeyed the voice of the good Angel Gabriel. These early Fathers already say that just as Eve became the mother of all sinners, so Mary, the new Eve, became the mother of the new redeemed mankind. Tradition has shown from the very beginning that this biblical account cannot be taken metaphorically in the sense of denying the historicity of Adam and Eve. Such an interpretation amounts to heresy and a rejection of both the New Testament and the Tradition of the Church.

Can we still talk about a Christian Europe? It seems that the Church has definitively lost the battle for the soul of Western man. The churches are increasingly empty. Two years ago, the oldest diocese in Germany, the diocese of Trier, had to close 96 percent of its parishes. Out of nine hundred three parishes, thirty-five are left. A similar process of a mass exodus from the Church can be seen throughout Europe. When John Paul II visited Ireland in 1979, there were a thousand seminarians studying there; today there are around twenty. You could get the impression that a mysterious illness is developing in the Church. A certain correlation can also be identified: the faster the rate of the liberalization of the Church in a country, the more dramatic the collapse. Those national churches that had the greatest influence on the Second Vatican

Council — German, Dutch, Belgian, French — are in a state of complete decline. Are we facing the final stage of Christianity's existence in Europe?

I would not say that this is the end of Christianity in Europe. But we can certainly speak of a spiritual virus that has infiltrated the Church after the Council, despite the expectations and intentions of many of the Council Fathers, who wished for the exact opposite — the renewal and strengthening of the Church. Let me emphasize that the Council documents include many valid and important points. But they also include some statements that have opened the door to ambiguity and relativism. If all religions have an alleged natural right of being freely spread, why should I get involved? What should be the source of the spirit of zeal, sacrifice, and devotion? Why make sacrifices such as, for example, celibacy? Why seek to save souls? To evangelize? Opinions never before found in the Church started to spread, such as the idea that everyone goes to Heaven, or that Hell is not eternal. Priests who spread such beliefs were subsequently appointed bishops, even cardinals. We can certainly speak of a grave responsibility of the Holy See for appointing bishops and cardinals from among those whose preaching was ambiguous and for whom there was no guarantee that they would faithfully teach the constant Faith of the Church. Men of the middle, advocates of compromise, in short, relativists, started being promoted. It was these people who were opening the doors of the Church wider and wider to the deluge of relativism. There is no denying that it was the hierarchy from whom those destructive actions came. Let me reiterate, the responsibility for this lies with the Holy See.

I am convinced that future popes will have to repent for this. I believe that a future pope will make a public confession of sins in which he will say: "We, Rome, the Holy See, are accountable for the disastrous regress of many local churches, for the destruction of the true Catholic life of faith, of dogmas, liturgy, and morality among so many Catholic nations, because we promoted and tolerated heretical and worldly bishops and cardinals." One of the future popes will follow in the footsteps of Pope Adrian VI from the times of the reformation, who in 1522 for the first time in the history of the Church (until now it has been the only time) wrote a letter in which he publicly admitted that all evil, all wrongs had spilled out onto the Catholic world from one source: from Rome. We are the great sinners, we are to blame for the evil in the Church. Adrian gave the letter to his envoys, who read it at the Imperial Diet in Nuremberg in 1522. I think this was an honest and proper attitude. Such a thing will also be necessary in the future.

Going back to your question, we must say that the destruction of Christian Europe began with the outbreak of the French Revolution. Or, if we are looking for the actual historical roots, the beginning of the decline of Christian Europe came with the Protestant Revolution. I am not talking about the Protestant "Reformation," but about the Protestant *Revolt*. It was then that an internal division of Christianity occurred, and the Thirty Years' War showed the immense and terrible consequences of that division. One of them was the invasion of Europe by Muslim Turks. Through God's grace, thanks to the heroic Polish king John III Sobieski, this invasion was eventually successfully stopped at Vienna in 1683.

Then there was another revolution, that of Freemasonry, which succeeded in slowly eliminating the influence of the Church from the educational system and from public life. Throughout the nineteenth century, Freemasonry conducted a very deliberate campaign whose main goal was to expel Christianity from the public square. The next stage on the road leading to the eradication of Christianity in Europe was the Communist October Revolution in 1917. In one fell swoop, the Communists destroyed the Christian religion in Russia, the most pious European nation at the time — the Orthodox have always been much closer to Catholics than to Protestants in matters of faith. The Orthodox Church was crushed and almost destroyed, and instead of religion, official atheism was introduced. After World War II, almost half of Europe — the entire Eastern Bloc under the hegemony of the Soviet Union — became officially atheist. Simultaneously, the process of eradication of Christianity by liberal and Masonic forces continued in Western Europe. Christianity was gradually excluded from schools. The new school curricula negatively portrayed the Church and the history of Christianity. This negative image was also promoted on a large scale by the film industry, with particular emphasis on Hollywood productions that reached the entire West and shaped its consciousness. The films produced there deliberately eliminated Christian values while promoting sexual promiscuity, immorality, and adultery. Abortion was also advocated there; it was always depicted in such a way as to arouse compassion, understanding, and support, all through a suitably chosen script, appealing to feelings and emotions. It's worth noting that these successive waves of the moral revolution seem to have been carefully orchestrated by someone: suddenly a movie is released, which reaches all corners of the world at the same time, with the same message. It's as if someone had pressed the right button. At the end of the twentieth century and now in the twenty-first, we are witnessing an increasingly aggressive campaign to promote homosexuality in movies. The latest fad is elevating animals and showing man as an animal. In this way, gradually, Christianity is being eliminated from the life of Western societies. We could say that we have hit rock bottom. We are in a situation where Christianity is increasingly being attacked openly and directly. It is being ridiculed in advertising and mocked in public life. We have, in fact, become a minority. Basically, Christian Europe does not exist, as there is less and less Christian influence in social and political life.

In historical and political terms, it can be said that Christian Europe disappeared after the French Revolution — with the Habsburg Empire and the Orthodox Russian Empire as its only remnants in the nineteenth century. They both came to an end during World War I. I have no doubt that an important motive leading to the outbreak of that war was the desire of the enemies of the Church to topple these last vestiges of Christianity as a political and public force.

And so now we are dealing with a Europe in which Christians are a minority. More and more often, they are ferociously attacked and even persecuted. We still can't talk about martyrdom, but we are getting close to it. For the time being, we have defamation campaigns, suppressing the freedom of speech, obstructing free expression. There is discrimination. I'm afraid we are not far from a historical moment similar to the Roman Empire, where a defamation campaign was followed by physical persecution. We now find ourselves in a neo-pagan society.

In your book *Christus Vincit*, you talk about how after several centuries in Russia your family returned to Germany. In the book we can read about the deep devotion and faith of the whole family. But when you came to Germany with your parents as a boy, you had to face a completely different model of Catholicism — liberal, progressive, post-conciliar German Catholicism. When did you notice these changes? I am asking about your personal experience. Obviously, a young boy raised in the traditional faith, devoted to Catholicism shows up and suddenly he is thrown into a new world. When did you notice that this German Catholicism did not resemble the religion in which you were raised under the Soviets?

As I said, we arrived in West Germany in October of 1973, when I was twelve and a half years old. Before we left Estonia, which back then was part of the Soviet Union, Germany seemed like paradise on earth to us. When we came to Germany, I was twelve and a half years old, my brother was eighteen, and my sisters were sixteen and fifteen. To be honest, I'm a little embarrassed to share my first impression: we arrived at the train station, walked out onto the platforms, and walked up to the newsstand — and there, in the window right in front of our eyes, we saw magazine covers with pornographic photos. It was an absolute shock. We couldn't believe this. It seemed absurd and horrible to us. Here we are, arriving in paradise, the land of freedom, and its first sign is publicly displayed pornography. My older brother was not as religious, but even he was repulsed by it. My parents didn't know what to say, either. How is it possible, we asked ourselves, for shamelessly public displays of licentiousness to be the face of freedom? The second impression was my encounter with the fashion, with a much more casual dress code.

In terms of the Church, it was a real shock to me when I was first exposed to the distribution of Holy Communion in the hand. It shook my world.

So this practice was already present in Germany in the 1970s?

Certainly. As I learned later, it became common practice in the '60s, and it was introduced *de facto* immediately after the Council. In 1973 it was already ubiquitous in Germany. I couldn't get over it. I kept asking, how is it possible? I still haven't been able to understand it. How can this be? How can they receive God in all His holiness, in all His grandeur and majesty hidden in the Eucharist, as if they were eating fruitcake or a doughnut?

Was this your first experience of Mass in Germany? Just a parish Mass and a discovery of how Communion was being approached?

Yes, exactly, as soon as we arrived we went to Church for Mass and we suffered a shock. The most shocking thing was the way of receiving Communion. But not only that. Also the way in which the liturgy itself was celebrated was depressing to me. In Estonia, the priest would still celebrate Mass facing the tabernacle, and here instead of the altar there was a table, and the priest was facing the people. He was also dressed differently, in a way that was somewhat less festive, less majestic. I didn't attend Mass at that parish for long. Soon I was sent to a boarding school run by the Pallottine Fathers. The school was only for boys from Communist countries — those who came from Romania, Poland, the Soviet Union. It was there that I saw priests without habits or cassocks for the first time. That was another shock. They were dressed like regular lay people, they wore jackets, shirts with ties. I asked myself, could they really be priests? I was just a boy, but I could sense that something was not right. Why did priests dress and behave like lay people? I remember that I even asked one of them about it. He replied, "Hey, kid, you are not here to tell us how to dress." The youth Mass, with guitars and practically secular music, was a new experience. I remember, when I was thirteen and fourteen years old, it really bothered me. Now I can see that paradoxically, thanks to my background, to the years spent under Communist rule and to the experience of persecution there, I was immune to all this progressive ecclesial liberalism. Thanks be to God this immunity has stayed with me my whole life.

You have emphasized, in talking about your family, how devout they were. They went to Mass every week, and they prayed frequently and fervently. In Germany, such devotion must have been rare. When did you start asking yourself about the origin of this

tremendous difference between the Catholicism passed down to you by your parents and ancestors and the Catholicism you encountered after your return to the fatherland? German Catholicism was extremely progressive. It was the German theologians, Karl Rahner, Hans Küng, young Joseph Ratzinger, who contributed most to the development of the Church in that direction. The German Catholicism of the late 1960s and early 1970s owes its special characteristics to them, and it was definitely distinct from the Catholicism in which you were raised. When did you realize that? How did you explain this discrepancy to yourself?

Of course, when you are fifteen you don't delve into theological treatises. When I was thirteen I already knew that I wanted to be a priest. That is why I read a lot. I was very familiar with the old, classic traditional German catechism, and I read the lives of saints. As I said, this secularization of habits and liberal approach to the liturgy were repugnant to me. That is why I was suspicious of change. I found the arguments of those priests unconvincing. I started reading good Catholic literature. These were the books I could find in Germany in the 1970s by good Catholic priests against modernism and in defense of Tradition. At that time, I was not yet familiar with the writings of Archbishop Lefebvre, but I read other texts criticizing modernism. I recall a book with quotations from Council documents, thereby refuting the teachings of modernists and liberal theologians. These were often very pertinent quotations. Thanks to these writings, I was armed against those theologians you mentioned.

A little later, when I was sixteen, I also started reading the writings of Archbishop Lefebvre. I didn't look for them myself, a neighbor probably sent them to me. They made a great impression on me. I remember that I found myself in a difficult situation then: on the one hand, I saw that what Archbishop Lefebvre wrote was right; on the other hand, I said to myself that the Council was, after all, infallible. That is, the Council could not have been wrong; that was what infallibility was all about. This meant that Archbishop Lefebvre must either have misunderstood its teachings or overstated his criticism. I was faced with a dilemma. I began to read the entire texts of the Council in the light of Tradition, as we say today. Using contemporary language, I employed a hermeneutics of continuity. Today, I have to admit, I can see that it involved a lot of mental gymnastics. Occasionally, what I was trying to do seemed like an attempt at squaring the circle; I can see it clearly now when I think about how I tried to interpret the statements on religious freedom. I was doing everything I could to turn off my reason, to avoid drawing definitive conclusions from the ideas presented in the documents. That would entail being unfaithful to the Church, I told myself. It really was a huge dilemma for me. My studies were a huge help. I was fortunate to receive a good, traditional education grounded in the theology of St. Thomas Aquinas. Thanks to my studies, I could see clearly that Rahner and others like him were Gnostics who developed their own vision of Christianity, radically different from the deposit of the Tradition of the Church. I was never attracted to it or convinced by it.

Occasionally, you also visit Poland. Our country so far seems to be immune from the religious crisis or apostasy. Some politicians and intellectuals believe that Poland will be the place from which the spark of the renewal of faith will come. What do you think about Polish Catholicism? Is a true re-Christianization of the West possible?

I have a great respect for Polish Catholicism. I also admire the fact that the Poles, despite such a difficult history and all the adversities, persevered courageously and preserved their faith. They became a real example for the world to follow, when they defended their faith despite the oppression of communism. The Polish people remained faithful. Based on my own experiences, I can say that I have a particular respect for the simple believers who, as a rule, are more devout and zealous than the clergy and priests. I am frequently edified by this faithfulness, purity of faith, and clarity of thought. I'm talking about Polish Catholics who are simple, yet educated. I can see a movement of renewal among Polish Catholics — primarily the lay faithful, less so among the clergy. Unfortunately, the Polish clergy have become too politically correct. Naturally, I am painting with a broad brush here, I am pointing out a tendency that doesn't apply to every individual. Many Polish priests have conformed themselves too much to the prevailing fashions, to whatever comes from the West. Sometimes I get the impression that many Polish priests feel an inferiority complex toward the Western Church. That's why they want to adopt everything that prevails there, at all costs. That is evident in liturgical changes: receiving Communion standing up, altar girls, lay ministers of the Eucharist. Similarly, Polish seminaries have welcomed fashionable, liberal theologians from the West. In recent decades, Polish clergy have been infected with this way of thinking. It saddens me to conclude that many Polish priests have succumbed to this tendency and that they uncritically accept the changes from the liberal Church in the West. Fortunately, I know several theologians and bishops in Poland who can clearly see that the Western Church has followed the false path of liberalism, and they are trying to defend the Church in Poland from a similar trend. May there be as many of them as possible! Together with the laity, they are forming a new force and making faith increasingly important in society, as well as in public life and politics. After all, politics is a part of social life — Jesus must reign again in the parliament. It's my hope and dream that the Polish government can completely abolish the law allowing abortion. It would be a great sign for the whole world. I hope that by God's grace Poland will make such a move.

We have talked about the situation of the Church in Europe, Germany, and Poland. Symptoms of the disease can also be seen in South America. More and more of the so-called "free churches" are being established there — evangelical communities in Brazil, Argentina, Peru, Mexico, and other countries. You worked as a professor in Brazil for seven years, and you are intimately familiar with the situation there. Why are so many South Americans leaving the Catholic Church and looking for new communities? Why are these "free churches" gaining so much popularity? According to the latest surveys, only around 50 percent of Brazilians remain faithful to the Church. What are the reasons for this?

One of the main reasons is that since the Council, a spiritual void has developed due to the new liberal approach, which could be found also in Brazil and throughout Latin America. I talked earlier about relativism regarding the belief in the truth of the revealed religion and changes in the liturgy. In general, there has been a wide-ranging process of making religion more worldly. All this has created a void, a vacuum, a spiritual desert zone — and it is here that Protestant sects have appeared with their message. By nature, man desires certainty and clarity. Even if a truth is just ostensible, it must be clear, it must embody ideals. Otherwise, it cannot conquer hearts and minds. And Protestant communities provide clear answers, have a transparent structure, preach clear ideals, and demand a commitment. Moreover, it's not about earthly and temporal matters but about spiritual and religious concerns. Man has a thirst for the supernatural. It's not enough for him to be constantly preoccupied with the things of this world; he keeps searching for more. These free churches understand it very well and deliver religious teachings to these people. The pastors are enthusiastic, and they ignite in the believers a willingness to commit themselves to Christ. They inspire generosity, preach the Gospel, and organize services that appeal to the feelings and emotions of the locals. They fill the void left by Catholic priests who were engaging in temporal activities for the improvement of lives. I saw it with my own eyes in Brazil. This means that the greatest responsibility for the collapse of Catholicism and the proliferation of Protestant communities falls on Catholic priests and bishops. After the Council, all their attention was turned to temporal matters. If they had not abandoned the teaching of the Faith, if they had not departed from the supernatural, from the transmission of the sacraments, from the sacredness of the liturgy, if they had not sunk into what is worldly, the Protestant communities would not have gained such influence. Similarly, if the religious had been giving witness to the supernatural life, there would have been no large-scale exodus from the Church and no flourishing of the cults.

Let me give an example from my life. I was working in Brazil at the time, in the state of Goiás. It's located in the central part of the country. Although the State includes the capital, Brasilia, and several other large cities, such as Goiânia with over a million inhabitants, it's not very developed in terms of infrastructure and roads. At least this was the case several years ago. Our monastery took care of several communities there. One community was located about thirty miles from my monastery, in a deserted and run-down area. Priests would hardly ever show up there. The whole diocese in general had very few priests, and they visited this area perhaps a few times a year. In the middle of the village, there was a beautiful Catholic church. So at some point Protestant preachers showed up in the village and started living there with their families. They started preaching, and the locals would come more and more often and listen to them. At that point, the bishop asked us to take care of this community. We agreed, and from then on we visited the village every week. I was a deacon, and together with other brothers we went there every Sunday. We always went wearing our cassocks. Previously, the priests who would show up there were dressed in civilian clothes, like the Protestant ministers. When we were walking through the village for the first time, my confrère and I, people would open their windows in amazement, look out, and stare, as if something unusual had happened: two Catholic priests were walking through a Catholic village in their cassocks. Some were saying: "Oh, you are priests, how wonderful. *Padre*," and they were asking, "Now, will you keep coming to us?" "Yes," we responded, "we will come every Sunday." "That's so good," came their reply.

In this way, gradually, thanks to our weekly visits to this village, after a year, the one half who had previously left to join the Protestants and the free church returned to the true faith, to the Catholic Church. We started visiting the families systematically. They saw that we always wore cassocks. We organized processions, and we prayed the Rosary together. People enjoyed all this very much. It reminded them of their youth, of the seriousness of the Faith, of the truth. We also preached and taught the catechism to them. We taught religion classes to the children. You could say that we systematically re-Catholicized the village. There were still Protestants in the village, but only those who had resettled there — the original inhabitants returned to the Faith. So I think that if young priests started to preach the Gospel again, lived out the Faith, and catechized, then re-Catholicization would take place all over Latin America.

We need a new apologetics, preaching the Catholic truth in the true sense of the word, and a worthy liturgy. I have seen how strongly the traditional liturgy with Gregorian chant can attract people, how sensitive they are when they hear Latin. I visit Latin America all the time: we still can't talk about a full re-Catholicization there, but there are first signs of a revival, especially noticeable among young people. The fruits of this revival would be much more abundant if it were not for the majority of the bishops who are still following a liberal course. A kind of temporal, superficial Catholicism is still more important to them.

Speaking of worldliness and secularism, the Jesuit order was the stronghold of Roman Catholicism in Latin America for centuries. Jesuits were in charge of schools, education, and intellectual life, and they ran the universities. They gave support to the bishops and the secular clergy. But the triumph of the "preferential option for the poor" completely changed the order. The 1960s and 1970s were a real turning point in the life of this congregation, and Marxism soon became rampant at Jesuit seminaries. How was this possible?

This phenomenon is not unique to the Jesuits, although it's true that their contributions to the evangelization of Latin America were exceptional. In Brazil, for example, Franciscans and Dominicans also played a significant role. The fact remains that the Jesuits controlled practically the entire educational system, including universities.

Prior to the Second Vatican Council, Jesuit schools and universities educated the Catholic elite of most Latin American countries. Catholic theologians were highly respected. Let me mention here the outstanding figure of Fr. Leonel Edgard da Silveira Franca, who died just after World War II. He was a great writer, a theologian, a defender of the Faith, who presented it in a clear and solid way. I didn't know him, of course, because he died in 1948, long before I was born or came to Brazil, but I read his books and valued them tremendously. Marxism forced its way into the seminaries and the minds of the Jesuits through liberation theology. We must remember, however, that it appeared in South America, and Latin America broadly, as an imported product, which came from Germany and other European countries. Marxism is the product created by Karl Marx and Friedrich Engels mainly in Germany. According to this ideology, all that matters is the material, the temporal, the worldly. All the focus is on action, on change. Truth doesn't matter, what matters is practice, *praxis*. The taking over of the seminaries by Marxists was a real masterstroke. They said: The Church must be the Church of the poor. We are here for the poor. And where are the poor? So they pointed to those areas of poverty and deprivation that were so plentiful in Latin America and to the misery that could be found there. At the same time, we must remember that the Church really did a lot for the poor prior to the Council — that was the goal of extensive charities. *Caritas Internationalis* was incredibly active, numerous welfare institutions were being established, and charitable works were flourishing. The poor in Brazil were surrounded by great care, and they could count on assistance.

After the Council, the slogan of "the Church of the poor" was announced, but the poor were understood here exclusively in social and political terms. I would go as far as to say that in this way the poor became even poorer, because they were deprived of the greatest treasure, the greatest wealth previously available to them: eternal life, grace, supernaturalism, the Gospel of eternal life, the forgiveness of sins, life with God. The new progressive theologians and bishops have outright robbed the faithful of these gifts. I witnessed this myself in Latin America at the time. Let me give you one example.

I came to the Diocese of Anápolis in early 1984. In Goiás, it was the heyday of liberation theology. The bishop who ordained me as a priest and was my teacher, Manuel Pestana — whom I consider a truly holy man (alas, he is no longer with us) — asked our entire community of canons regular for help. He told us that when he was ordained bishop in 1979, his whole diocese was, in a spiritual sense, nothing but a ruin. It had been destroyed by liberation theologians and by priests interested mainly in politics and social issues. They represented a Marxist approach; they preached a completely new secular gospel of materialism, which was all about deliverance from material poverty. They were only concerned with the question of liberation from social structures. All their attention was focused on sociology. These priests, for example, erased auricular sacramental Confession in the diocese. They claimed that the poor didn't need any Confession or Penance because they were being oppressed by the rich in any case. If anyone were to go to Confession anymore, it should only be the rich. They taught that, as a rule, man doesn't need the sacrament of Confession, for he can liberate himself through his actions, through becoming active. If he did something good and served the cause of liberation, this would already cleanse him of his sins. So for years, only general Confession was available in the whole diocese; priests no longer offered auricular Confession. In the same way, the adoration of the solemnly exposed Blessed Sacrament was suppressed in the diocese, seminaries were dissolved, and all religious life was focused on the temporal. Everything sacred and supernatural was eliminated. Priests didn't wear cassocks, they only dealt with sociological problems and trade unions. I saw it all with my own eyes when I arrived there.

Then Bishop Manuel Pestana came and saw this devastation. The first thing he did was to restore auricular Confession. The vicar general gave him the greatest resistance at that time. When the bishop told him to go to the cathedral to hear confessions, he replied that it was not for him. "It's not for me," said this priest. To which the bishop replied, "As of today, you are no longer the vicar general." The next step was establishing a completely new seminary and inviting orthodox priests to work with him. That is why the bishops turned to our congregation of canons regular, entrusting us with the formation of new seminarians. I was in the first group that our congregation sent to help. Along with my confrères who were already priests, we came to offer assistance. They became professors at the seminary, and the bishop also taught there. During the seven years, I watched as the diocese was being revitalized and continued to regain its Catholic identity. The seminarians, educated by the bishop himself, had the Catholic spirit in them. After six years of studies, they became priests and wore cassocks, or at least clerics. In their sermons, they preached again about the supernatural, organized prayer services, arranged solemn expositions of the Blessed Sacrament, led community Rosary and Eucharistic processions. Confessions returned to the cathedral.

The bishop even introduced all-day Confession: from early morning until late in the evening, there were always priests hearing confessions in the cathedral. When I became a priest, I myself heard confessions there, and I also worked for the Diocese of Anápolis. Every day, all day, from morning until evening, there were lines of penitents. It was a big city, about three hundred thousand people, but I saw the faces of those people when the priests returned to them. They were happy, they longed so much to be allowed to go to Confession. How long were these people being robbed? How long did the liberation theologians and earlier bishops take away what was most important to them? To my mind, what they did to these simple people was a spiritual crime, perpetrated by liberation theologians. After all, they were deprived of all those graces that Christ obtained for them on the Cross through His suffering. This was all the result of the intrusion of Marxism into the Church through liberation theology. The basic trick was to consider as the poor only those who were poor in the material sense. Hence the distortion in the slogan "the Church of the poor." However, it's those who don't have the grace and life of God who remain the true poor, indeed, the destitute.

But how exactly did the penetration of Marxism into the seminaries happen? For a Pole, this is still difficult to comprehend. In Poland, Marxism was literally synonymous with an anti-religious, anti-Catholic ideology. How is it possible, then, that so many priests were deceived by it? That so many priests found Marxism and liberation theology credible? Do you think that this was the result of infiltration? Can we talk about a covert operation, an attempt, planned by the Communists, to take over the government of souls?

I don't think that this development can be attributed solely to a conscious, intentional, external infiltration. Rather, it originated from a false theology of relativism and the tendency toward temporality. With the Second Vatican Council, the Church gave more attention to the earthly, the temporal, the transient. The zeal for the supernatural, eternal perspective was diminished. A new Pelagianism developed, which claimed that man is saved by his natural faculties. In this sense, it was implicit materialism.

We had a neighboring diocese, formally a prelature, in which liberation theology completely prevailed. It was ruled by the famous Bishop Pedro Casaldáliga Plá, who was the prelate of São Félix. He was a Spaniard and a member of the Claretian congregation, so formally a son of St. Anthony Maria Claret, the great apostle of Catalonia. Well, Bishop Casaldáliga was a real Communist. His sermons were exclusively about social injustice and wages. They were effectively rallies against the rich. He believed that the mere fact of being poor was sufficient for salvation. He preached a Jesus who had nothing in common with the one presented in the Gospels. Once, some time in the late 1980s, Fidel Castro came to São Paulo. When the bishop heard about it, he got on a plane and flew almost nine hundred miles to meet Castro. At that time, Communists used to wear sweatshirts with five-pointed stars and an inscription reading that communism was liberation. As soon as he arrived, the bishop immediately put on that sweatshirt. It caused a huge uproar. He said then that he felt better in this sweatshirt than in a chasuble. There was no serious reaction from the Vatican. But this bishop should have been removed from office immediately. No such thing happened. The whole time he was being tolerated and ruled the prelature, unfortunately also during the pontificate of John Paul II. All despite the fact that his Marxist views were common knowledge and that he systematically destroyed religious life in his prelature. There were many like him. Another diocese near us was headed by a Dominican bishop only slightly less radical. These were the two most extreme neighbors of our Bishop Manuel Pestana. After twenty-five years of his rule, the diocese returned to its former catholicity. Beautiful, traditional churches were being built. I witnessed with my own eyes the increase of faith and piety. In the churches, high altars were re-erected and tabernacles were placed in the center, and altar rails and kneelers were brought back. Numerous vocations also sprang up. This shows how much one good bishop can accomplish.

The enemies of the Church know this and understand perfectly well how important controlling episcopal appointments is. From a strategic point of view, the policy of appointing bishops is crucial. Unfortunately, the Vatican has often pursued a policy of compromise. A liberal bishop on the one hand and a conservative on the other. My bishop Manuel Pestana was accused of being too traditional all the time, to which he replied that he was not doing anything other than what the Church demanded.

5

Protestant Sources

I would like to talk about Martin Luther. Klaus Berger, a prominent German theologian, talked about the ecumenical myth, which has actually turned into a delusion, a mirage of sorts. "The more the faithful leave the Church, the louder the talk of the successes of ecumenism. The more the Church conforms to the world, the more often unity is mentioned. The myth of ecumenism generates a phenomenon of mass intoxication."[15] Isn't this intoxication exemplified by the new attitude of the pope and many members of the hierarchy toward Martin Luther? More and more, he is being portrayed as a model of true faith. It's been said that Martin Luther is a "father of the Church." Some claim that he is the "new Francis of Assisi." Others claim that he is an authentic "witness to the Gospel." All this combined does give the impression of some kind of mass intoxication, a separation from reality. What do you think about these statements?

> In short, it's a betrayal. It's a betrayal of our Catholic beliefs. These opinions create a new myth that has nothing to do with the facts. It's a fairy tale about Luther. The Luther that Pope Francis says was a model of faith didn't exist. He was in no way a model of the Faith. How can we take as a model the man who first took solemn vows and then broke them? How can we call a model the man who was ordained a priest and then abandoned the priesthood? Not only did Luther do this, but he was proud of it. He would say, I am proud that I broke my religious vows.

[15] See Georg May, *300 Jahre Gläubige & Ungläubige Theologie* (Stuttgart: Salto Verlag, 2017), 934.

How can you be proud of having made a vow to God and not having kept it? This can't be good in any way. There are no circumstances that could justify such conduct. Not only did Luther break his word, break his vows, but he urged and encouraged others to do the same. Luther was also notorious for his hate-filled speeches against the pope, the successor of St. Peter. He attacked popes in his writings and sermons, in every possible way. There is no doubt about it. He preached that the pope is Antichrist and that he would have been glad if the pope had been hanged and killed. Saying that he was a model of faith sounds like a joke. I don't understand it, I can't fathom it, it just seems absurd to me. How could Luther be extolled in this way, when we know that he would say that the Mass was invented by the devil? So in his view, the sacramental sacrifice of Christ, the heart of our Faith, was from the devil. The belief that the Mass is the heart of the Faith is not just part of the Catholic tradition, the Orthodox also believe this. From the beginning, the Church saw the Mass as a sacramental sacrifice. How, then, could you claim that it's the devil's invention? This is a blatant ridicule and mockery of our Faith.

Luther was also one of the greatest anti-Semites in all of history. For strategic reasons it's never mentioned today. But it's enough to consult the critical edition of Luther's writings, the so-called Weimar edition, to find enough evidence to support this claim. After all, toward the end of his life, Luther encouraged his supporters to burn synagogues! He used truly horrifying names for the Jews. And this is supposed to be a "model of faith" for us? Both Hitler and his anti-Semitic propagandists appealed to Luther, reprinted his writings, and referred to them. A concrete example of such an inspiration are the events of *Kristallnacht*, which took place on November 9 and 10 of 1938. It was then that mass arson attacks on synagogues took place. Let me quote here the words of the Evangelical Lutheran Bishop Martin Sasse of Eisenach:

> On November 10, 1938, Luther's birthday, synagogues are burning in Germany. The German people have finally broken the economic grip of the Jews in the new Germany, thus honoring the Führer's struggle, blessed by God, "for the complete liberation of our people." At this very hour we must listen to

the voice of the man who, as a German prophet of the sixteenth century, started out as a friend of the Jews, and who, guided by conscience, guided by experience and realism, became the greatest anti-Semite of his time, a living warning to his people against the Jews.[16]

Many such examples could be found.

Martin Luther holds responsibility for the great schism in Christianity. We must also remember that the religious division was followed by religious wars. Had it not been for Luther's speech, which led to a breakdown of unity and to sudden divisions, the religious wars, which were a real disaster for the West, would not have occurred. Christianity would have stayed united. All those dramatic ruptures, family breakdowns, feuds, and dissensions would not have occurred. He bears responsibility for all that as well. How, then, can we speak of a model?

Further, if someone rejects the priesthood, denies the hierarchical and sacramental structure of the Church that Christ gave us, and rejects the sacraments, except for the two he kept according to his understanding, how can he be a witness to the Faith, or a Father of the Church? Of course, we can also find good and wise statements in his writings. Even a broken clock is right twice a day. But we must look at the man holistically and see his influence, his legacy, what he has left behind. Beautiful statements can be found in Luther's commentaries on the Magnificat when he writes about Mary, the Mother of God. But on the other hand, he rejected the veneration of the Mother of God. He picked and chose aspects of the Faith. He didn't accept it in the Catholic way, he did not venerate the Mother of God as it should be done.

Pope Francis has said that Martin Luther was not mistaken regarding the doctrine of justification.[17] How can we assume that Martin Luther was right and that his teaching on

---

[16] M. Sasse, *Martin Luther über die Juden: Weg mit ihnen!* (Freiburg: Sturmhut Verlag, 1938), 2, quoted by A. Paprzyca, *Noc kryształowa*, in *Deutsche Welle* (November 9, 2010), www.dw.com/pl/noc-kryształowa/a-6209233.

[17] Pope Francis, In-flight Press Conference of His Holiness Pope Francis from Armenia to Rome (June 26, 2016), www.vatican.va/content/francesco/en/

justification is correct, if the result of that teaching was a rejection of the Magisterium of the Church? According to a German theologian Paul Hacker, who is one of the leading experts on Luther's thought, as early as 1518 Luther believed that faith was not an obedient acceptance of revelation, based on the authority of the Church, but rather a manufacturing of certainty, a creation of a feeling of consolation. "A man is justified in the eyes of God if a man believes that he is justified." This is completely incompatible with the Catholic understanding of faith, which rejects all absolute certainty.

> In Luther's thought we find subjectivism: ultimately I determine the truth on the basis of my inner disposition. It is I who acknowledge and decide what is true and what divine revelation is. But the Catholic understanding is completely different: revelation is not given to each of us directly, but through the apostles and handed down by the Church. The guarantee of the truth of revelation is the teaching office of the Church. Luther wanted to set it aside and interpret God's revelation himself. Such an approach must mean that everyone receives revelation from God as his own. Luther said that he received the Gospel directly from Heaven.[18] In another place Luther said that not even the earthly personality of Jesus or His miracles were the ultimate basis of faith in the word of the Bible, but the word taken *in itself* should be sufficient for the heart and make a person feel and understand the truth of this word — even if the whole world and even if God Himself would say something different.[19] The influence of gnosis is clearly evident here. Everyone experiences the spirit, God, in his own inner self. There is no need for intermediaries, apostles, and ultimately, no need for the Church. You are your own teacher. It's a completely non-Catholic attitude, which is also contrary to the words of the Lord Jesus Himself, who said to His apostles: "He that heareth you, heareth me" (Luke 10:16).
>
> So this is an example of extreme subjectivism in matters of religion. The most important thing is that I feel comforted, that I feel liberated. Faith is determined by imagination, fantasy, the strength with which

---

speeches/2016/june/documents/papa-francesco_20160626_armenia-con-ferenza-stampa.html.

[18] See *Weimar Ausgabe* [*WA*], 5, 324.

[19] See *WA* 10, I, 1, 130, 14.

I am able to impose this imagination on myself. But this is a vicious circle. It's subjectivism that rejects the objectivity of God's revelation, accepting only certain parts of it that suit a given "I." A Catholic, on the other hand, must accept the whole of revelation and must obey the mediator, Jesus Christ, and His Church, which is nothing but the living Christ, His mystical Body. This is Luther's fundamental error — this private, personal, subjective understanding of faith. Although Luther defended himself against this accusation, and claimed that the Gospel and the Word of God should be the measure, still, he always ended up contradicting himself. For how can you interpret this word if you reject Tradition through the mediation of the Church? All that is left is the subjective "I." After all, there are always different possible interpretations and explanations of the Gospel. So who is to decide which is the right one? Based on what principle? Calvin believed one thing, Zwingli believed another. Each interpreted the Gospel in his own way. You can clearly see the contradiction here.

Luther simply refused to accept that God saves and justifies and cleanses us from sin through a visible mediation — through visible means of mediation, through visible and sacred rites, the sacraments. That is why the Incarnation, through which God became visible and tangible, is so crucial and fundamental. This Incarnation continues in a way through the Church, which is the Mystical Body of Christ. The forgiveness and remission of sins that Jesus brought are still available to us through the Church's sacraments.

After fifteen centuries, Luther was the first to adopt again the principle of gnosis: I am justified by my own interior attitude, by faith alone (*"sola fide"*), without an external, visible mediator of the Church's sacraments. This is ultimately gnosis. When we examine his understanding of justification, Luther turns out to be more Gnostic than Christian. Pope Francis is therefore wrong to regard Luther's doctrine of justification as correct. We can find correct statements in Luther, when he says that God offers us forgiveness regardless of our past merits — Scripture and St. Paul say the same. But Scripture also says that faith without works is dead (see James 2:14–26). And Luther rejected that, which is also why he dubbed the Epistle of St. James "an epistle of straw." This is a sin against the Word of God, for the Epistle of James is the Word of God and it's inspired by the Holy Spirit. You can see how subjectivism must have led Luther to selectivism, to private choice. Luther began to decide what is and what is not part of God's revelation, and yet the entire New Testament is part of God's revelation. Divine revelation is contained not only in the text of the Holy Scripture, but also in the oral teachings of the apostles, in Sacred Tradition. By rejecting the Epistle of St. James, Luther committed a sin against revelation. He revealed that he picks from revelation whatever suits his personal convictions. He picks what he likes, and what he doesn't like he rejects. This is typical sectarian behavior. So Luther was more like a Gnostic and a sectarian. He was, strictly speaking, a heretic, because the Greek word *hairesis* means choice, selection.

Going back to these different commendations of Luther, I agree that some good qualities can be found in every person. Yes, even a mafioso can have something good in him; for example, concern for his family, his wife, or his children. He may be faithful to his wife. He can also be kind to the poor. But am I allowed to say, then, that this mafioso is supposed to be a role model? Despite the fact that he steals, corrupts, and kills? It's impossible. The fact that something positive can be found in a person doesn't mean that he can be presented as a role model in everything — especially if he is to be a model of faith.

I would like to mention one more thing. Years later, long after he broke away from the Church and when he was leading a Protestant community that he founded, Luther preached a revealing sermon. It was about twenty years after his rebellion, and a new generation, unfamiliar with life in the Church, had already been born. At that time, he said, "We evangelicals have now become worse than when we were under the pope." These are his own words. Luther himself gave the best account of the fruits of the Reformation. He went on to say, "We have cast out one demon — meaning the Catholic faith, the papacy — and seven other, more evil demons came to us."[20] That is Luther's own sermon. Also, in a letter to his close friend and advisor Philip Melanchthon he wrote that when he was still a Catholic monk he was a much better

---

[20] *WA* 28, 763.

man. He wrote that he prayed much more and that he lived a much
deeper spiritual life than afterward.[21] How, then, can we present him
as a father, a teacher in faith? How can we speak of his statement as
progress? It was no progress, but, on the contrary, a regression.

According to Pope Francis, proselytizing among Christians, in any form, is a mortal
sin.[22] This also applies to Protestants. Does it mean that the great teachers of the Church,
such as Peter Canisius, Piotr Skarga, and Robert Bellarmine, who converted Protestants
to Catholicism, actually sinned? Isn't a refusal to convert Protestants an indication of a
lack of love for them? If the fullness of truth resides in the Catholic Church, why would
Catholics not share that truth?

Precisely, that's exactly the case. We must first begin by defining exactly
what proselytism is. It's not honest or fitting to use the term without
defining it. We must be very careful what we want to convey, how we
use words, what meaning we attach to particular concepts. In today's
terms, proselytism means a situation in which people are persuaded by
dishonest means to adopt the religion of the persuader. In exchange for
accepting the religion, they are offered various benefits, money or other
material incentives. The goal is to entice and deceive them. This is how
sects work. Alternately, attempts are made to force others to adopt one's
religion. Pressure and coercion are employed. This is what proselytism
involves. The apostles never acted in such a way. Neither did any of the
great missionaries of the Church. None of them attempted bribing or
offering material gains to solicit conversions. This doesn't add up. The
Church has never done anything like this. The charge that Catholics
have been conducting missions in this way is false.

If, on the other hand, proselytizing means preaching the Catholic
faith to non-Catholics with zeal and conviction, then we would have to
conclude that the apostles were also wrong. If by proselytizing, then,

---

[21] See *Briefe, Sendschreiben und Bedenken,* ed. De Wette, 2, 22.

[22] See Pope Francis and Stefania Falasca, "L'intervista ad Avvenire. Papa Francesco: non svendo la dottrina, seguo il Concilio," in *Avvenire* (November 17,
2016), www.avvenire.it/papa/pagine/giubileo-ecumenismo-concilio-intervista
-esclusiva-del-papa-ad-avvenire.

we were to understand someone's willingness to preach the truth — as Christ commanded us to do when he said, "Going therefore, teach ye all nations; baptizing them in the name of the Father, and of the Son, and of the Holy Ghost. Teaching them to observe all things whatsoever I have commanded you" (Matt. 28:19–20), and as all the apostles and great saints and great missionaries did — it would follow that they all committed the crime of proselytism. So the question arises: what do those who use this term today mean by it? Do they mean to condemn proselytism in the first sense or in the second? Is preaching, announcing, and proclaiming the truth to non-Christians, non-Catholics, proselytism in itself? Is it proselytism to believe that you are right? Does the Faith proclaimed with this conviction, even with respect for the freedom of others, become a form of proselytism? As a rule, the Church has always acted this way. There have been exceptions, but the principle has been just that. If it turned out that we were denied the right to proclaim the Faith and to convert — let me repeat, while respecting the freedom of others — I would have to protest against it. That is not proselytism. Could the pope say that the zealous preaching of the Faith to non-Catholics is wrong? I would question this. It's really impossible.

In your opinion, can we invite non-Catholics to receive Holy Communion? Cardinal Walter Kasper calls it a sign of hope. The German bishops are also inviting Protestants to receive the Eucharist. How can this be accepted? After all, Protestants don't believe in the Real Presence of Christ in the Eucharist, and they also have a completely different understanding of the sacrament than Catholics. What do you think about this behavior of the German bishops?

It's a big gimmick, a big scam. It's simply fraudulent. At the same time, it's a betrayal of the Faith. It's a double deception. Man is deceiving himself and others. A great betrayal of the Faith is taking place here. Those bishops who invite Protestants to partake in Holy Communion must not have the true faith, the Faith that the Church has always professed in teaching about the sanctity of the Eucharist. Nor do they understand what the Church is. For them, the Church is merely a certain social community. Truth is no longer the criterion for belonging to the Church, as our faith teaches. They can no longer distinguish between truth and erroneous teaching, between orthodoxy and heresy. As a result, neither can they distinguish between the life of sin and the life of sanctifying grace. In their eyes, the Eucharist is no longer the true presence of the Lord, there is no actual transubstantiation of bread into the Body of Christ. In the end, they view the Eucharist as a symbol. In this way, the Eucharist is being degraded, reduced to the level of an ordinary meal to which you invite friends, acquaintances, or other guests, just as you invite guests and friends to dinner at home. I may want to form a friendship over dinner. Such an invitation of Protestants to receive the Eucharist is a way of degrading it. The Most Holy Eucharist, the precious Body and Blood of Christ, that which is most sacred in the Church, is relegated to the level of a common symbol, an ordinary dinner. I am using stark, vivid comparisons, but ultimately that's how it is.

For me, this is a defection from the true Faith of the Church, from what the Church is, what the Eucharist is, and, finally, from the truth. As I said, the criterion of truth is no longer relevant. So again we are faced with relativism. Again we are faced with disobedience to the words of Jesus and the apostles, disobedience to the constant, let me emphasize, *constant* Tradition of the Church. Jesus said:

> But if thy brother shall offend against thee, go, and rebuke him between thee and him alone. If he shall hear thee, thou shalt gain thy brother. And if he will not hear thee, take with thee one or two more: that in the mouth of two or three witnesses every word may stand. And if he will not hear them: tell the church. And if he will not hear the church, let him be to thee as the heathen and publican. (Matt. 18:15–17)

Jesus is clearly saying here that if the brother doesn't listen to you, or you and your witnesses, you are to appeal to the Church, and the Church must rebuke such a person. And if he doesn't listen to the Church, "let him be to thee as the heathen." Such a man must be excluded from the Church's communion. These are clearly the words of Jesus, the words of God. We must not put ourselves above God, we must not give ourselves power over God.

The Church has preserved this teaching, and St. Paul, whose words are inspired by the Holy Spirit, also teaches it. He writes:

> Therefore whosoever shall eat this bread, or drink the chalice of the Lord unworthily, shall be guilty of the body and of the blood of the Lord. But let a man prove himself: and so let him eat of that bread, and drink of the chalice. For he that eateth and drinketh unworthily, eateth and drinketh judgment to himself, not discerning the body of the Lord. (1 Cor. 11:27–29)

The apostle clearly indicates that whoever partakes of the Eucharist unworthily passes judgment on himself. If he is not worthy, it would be better for him not to receive Communion. So bishops who invite Protestants or divorced people living in new relationships to receive Communion, these bishops are doing great harm to them. They are exposing and subjecting these people to God's judgment. This is cruel. They will certainly be held accountable before God's tribunal, since by acting in this way they are actually denying the true meaning and the holiness of the Eucharist. They are acting against the entire Tradition of the Church, which has unequivocally stated that whoever professes false doctrine, whoever stubbornly insists on it and doesn't convert, must be excluded from the communion of the Church.

If the bishops in question could hear these words, they would probably reply by saying that you are a rigid, dogmatic fundamentalist. That you lack sensitivity and empathy, but instead are guided by strict doctrine that has been replaced. They claim that the words of Scripture can't be taken literally, or else it's fundamentalism. Human awareness changes over time. We are currently living in a different cultural context, and that's why we should not take literally the words of St. Paul or any teaching of the New Testament.

Such an opinion contradicts the facts. The two-thousand-year-old Tradition of the Church stands against such a position. First, the apostles received the word and teachings from Jesus Himself, and then they passed it on to their disciples, faithfully and exactly as they had received it. The Word of God was transmitted uninterruptedly from generation to generation, through bishops, popes, saints, and Doctors of the Church. This transmission of the Word has also been accompanied by practice. If, therefore, the whole Church has understood the same doctrine in the same way for two thousand years and has continuously passed it on, it could not have been wrong all the time. The Church could not have been wrong all along in her interpretation. It's the people of today, those who say that we have a new awareness, who must be wrong. They mistake their new awareness for Church teaching. In fact, it's not new awareness, but gnosis. It's a new Gnostic Christianity that doesn't come from Christ's Church. These are their own ideas, radically different from the teaching of the apostles and the Faith of the whole Church for twenty centuries. Continuity and immutability — these are the criteria. The absolutely indisputable criteria for the validity of the Faith are the constant, continuous, immutable, same interpretation and actions of the Church over two thousand years. For Jesus said, "And behold I am with you all days, even to the consummation of the world" (Matt. 28:20). Similarly, in the Gospel of John, he explained, "But when he, the Spirit of truth, is come, he will teach you all truth. For he shall not speak of himself; but what things soever he shall hear, he shall speak; and the things that are to come, he shall shew you" (16:13). Thanks to the Holy Spirit, the Tradition of the Church is preserved and transmitted in an infallible way. The Spirit "shall not speak of himself; but what things soever he shall hear, he shall speak." We can see here the complete unity of the Word of God, the word revealed by Jesus and the word preached by the Church. Thanks to the Spirit, the Church is able to go deeper and explain better the same words of Christ. Thanks to the Spirit, the Church preserves this immutable meaning and is able to pass it on.

Perhaps never before have so many Catholics differed so much in their assessment of a single pontificate as they do now. There are authors, writers, and columnists who see Francis as a true prophet. I am thinking for example of Austen Ivereigh, Andrea Tornielli, or Andreas Englisch. They believe the Church must be more modern and that the current pontificate and the teachings of the pope are the correct response to what is new, to the modern world. They believe it's Pope Francis who accurately reads the signs of the Holy Spirit, and therefore he represents a truly open and modern Catholicism.

Many commentators see it very differently. In recent years, several very critical books have been published about Francis's time in office. I am talking about books such as *The Dictator Pope* by Marcantonio Colonna, *Lost Shepherd* by Philip Lawler, and *The Political Pope* by George Neumayr. Highly critical texts, articles, and books have also been written by such well-known authors as Antonio Socci, Sandro Magister, Roberto de Mattei, and Enrico Maria Radaelli. What do you think about this dispute? How do you assess the current pontificate?

> Well, the authors you mentioned at the beginning, those who see Francis as a prophet, would clearly want a different, new Christianity, different from the one Jesus brought, the one handed down by the apostles. They would like a Christianity in which truth is relative and in which relativism reigns. They would like a Church that has perfectly adapted herself to the world, has rejected God's revelation, and is creating truth for herself as she pleases. That's why they would like the highest offices in the Church to be held by people who will carry out such an agenda of adapting to the world. This is a Christianity that will allow sin, won't care about truth, won't defend it, and won't speak out against error or falsehood. Such an approach can receive approval and be supported by these authors. If it seems to them that this is how Church representatives are acting, they call them "prophets," and in their actions they recognize signs of the work of the "Holy Spirit." They are prophets of a fake church of this world, prophets of temporality, of what is worldly. And even if they are writing about the Catholic Church, they are talking about a different Church, not the one Jesus established and about which He taught.
>
> It's not enough to say that something is "Catholic." Something is Catholic only if it is in fact Catholic. The best definition of what is Catholic was given by St. Vincent of Lérins. In his famous *Commonitory* (2, 6), he assumes with absolute certainty that
>
>> in the Catholic Church itself, all possible care must be taken that we hold that faith which has been believed everywhere, always, by all. For that is truly and in the strictest sense Catholic.... This rule we shall observe if we follow universality, antiquity, consent. We shall follow universality if we confess that

one faith to be true, which the whole Church throughout the world confesses; antiquity, if we in no wise depart from those interpretations which it is manifest were notoriously held by our holy ancestors and fathers; consent, in like manner, if in antiquity itself we adhere to the consentient definitions and determinations of all, or at the least of almost all priests and doctors.[23]

Let me repeat: what is Catholic is that which has always, for two thousand years, been believed, that which has always been interpreted in the same way and with the same meaning, that which has always been understood the same way and has been taken as a guide to act the same way. And it has been that way everywhere, for all the teachers of the Church.

If we abandon this belief, our approach is no longer Catholic. Then the above-mentioned authors would have to speak of "Pope Francis's Catholicism." It would no longer be Roman Catholicism, but Pope Francis's Catholicism. A new Catholicism, not the apostolic Catholicism of all the centuries. Or perhaps some modernized, modified version of today's Catholicism. In fact, many journalists apparently understand it this way. I myself have read articles explicitly talking about "the Church of Francis." It is fundamentally false. There is only one Church, the Church of Jesus Christ. When we say "the Catholic Church" and "the Apostolic Church," our language is based on the creed. These authors have a completely secular, worldly, political understanding of the Faith and the Church. They are writing as if the Church were the personal property of Pope Francis. But the pope can't do as he pleases with the Church. He can't change this constant, immutable understanding, which is expressed in the sacraments, in celibacy, in doctrine, in the proven practice of the Church. It's not enough to invoke the expectations of our contemporaries or cultural and social needs and developments of one kind or another. If this were done, it would be a clear

---

[23] The English translation of the *Commonitory* is taken from https://www.newadvent.org/fathers/3506.htm.

abuse of power. This is precisely what these authors fail to notice. They ascribe to the pope the authority and power of a political leader who can indeed change the platform of a party, introduce new proposals, and enter into coalitions first with one party and then with another. That is not the case for the pope. In the proper sense of the word, the pope is the man in the Church with the least power. In the proper sense of the word, he is the one who must be most obedient. Ideally, he is the one who must show the greatest fidelity to the deposit handed down to him by his predecessors — a deposit that has reached him after two thousand years. And he must continue to pass it on to those who will come after him without violating, distorting, or destroying it. Instead, these authors are writing about a prophet-pope who can make changes in the Church as if it were the State or a secular institution.

As far as the latter group of authors is concerned, I consider their voices, which are different from each other, extremely important. They seem to have one thing in common: they are all saying, "Stop, we cannot go in this direction. It would be a betrayal of the true Church founded by Christ and entrusted by Him to His apostles. It is this Church that Jesus said would last until the end of time."

Three years ago, sixty-two people (including prominent theologians) published a letter accusing the pope of heresy. The reason for writing and publishing this letter was the papal document *Amoris Laetitia*. In April 2019, another open letter was published, partly with new signatures. Among the signatories were such notable theologians as Fr. Aidan Nichols, O.P.; Professor John Rist, a well-known historian of philosophy; Fr. Thomas Crean, O.P.; Fr. John Hunwicke, former Senior Research Fellow at Pusey House, Oxford; and Dr. Peter Kwasniewski. They believe that the pope's words and actions are a denial of Catholic doctrine and Catholic dogma. They wrote that they must react to "the manifold manifestations of Pope Francis' embrace of positions contrary to the Faith and his dubious support of prelates who in their lives have shown themselves to have a clear disrespect for the Church's faith and morals."[24] Two other quotes

---

[24] See Maike Hickson, "Prominent clergy, scholars accuse Pope Francis of heresy in open letter," *LifeSiteNews* (April 30, 2019), www.lifesitenews.com/news/prominent-clergy-scholars-accuse-pope-francis-of-heresy-in-open-letter. The

from the summary of the letter: "The words and actions of Pope Francis amount to a comprehensive rejection of Catholic teaching on marriage and sexual activity, on the moral law, and on grace and the forgiveness of sins,"[25] and further, "This protection and promotion of clerics who reject Catholic teaching on marriage, sexual activity, and on the moral law in general, even when these clerics personally violate the moral and civil law in horrendous ways, is consistent enough to be considered a policy on the part of Pope Francis. At the least it is evidence of disbelief in the truth of Catholic teaching on these subjects."[26] What do you think about these letters and the accusations against Pope Francis that they contain?

> I think that if lay people and theologians speak up in the face of the current crisis of the Church, this is in itself a good thing. Assuming that these letters are written in the right tone, showing respect and reverence for the pope, I would not consider such actions to be schismatic or worthy of immediate condemnation. If I were to sign them myself, I would certainly attempt to show respect more clearly in the letter. Besides, I have the impression that in the second letter, the authors didn't focus sufficient attention on specifying what exactly constitutes heresy. According to the constant teaching of the Church, heresy is a situation in which someone directly and persistently denies a revealed truth of God or deliberately questions it. It has been Church practice to admonish the person before publicly declaring him a heretic. He was given a chance to explain himself. He was asked how he understands those propositions. He may have been misunderstood. If his reply indicated that he understood them in a way contrary to revelation, he was exhorted to recant his teachings. This is what happened in the case of Luther. The bull *Exsurge Domine* issued by Leo X contained only

---

documents mentioned here and others related to them, as well as extensive commentary, may be found in the book *Defending the Faith Against Present Heresies*, ed. John R. T. Lamont and Claudio Pierantoni (Waterloo, ON: Arouca Press, n.d.).

[25] See "Open Letter to Bishops of the Catholic Church: A Summary" (Easter Week, 2019), www.documentcloud.org/documents/5983408-Open-Letter-to-the-Bishops-of-the-Catholic.html; also contained in Lamont and Pierantoni, *Defending the Faith*.

[26] Ibid.

a list of condemned propositions and a warning. Luther was given a specified amount of time to recant his teachings, and it was explicitly stated that he would be excommunicated only should he fail to do so. And this is what happened when Luther disobeyed. Even among those propositions condemned by the pope, not all were heretical. They fell into different categories: some were directly heretical, others were suspected of heresy, and still others may have been dangerous.

The authors of this open letter don't show what precisely heresy consists in, and neither do they show whether we are dealing with a so-called persistent, obstinate, repeated rejection of the truths of revelation. Additionally, another important question is at stake here: the pope is the supreme authority in the Church. He has no superior on earth. In special situations bishops and cardinals can and should respectfully approach the pope and tell him that some of his statements contradict or undermine the divine truth of revelation, demanding that the erring pope retract them. If it were so, if such an error could be proven, then all the bishops and cardinals could request, with full respect, that the pope retract his false teaching. In any case, I would look for a different word in that letter than "heresy" because, as I said, it has a very specific, clearly defined meaning. Even if their concern is justified, it's important to choose words carefully.

In 2019, you also published a very detailed analysis on the question of whether the pope can be a heretic. I'm not sure if I understood the point of the argument correctly, perhaps I am mistaken, but I was under the impression that the overall conclusion was as follows: even if theoretically the pope could be a heretic, there is no authority that could determine this in practice. For the pope cannot be judged by anyone.

This is not quite what I wanted to convey. I think that it is possible that a pope could affirm a heresy in his daily teachings, or when he is clearly not intending to teach infallibly ("*ex cathedra*").

Well, yes, but there is a difference between a private statement and an official acknowledgment of error with an implementation of the removal procedure. In the case of the pope, this seems to be impossible.

If it turned out that the pope were publicly acting in a way contrary to the Faith or harming the Faith, we have the college of cardinals, which, theoretically, should assume responsibility and bring it to his attention. For example, send him a letter and point out dangerous errors.

That is what was done by the four cardinals who addressed their *dubia* to Pope Francis regarding *Amoris Laetitia*. However, there were only four of them.

I am not commenting on this particular case here, but talking about the procedure. If such a situation were to arise and the cardinals were to send a similar letter to the pope and he would not respond, they should make such a letter public. They should do so for the good of the Church and the good of the faithful, who should be publicly warned against the spread of erroneous teaching. The Church is not the property of this or that pope. And then, if it turns out that such a publicly released letter from the cardinals receives no response either — nothing more can be done. Legally, there are no more options.

That is exactly what I said earlier: essentially, it means that there is no authority that could judge the pope.

This is a fundamental principle of the Church: the first episcopal see cannot be judged by anyone. *Prima sedes a nemine iudicatur.* All we can do is pray that God may enlighten the erring pope or intervene in a way known to Him. That the pope may be converted and that he will start preaching the truth to the faithful in place of the previous errors. Besides, we must remember that we have sufficient means of defense. After all, in such a situation, even if the pope were to err, both bishops and priests can continue to preach the sound, true teaching that has always been preached by the Church. In this way, they remain united to the Church and to the teachings of all the popes, even if the current pope during whose reign they live is teaching falsehood. They have the means to restore equilibrium here. In such a situation of conflict or contradiction, they must adhere to the constant, immutable teaching of the Church. They can do this in sermons, they can write articles or books. They must also pray. No single pope is eternal. We must have enough faith, enough patience to endure until God summons him or grants him conversion. History knows such cases.

This makes sense only if we assume that the succeeding pope will be better than the one teaching error. And yet, given that it's the pope who appoints cardinals and bishops, we might fear that the error will thus be perpetuated.

But the Church is holy, the Church is in the hands of God!

Of course. I'm just talking about a hypothetical situation.

We must keep emphasizing this: the Church is not in our hands. It's an act of faith. Ultimately, the Church is not a human institution. So if it happens that a pope who has made mistakes dies without revoking them before dying, without repenting of them, then after his death the next pope or the pope together with a council will undoubtedly denounce the mistakes and condemn the one who preached them. That was the case with Pope Honorius. The Church is the Church of God and can't approve error. God can't approve error, for it's contrary to His nature.

On the subject of contradictions, the question emerges: is it possible to reconcile two papal documents, *Amoris Laetitia* and *Veritatis Splendor*, with each other? In the latter, John Paul II taught that there are intrinsically evil acts that can never be justified; according to the former, as numerous commentators believe, ultimately everything depends on the private judgment of conscience. Professor Josef Seifert, for example, has argued that by embracing the reasoning of *Amoris Laetitia* the Church is falling into relativism and it's not impossible that at some point in the future she would accept abortion and euthanasia. Seifert is referring to paragraph 303 of the exhortation, which states the following:

Recognizing the influence of such concrete factors, we can add that individual conscience needs to be better incorporated into the Church's praxis in certain situations which do not objectively embody our understanding of marriage. Naturally, every effort should be made to encourage the development of an enlightened conscience, formed and guided by the responsible and serious discernment of one's pastor, and to encourage an ever greater trust in God's grace. Yet conscience can do more than recognize that a given situation does not correspond objectively to the overall demands of the Gospel. It can also recognize with sincerity and honesty what for now is the most generous response which can be given to God, and come to see with a certain moral security that it is what God himself is asking amid the concrete complexity of one's limits, while yet not fully the objective ideal. In any event, let us recall that this discernment is dynamic; it must remain ever open to new stages of growth and to new decisions which can enable the ideal to be more fully realized.[27]

According to the logic of *Amoris Laetitia*, Seifert believes, if adultery is accepted as morally good in certain situations, then similarly abortion, euthanasia, suicide, lying, stealing, perjury, and treason can be justified in some instances and "be what God himself is asking amid the concrete complexity of one's limits, while yet not fully the objective ideal."[28] Many theologians argue that the document written by Francis makes the claim that God can command sin. This would be, in principle, exactly the same teaching as that propagated by Martin Luther. What do you think about this?

There is no way to reconcile *Amoris Laetitia* and *Veritatis Splendor*. We must remember that the teaching of *Veritatis Splendor* is not an original teaching by Pope John Paul II; he merely confirmed the constant teaching of the Church. I want to emphasize: this is not about the teaching of John Paul II, as many claim. It's a confirmation of the constant teaching of the Church. Certainly there are expressions in *Amoris Laetitia* that contradict truth and faith and divine revelation. This is especially true of the paragraph that you quoted. It maintains that something objectively forbidden — the sin of extramarital sexual intercourse — can be subjectively commanded by conscience. So one can simultaneously sin and offend God objectively while subjectively considering it a command of God to sin in this particular case. This is certainly against the Church's teaching on the indissolubility of marriage

[27] Pope Francis, Apostolic Exhortation *Amoris Laetitia* (April 8, 2016), www.vatican.va/content/francesco/en/apost_exhortations/documents/papa-francesco_esortazione-ap_20160319_amoris-Laetitia.html.

[28] See Josef Seifert, "Does Pure Logic Threaten to Destroy the Entire Moral Doctrine of the Catholic Church?," www.catholicculture.org/culture/library/view.cfm?recnum=11720.

and the absolute validity of the sixth commandment of the Decalogue. Sinning and offending God can never be accepted as means to a good end. We can't condone the abrogation of the sixth commandment.

This sentence from *Amoris Laetitia* is very dangerous indeed, as it contradicts the Church's constant teaching regarding the absolute unacceptability of certain acts that are by their nature always and in all circumstances morally wrong, such as having sexual relations outside of a valid marriage. The sixth commandment was given to us by God, not invented by the Church. Therefore, we shouldn't be talking about "Church teaching" here. No, this is divine revelation. This is God's commandment. The Church is merely passing it on and preserving it. Whoever disagrees with it must say that God Himself has made a mistake and has given us a false commandment. It's therefore completely impossible to reconcile with God's revelation the relativism contained in *Amoris Laetitia* regarding the judgment of moral acts.

What do you think about the reports regarding the "St. Gallen Mafia," a group of cardinals who would have been meeting in the Swiss diocese of that name at the invitation of the local bishop Ivo Fürer to develop plans of introducing their candidate for the papacy? This was believed to have been taking place as early as the end of John Paul II's time in office, and then again after Benedict XVI announced his decision to abdicate. At that time, meetings were reportedly being held to ensure that Cardinal Bergoglio would be elected at the conclave. The name of the group comes from the Belgian cardinal Godfried Danneels, who was so proud of his success in getting the Argentinian cardinal elected that he told his biographers all about it. Did such a group exist? What influence could it have had over the election of the pope?

I don't know much about this topic. All I have to say is based exclusively on what I have read and what was shared in the media, or what Cardinal Danneels wrote in his autobiography. He himself listed the names of the bishops and cardinals who met in Sankt Gallen. This is a clear testimony that they did indeed meet there. And the cardinal himself used the term "mafia," as you pointed out. According to various reports, this group, to use a neutral term, wanted to promote their cardinal as early as the 2005 conclave. Already then, Cardinal Bergoglio was a contender against Cardinal Ratzinger. At that time, however, conservative cardinals held the majority in the college of cardinals and so the operation failed. Following that, the members of this group decided to do everything in their power so that newly appointed cardinals would have views similar to theirs. And they succeeded. I am surprised about the carelessness with which Benedict XVI sometimes appointed cardinals, selecting also liberal, in some cases even extremely liberal, candidates. Every reasonable person must have understood what this would lead to: at the next conclave, these people would constitute the majority.

I don't really understand all this. You yourself mentioned your experience in Brazil, where two dioceses neighboring the one in which you served as a priest were led respectively by an open Communist and by a strong supporter of liberation theology. The cardinals would meet in Sankt Gallen for years, apparently forming something akin to a political party. The simple question is: what happened to authority in the Church? Why is there no reaction from anyone even in a situation where Communist ideology is openly preached?

That's what infiltration in the Church is all about. Of course that is what it's all about. One can't deny this unless one is completely naive. The paralysis of ecclesiastical authority is nothing new, it's a phenomenon that has been around for many, many years. If we wish to refer to specific publications, it's described in Taylor Marshall's book *Infiltration*, to which I wrote the foreword. It shows the growing influence of modernism and partially also of Freemasonry on the life of the Church. I don't want to say that modernists were simply Freemasons — that was not the case. It could occasionally happen that these groups came into contact with each other and these ideologies intermingled. But as a rule, they were parallel currents of thought. If we are looking for their origins, then in the historical sense, the first attempts of these movements to penetrate the Church took place under Leo XIII. On the one hand, he was a great pope. He wrote wonderful, clear, unequivocally traditional encyclicals promoting and defending the Catholic faith. He also explicitly condemned Freemasonry and the ideology proclaimed by Freemasons. However, all this happened at the level of doctrine. The practice was somewhat different. It was then that noticeably liberal bishops first emerged. This was the beginning of the great process of infiltration. His Secretary of State, Cardinal Rampolla, was perceived as a liberal by his contemporaries. He maintained exceptionally close and friendly ties with the radically anti-Catholic government of France, which was controlled almost exclusively by Freemasons. At the same time, his policy toward the Austrian Emperor Franz Joseph, who was Catholic, was not very favorable.

Can this, however, be compared with what is happening in the Church today? In the end, it was probably a matter of politics. And the Church has shown over the centuries that she can enter various alliances and that practical considerations don't always go hand in hand with religious concerns.

Politics is obviously of paramount importance for the life of the Church as well. Let's take another example. During the Kulturkampf period, when Chancellor Bismarck attempted a complete political subjugation of the Church, the German bishops demonstrated great courage and strength of character. In a truly heroic fashion, they defended the rights of the Church and didn't yield under persecution. Unfortunately, Pope Leo XIII didn't make use of this will to resist and quickly reached a compromise. Thus, we could even say that by seeking compromise at all cost, he broke the will of resistance of the German Catholic bishops. By making a deal with the German government, he gained peace, but weakened the spiritual strength of the Church in Germany. As a result, the cardinals he appointed in Germany were very moderate, even politically correct for their time. One such example was Cardinal Georg von Kopp of Breslau (d. 1914), who was in fact the candidate of the Protestant Emperor. We must remember that during the Kulturkampf he was the bishop of Fulda and was one of the very few who tried to reach an agreement with Chancellor Bismarck, often going against the position of the other hierarchs. And for this, for his willingness to make concessions to the Protestant State, Pope Leo XIII later rewarded him with the cardinalate. Please note the moral of the story here: resistance and opposition to the State doesn't pay off, because

in the final reckoning Rome rewarded oftentimes not those who faithfully defended the rights of the Church, but people of compromise,
submission, and subordination.

The policy of so-called *ralliement* toward the government of France
had a similar dimension. On February 16, 1892, Pope Leo XIII addressed his encyclical *Au Milieu des Sollicitudes* to the French Catholics,
and in it he encouraged their "joining" (*ralliement*) of the French Republic. French Freemasons interpreted this papal move as a surrender. With
Leo XIII, for the first time in history a pope used the term "Christian
democracy" in a positive sense. The goals were commendable: the pope
believed that by withdrawing his support for the monarchist movement
and entering a compromise with the anticlerical French Republic, he
would succeed in decreasing their openly anti-Catholic policies. He himself contributed to the collapse of the legitimate democratic resistance.
Previously, Catholics would say: we don't recognize this government.
Yes, we are conforming to the laws, but we don't recognize the anti-
Christian laws. Leo XIII weakened this force of political Catholicism and
its unity. As a result of the *ralliement*, the united Catholic bloc fell apart.
The pope became so involved on the side of the French Republic that
Catholics opposed to the agreement were threatened with being denied
absolution in Confession. To me, this was an example of a grave abuse
of papal power: faithful Catholics were forced to accept a government
hostile to them. The anti-clericals felt empowered and, with no serious
opposition at this point, they kept introducing further anti-religious
legislation. By speaking about the separation of State and Church, they
actually wanted to eliminate Christianity from the public square.

It was also during the time of Pope Leo XIII that the first instances of
modernists infiltrating the Church and gaining influence and positions
occurred. This is what infiltration was all about. Pope Pius X was the one
who decided to oppose it. He saw the extent to which modernism had
infiltrated the seminaries. Of course, this influence was not as strong
as it is today, but the early indications were already clear. So while Leo
XIII in theory was extremely strict and kept the deposit of the Faith
intact, while he published excellent texts and was a great defender of
Catholicism, in practice he made decisions that were difficult to defend,

opening the Church to the influence of her enemies. Let's say that it was flexible politics. It was then, during his time in office, that bishops and cardinals with more liberal views first appeared. They were certainly not modernists — perhaps more supporters of a "third way," of moderation and compromise with the world. Fortunately, Pius X put a stop to that and took a determined stance against modernism, but looking from a broader perspective, his reign was only a transitional period. It was almost forgotten. After his death, Benedict XV was elected to the throne of Peter, and it was common knowledge that he was not a fan of Pius X and that he didn't want to follow his firm, anti-modernist course. That's why some of his nominations for bishops and cardinals went to men who didn't perceive modernism as a great danger. Gradually, they became increasingly numerous in the episcopate. They were not quite modernists, but neither did they want to commit themselves forcefully to the defense of the Faith. The same was true during the pontificate of Pius XI. On the one hand, he wrote wonderful encyclicals like *Mortalium Animos*, but on the other, he didn't take the modernist threat as seriously as his great namesake. Like Leo XIII, he also sought political compromise. For this reason, he withdrew his support for the *Cristeros* in Mexico and supported a peace agreement that was extremely unfavorable to Catholics. Also during his time, some candidates for the episcopate were cautiously liberal in their views.

Generally speaking, in terms of teaching the Faith, all of these popes were staunch defenders of Catholic doctrine. In matters of faith and morals, they were uncompromising in principle and proclaimed the true doctrine of the Church clearly, unambiguously, and without any concessions. However, their personnel decisions and appointments, and the compromises they made in these cases, allowed outside and worldly forces to grow within the Church. Words contained in documents are one thing, but people are another. Thus the ground had already been laid before the Second Vatican Council. Many of the bishops and cardinals were rather liberal, with, we could say, flexible thinking. They were still not the majority, but their influence was growing.

I believe that from this standpoint John XXIII's decision to convene the Council was a big mistake. What was the need? To prepare pastoral instructions? You don't need a council for that. It is worthwhile to recall here also the following apt observation of Cardinal Joseph Ratzinger: "Not every valid council in the history of the Church has been a fruitful one; in the last analysis, many of them have been a waste of time."[29] Furthermore, in the late '50s, the bishops were already clearly divided internally. It was perfectly obvious at the time. It was also easy to predict that if a council were to be called, a well-organized liberal force would play a huge role in such a large gathering.

Theologians who were suspected of questioning orthodoxy played a significant role at the Council.

This is precisely the perfect example of what I have called infiltration, a misguided personnel policy. The real breakthrough came when Pope John XXIII announced the decision to convene a council. Those theologians who for years had been suspected of modernist tendencies, who were often viewed as unclear and dangerous, suddenly regained their lost positions. Thanks to their appointments to conciliar commissions, they started to play prominent roles. A conscious political strategy is clearly evident here. There is no other explanation for what happened. It was a political strategy. This tendency to appoint true, committed liberals to crucial ecclesiastical positions only intensified during the pontificate of Paul VI. It was then that the idea of the "spirit of the council" and the expression "the conciliar Church" (*"Chiesa conciliare"*) emerged. Alas, this spirit of the council was also manifest during the pontificate of John Paul II. Over and over, important Church positions were assumed by people known for their doctrinally ambiguous (at very least) positions. Suffice it to recall the careers of Cardinals Walter Kasper and Karl Lehmann. It would be worthwhile to conduct a detailed analysis of episcopal appointments since the Second Vatican Council.

Let me use another example from Brazil. In 1954, toward the end of the pontificate of Pius XII, Archbishop Armando Lombardi was

---

[29] *Principles of Catholic Theology: Building Stones for a Fundamental Theology* (San Francisco: Ignatius Press 1987), 378.

appointed apostolic nuncio there. Even then, he was generally considered liberal, although he kept his views to himself until Pius XII's death.
As it turned out, he was a close friend of Archbishop Hélder Câmara,
who later gained notoriety as the promoter of liberation theology. Both
during the Council and afterward, Archbishop Câmara proclaimed truly
revolutionary ideas. As a young priest, he was a fascist, committed to
the point of wearing fascist insignia beneath his cassock. In the 1940s
and 1950s he "converted" to communism, Marxism, and the fight for
social justice. It was then that nuncio Lombardi met him in Rio de Janeiro. He used his influence to have Câmara nominated as an auxiliary
bishop of Rio de Janeiro soon afterward. All episcopal nominations in
Brazil from 1954 till the time of the Council substantially depended
on these two — on Nuncio Lombardi and Bishop, later Archbishop,
Câmara. It was during this period that a large cohort of priests with
liberal, leftist, and Communist views became bishops. His successor,
Nuncio Sebastiano Baggio, was equally progressive and liberal. He
was commonly believed to be a Freemason. And Brazil was not just
an isolated case.

The Vatican's personnel policy was the same everywhere. Nuncios
played a major role in the appointments. They are responsible for the
disastrous condition of many local churches that previously flourished.
Of course, I don't mean all of them, but many — it pains my heart to
say it — pursued such a personnel policy, with the support of the Holy
See. Some of the nuncios were the most secular and worldly among
the hierarchy and behaved like secular, liberal, progressive politicians.
This was also the case in the United States during a certain period of
time. These are the sad facts. You can't escape them. Again, it would
be worthwhile to prepare a thorough analysis of the personnel policy
carried out by the nuncios just before and after the Council, to show
which candidates were being supported. The policy of cardinal appointments was not much different, particularly after 1965, under
Paul VI. Almost all the major capitals of the world were filled by liberal
candidates. There were exceptions, of course, as always. But the rule
was well-known. When I worked in South America, the cardinals in
Brazil, Chile, or Peru were extremely progressive.

In fact, Pope John Paul II continued such a policy. As a result, the group of cardinals committed to Tradition and willing to defend the Faith and its immutability at all costs steadily decreased. The creation of the influential group in Sankt Gallen was precisely the result of such a personnel policy in the pontificate of Pope John Paul II. After all, a dozen or so exceptionally influential cardinals belonged to it. They had so much power that, as it turned out in 2013, they were able to arrange the election of their candidate and stage everything accordingly.

A glaring indication of the current crisis in Catholicism is the number of pedophilia scandals that have been plaguing the Church over the past few decades. Shortly after his election, Pope Francis promised that the fight against this scourge would be one of the main goals of his pontificate. In your opinion, has there been a major change in this area? In February 2019, a summit was held at the Vatican on the fight against pedophilia and crimes against minors. At the end of that meeting, Pope Francis gave a speech in which he spoke once again about the evil of the scourge of pedophilia. "Our work has made us realize once again that the gravity of the scourge of the sexual abuse of minors is, and historically has been, a widespread phenomenon in all cultures and societies."[30] The pope also said that the currently available statistics on the sexual abuse of minors, compiled by various national and international organizations and agencies, including WHO, UNICEF, Interpol, and Europol, "do not represent the real extent of the phenomenon, which is often underestimated, mainly because many cases of the sexual abuse of minors go unreported, particularly the great number committed within families." He concluded by declaring that "we need to be clear that this evil, while gravely affecting our societies as a whole, is in no way less monstrous when it takes place within the Church." Other participants in this meeting also called for defending the victims and helping them. However, many critics claim that the practical effects of these deliberations were rather insignificant.

To me, it was all done for show. It was merely cosmetic. Unfortunately, these deliberations didn't lead to the adoption of any concrete plans to counter this phenomenon. No adequate measures were developed.

[30] Pope Francis, Address at the End of the Eucharistic Concelebration, www.vatican. va/content/francesco/en/speeches/2019/february/documents/papa-fran-cesco_20190224_incontro-protezioneminori-chiusura.html.

No effective and serious attempt was made to get to the root of the evil and wickedness, which Pope Emeritus Benedict XVI so aptly described in a subsequently released letter.[31] The real root of the evil is the moral relativism that has invaded theology departments and seminaries. According to these widespread views, it's no longer possible to clearly define good and evil, and no permanent truth regarding the question of morality can be discerned. It's been claimed that a sin against the sixth commandment is nothing serious. For example, masturbation, premarital intercourse, and other non-marital sexual acts are no longer to be considered sins.

Sexuality came to be viewed exclusively through the lens of an individual's private satisfaction and gratification. Sexual pleasure was a sign of maturity. In a sense, the gravity of sins against this commandment has been gradually abrogated. This is the actual root of the evil — the complete downplaying of this sin, the treatment of impurity as something insignificant, neutral, and inconsequential. This way of thinking, which first infected lecturers and teachers, immediately extended to the training of seminarians and future priests. For decades, priests were educated in a superficial way, without being taught the full theological truth about the significance of sin. Similarly evident were the deficiencies in their spiritual lives, manifested by the lack of formation of a personal relationship with Christ. Instead of showing them that the priesthood is first and foremost an imitation of Christ, an acceptance of His Cross in conformity with the model He gave us, the priesthood began to be treated as a profession, as an administrative and social function.

Not surprisingly, in such an environment few were able to remain chaste. How could they? Normal young men who are taught that the sin of unchastity is irrelevant, that having sexual activity is a sign of

---

[31] "Die Kirche und der Skandal des sexuellen Mißbrauchs," *Klerusblatt*, Zeitschrift der katholischen Geistlichen in Bayern und der Pfalz, April 15, 2019; in English, "The Church and the Scandal of Sexual Abuse," www.catholicworldreport.com/2019/04/10/full-text-of-benedict-xvi-the-church-and-the-scandal-of-sexual-abuse/.

maturity, and that virginity is old-fashioned, began to behave according to these principles. Without a personal relationship with Christ, convinced that the sin of unchastity is inconsequential, that by committing it we don't offend God, these people easily succumbed to evil temptations. Overcoming them, after all, requires both clear rules and strong willpower, and above all the conviction that evil must be avoided at all costs. To maintain sexual purity, you must have spiritual purity within. This is achieved through prayer, spiritual exercises, but also asceticism, corporal mortifications. The latter were eliminated altogether. It was against the whole wisdom of the Church, against everything that Jesus and the apostles passed on to us, against centuries of knowledge about human nature and its weaknesses. Still, the effects of original sin are in us and in order not to succumb to them, in order to overcome the inner wickedness and disordered desires, man has to fight. That is why asceticism, fasting, renunciations, practicing mortifications, and obedience to discipline are so vital. All this, of course, for the sake of love of Christ — renunciations and asceticism are nothing other than means to it.

Out of political correctness, the most important problem was not mentioned at all during this summit in Rome: the problem of homosexuality. As various studies have shown, over 80 percent of pedophilia cases in the Church are actually homosexual acts. This is exactly the issue they refused to acknowledge. That is why I mentioned cosmetic changes, doing things for show. If over 80 percent of pedophilia cases are homosexual, then the issue of homosexuality should be central. Instead, it was not mentioned at all.

As far as Church regulations are concerned, it seems to me that there is a loophole here. I mentioned this in my published articles. I believe that clear and rigorous norms should be introduced, explicit regulations that exclude men with evident homosexual tendencies from the priesthood. Such men should never be ordained. This should be introduced as an explicit norm of canon law: if there is a clear proof and evidence that a man has homosexual tendencies, he must not be admitted to the priesthood. This should be the case even if such a person has undergone therapy. It must be clearly spelled out, with no exceptions. This should happen for the sake of the whole Church, all the faithful. We cannot allow affectively unstable people to become priests.

Homosexual inclinations in adults signify a certain immaturity, a disability. I would even call it a type of pathology. Therefore, we can't allow a man who is internally immature, who has problems with his own identity, to be admitted to the priesthood. If a man feels erotic attraction to another man, it's against nature. Such a man is in a state of inner rupture. He is male by nature, yet his sexual attraction, instead of being directed toward the opposite sex, remains directed toward his own. He remains focused on himself, on his own sexuality. Such people, even if they are good and pious, should not be ordained. They should remain in the world, where they can do much good outside of the clerical state. Ordaining them involves a tremendous risk. It's better to have fewer priests in the Church than to have homosexuals among them with an immature personality. Only psychologically healthy men should be ordained as priests. We must not ordain people burdened with this or any other pathology. It's as if someone were to say that we should ordain kleptomaniacs, because they are generally good and pious people, intelligent, kind, who help the poor, but who just have this affliction whereby they are inclined to steal and do sometimes steal.

We need to be completely clear here: since homosexuality is a form of pathology, such men cannot be ordained to the priesthood under any circumstances. This rule should be codified in canon law. We must be very explicit here. Of course, we can't always have absolute certainty regarding the presence of such inclinations, and we can't hold everyone in suspicion. However, the principle should be this: if clear evidence is found against a candidate for the priesthood in the seminary, if we can point to concrete behavior that indicates a homosexual inclination, he should be expelled from the seminary immediately. I am referring to specific, external manifestations, such as watching homosexual pornography, attempted seduction, or other similar behaviors. Of course, we should show love and respect to such a person and offer help, but he has no place in a seminary.

We should say to such a person: go out into the world and be a good Christian. We can discreetly offer you help to cure this affliction. We can help you find psychotherapists, and we can point you to the right methods of therapy. Fortunately, today we have methods of therapy that help people with homosexual tendencies to come out of this situation, so that some of them can later have wives and start normal families. A cured homosexual man can receive from a good wife and from his own children the necessary human affections for his psychological stability. So we should say to such a seminarian: go out into the world, start a family, we will help you. But even if you have been cured, the path of the priesthood is not for you. This way we can have certainty. And the priesthood, in which everything is based on the trust of the faithful in the priest, must be something certain. So become a good father of a family. Such a man must have enough humility in himself to accept it, to say, yes, I accept it. To tell himself that he is a believing Christian, that he has no right to the priesthood. After all, there are other ways of living a good Christian life.

Such norms outlining the procedures for dismissal from a seminary should be developed in as much detail as possible. They should be introduced in seminaries all over the world. I'm convinced that such a measure alone would contribute to a huge decrease in the cases of pedophilia among the clergy. I'm certain that the effects would be visible immediately and that it would be a huge breakthrough in the fight against the scourge of pedophilia. Of course, we can never completely eradicate sin, weak human nature being what it is — we are not yet in Heaven — but we should do everything we can to reach that goal. Even if there are still cases of pedophilia, they will definitely be far less numerous.

The extent to which Catholic seminaries have been infiltrated by homosexuals is brought to light fully in the book *Goodbye, Good Men* by Michael S. Rose. I could not believe my eyes when I was reading it. Not only did it reveal the scope of the phenomenon, that is, the infiltration of numerous homosexuals into seminaries in the United States, but it also showed its consequences: moral decay, cynicism, tolerating evil, and passivity. When such behavior is tolerated, the plague of relativism immediately takes over the whole seminary. Everything is allowed. Religion becomes a façade. Rose showed an exact, precise plan for the destruction of the Church, in which the method was to allow or encourage depravity among priests and to deliberately attempt to create a situation where candidates who believe, who are orthodox and devoted to the Church and the pope, are harassed, discouraged, and even persecuted, while those who are mediocre, pathetic, and cowardly — those who just want to fit in and not ruffle any feathers — are promoted. "In short, many have hijacked the priesthood in order to change the Catholic Church from within," Rose wrote. It turns out that since the 1960s some Catholic seminaries, at least in the United States, instead of training priests of Christ — men who would want to offer their whole lives as sacrifices to the Lord, serving their neighbors to save their souls from damnation — have been producing unfulfilled revolutionaries, failed reformers, aspiring rebels. Rose reveals the deliberate infiltration of Catholic seminaries by "'the Lavender Mafia,' a clique of homosexual dilettantes, along with an underground of liberal faculty members determined to change the doctrines, disciplines, and mission of the Catholic Church from within."[32] Do you agree with the claims of this book?

> Yes, it's a very important book. It documents meticulously what I have talked about here. It contains very detailed data. However, it describes this phenomenon in detail in only one country, the USA. We can suspect that in other countries things are not very different. The infiltration and condoning of the homosexual subculture is a terrible threat. It's awful, but it has spread into multiple seminaries and has even reached Rome and the Vatican. We have no choice but to get to the root of evil. Evil must be uprooted, otherwise we will only continue to fight its effects. We'll stay on the surface. Our efforts will be merely superficial. Therefore, I am proposing that these standards be adopted and that various situations be described in detail. It's not enough to have a general statement that homosexuals must not be admitted to the seminaries; we need a precise description of such situations. Today we say that men who are found to have "deep-seated homosexual tendencies" should not be admitted to the seminaries. But what does "deep-seated" mean in practice? Everyone can interpret it in his own way. And this freedom of interpretation will make it possible to circumvent the rule.

---

[32] Michael S. Rose, *Goodbye, Good Men* (Washington, DC: Regnery Publishing, 2002), xii.

This way, homosexuals will continue to be admitted to seminaries. The homosexual subculture will not be eradicated and the threat against children and adolescents will not be eliminated.

In this day and age, can we still have any confidence that we can really know God? Or do we live in an age where we can only be skeptics when it comes to God's existence? "If a person says that he has met God with absolute certainty and is not touched by a margin of uncertainty, that is not good.... If someone has an answer to all questions, well, that is the proof that God is not with him."[33] These are the words of Pope Francis from his interview with *La Civiltà Cattolica*. In the foreword to the book *Martini e noi* [*Martini and Us*], the pope remarks that both believers and non-believers are seeking the truth at the same time and nothing is settled.[34] Such statements, and I could quote many more, seem to represent a certain declaration of skepticism.

> Certainly. This, however, is contrary to the Gospel. The statements you have just quoted are also inconsistent with the constant and immutable teachings of the Church. The apostles were already certain that they had found the Messiah. Take, for example, the description of the calling of the apostles in the Gospel of St. John:
>
> > On the following day, he [Jesus] would go forth into Galilee, and he findeth Philip. And Jesus saith to him: Follow me. Now Philip was of Bethsaida, the city of Andrew and Peter. Philip findeth Nathanael, and saith to him: We have found him of whom Moses in the law, and the prophets did write, Jesus the son of Joseph of Nazareth. And Nathanael said to him: Can any thing of good come from Nazareth? Philip saith to him: Come and see. Jesus saw Nathanael coming to him: and he saith of him: Behold an Israelite indeed, in whom there is no guile. Nathanael saith to him: Whence knowest thou me? Jesus

---

[33] See Pope Francis and Antonio Spadaro, S.J., "Intervista a Papa Francesco," in *La Civiltà Cattolica* (September 19, 2013), www.laciviltacattolica.it/articolo/intervista-a-papa-francesco/.

[34] See Marco Vergottini, ed., *Martini e noi. I ritratti inediti di un grande protagonista del Novecento* (Milano: Piemme ed., 2015).

> answered, and said to him: Before that Philip called thee, when
> thou wast under the fig tree, I saw thee. Nathanael answered
> him, and said: Rabbi, thou art the Son of God, thou art the
> King of Israel. Jesus answered, and said to him: Because I said
> unto thee, I saw thee under the fig tree, thou believest: greater
> things than these shalt thou see. (1:43–50)

Here we can clearly see the certainty of faith. Philip says to Nathanael,
"We have found him of whom Moses in the law, and the prophets did
write." And later Nathanael concludes, "Rabbi, thou art the Son of
God." There is no admixture of doubt, hesitation, or uncertainty here.

We also find such absolutely certain faith in the description of the
healing of the man born blind. Jesus says to him, "Dost thou believe
in the Son of God? He answered, and said: Who is he, Lord, that I
may believe in him? And Jesus said to him: Thou hast both seen him;
and it is he that talketh with thee. And he said: I believe, Lord. And
falling down, he adored him" (John 9:35–38). Confession of faith is a
recurring theme in the Gospels. Paul also had such absolutely certain
faith when he met Jesus on the road to Damascus. Similarly, we see
absolutely certain faith in Thomas. When Jesus says to him, "Put in thy
finger hither, and see my hands; and bring hither thy hand, and put
it into my side; and be not faithless, but believing. Thomas answered,
and said to him: My Lord, and my God" (John 20:27–28).

The very same faith was also transmitted by the apostles to their
disciples, to the Church. Each of us, when we have reached maturity,
can say with certainty that we have found God. After all, we profess one
Faith with the Church and do so with absolute certainty. This is exactly
what St. Peter taught when he wrote, "For we have not by following
artificial fables, made known to you the power, and presence of our
Lord Jesus Christ; but we were eyewitnesses of his greatness" (2 Pet.
1:16). We can see the same absolute certainty in the First Epistle of
St. John, "[That we announce to you] that which was from the beginning, which we have heard, which we have seen with our eyes, which
we have looked upon, and our hands have handled, of the word of
life" (1:1). We are talking about absolute certainty here. We are not

following fairy tales. We don't wander in uncertainty. No. We have seen, we have touched, we have heard. This faith gives us the greatest possible certainty that we can have on earth. It gives us truth spoken by God. He said that, so it must be true. God Himself, the source of truth, said so — then it must be absolutely true. We accept this word on the authority of God Himself. He alone is truly credible. Since He has given us the word, we can trust Him unconditionally.

Further, Jesus made it clear that He has built His Church on a rock. Not on sand, not on marshes, but on rock. God, then, gives us the greatest possible assurance of the truth of His revelation. Christ is that revelation, He is the light which shines, without which we would indeed wander in darkness and uncertainty. "The people that sat in darkness, hath seen great light: and to them that sat in the region of the shadow of death, light is sprung up." Those words of the prophet Isaiah were quoted by Matthew the Evangelist (Matt. 4:16) to show the clarity and magnitude of the Truth of revelation that came with Christ. Another crucial passage, this time from the Gospel of St. John: "No man hath seen God at any time: the only begotten Son who is in the bosom of the Father, he hath declared him" (1:18). So what Jesus taught us, His teaching, has absolute power and truthfulness. The same is expressed in the first verse of the Epistle to the Hebrews, which reads, "God, who, at sundry times and in divers manners, spoke in times past to the fathers by the prophets, last of all, in these days hath spoken to us by his Son" (1:1–2). Because of these words we can have certainty that our faith, based on the Son's revelation, is absolutely true.

Of course, faith doesn't offer easy answers to all questions, and in this sense the latter part of the pope's first sentence is true, but the former certainly is not. This kind of mixture has been a constant problem since the Second Vatican Council. Already in some conciliar documents the first part of a sentence may be true, while the second part is ambiguous, or the other way around. Often, a comma or a "but" introduces additional content that makes the entire statement unclear. That's why we must examine each part of a sentence separately and only then can we say whether something is true or not.

It's also true that we are still on the way, so we have *faith*, not knowledge.[35] The apostle Paul speaks of this in his Epistle to the Corinthians:
"We see now through a glass in a dark manner; but then [we will see]
face to face. Now I know in part; but then I shall know even as I am
known" (1 Cor. 13:12). So not until after death will the saved attain a
full vision of God, much fuller than what is available to mortals. But
what we currently know of God is true and certain. We don't have the
fullness of the knowledge of God, which we can attain only in eternity,
although even then our knowledge will not be completely exhaustive.
God is God. But that which God has revealed to us through His Son,
through Christ, that which the Church teaches — that is certain and
true. We can be certain of the truthfulness of this claim because it's
based on the credibility of God Himself.

**You speak of the certainty and truthfulness of knowledge based on the authority
of God. But such language is extremely rare nowadays. Even the highest-ranking
Church officials speak more often of doubts, ambiguities, and problems with the
Faith rather than its certainty. The Jesuit superior general, Fr. Arturo Sosa Abascal,
during the debate on *Amoris Laetitia*, questioned not only the truthfulness of the
Church's Tradition, but also the text of the New Testament, especially the words of
Jesus as conveyed in the Gospels. In his opinion, at the time of Jesus there were no
recording devices, so we can't be sure what Jesus actually said. Hence, we don't have
any certain knowledge about the authentic teaching of Jesus, but are left only with
conjectures and hypotheses.**

This contradicts the clear message of the Gospel itself, the words of
Jesus to the apostles. I have already quoted them once in our conversation, though in a different context. Jesus said to the apostles, "He that
heareth you, heareth me" (Luke 10:16). Here we should also turn to
other words of the Lord, which I also partially quoted, "All power is
given to me in heaven and in earth. Going therefore, teach ye all nations; baptizing them in the name of the Father, and of the Son, and

---

[35] *In via* (on pilgrimage in this life), one has *fides*, the acceptance of a truth on the
basis of another's word, not *scientia*, the immediate vision or apprehension of
the truth, which is God's by nature and ours in the Beatific Vision. — *Ed.*

of the Holy Ghost. Teaching them to observe all things whatsoever I have commanded you: and behold I am with you all days, even to the consummation of the world" (Matt. 28:18–20). These statements justify the existence of the Church's Magisterium and, at the same time, they are the words handed down to the Church by the apostles. The claim of the Jesuit superior general, therefore, contradicts the entire Tradition of the Church and actually challenges the very existence of the Magisterium.

Frankly, I think that even if there had been recording devices at the time of Jesus, such people would still not believe what was recorded. I think they would say, "Well, yes, these words were recorded, but that was then, a long time ago. They are no longer relevant, no longer binding." For this attitude arises not from the lack of recordings, but from the relativism and Hegelianism that many Catholic theologians have adopted. The entire argument that you have cited is not serious and demonstrates a lack of faith. It only serves to support the claim that in matters of faith and morals man can have no certainty. But this claim is absurd not only in a theological sense; the entire history of the Church also speaks against it. If there were no certainty in matters of faith, there would never have been any martyrs in the Church. How can I give my life, sacrifice it, if I am not sure that this is right? How can I suffer for Christ if I don't know whether He wants that? The martyrs are proof that such skepticism is not true.

The skepticism that the new theologians have for the Gospel accounts and Tradition is also demonstrated with regard to other truths of faith. The Jesuit superior general I mentioned above also claimed that Satan is a merely symbolic figure. Two years later, in another conversation, he maintained that the devil "exists as the personification of evil in different structures, but not in persons, because [he] is not a person, [he] is a way of acting evil. He is not a person like a human person. It is a way of evil to be present in human life."[36]

---

[36] See CNA, "Jesuit Superior General: Satan Is a 'Symbolic Reality'" (August 21, 2019), www.catholicnewsagency.com/news/jesuit-superior-satan-is-a-symbolic-reality-60691.

This is exactly like other situations in which various contemporary theologians express opinions that contradict divine revelation. A classic text describing the personhood of Satan is in the twelfth chapter of the Book of Revelation:

> And there was a great battle in Heaven, Michael and his angels fought with the dragon, and the dragon fought and his angels: and they prevailed not, neither was their place found any more in Heaven. And that great dragon was cast out, that old serpent, who is called the devil and Satan, who seduceth the whole world; and he was cast unto the earth, and his angels were thrown down with him. (12:7–9)

Scripture clearly speaks of the battle of the Archangel Michael and his angels against Satan and his angels. But how could we possibly think that we are dealing here with a battle of personifications, structures, or symbols? Just as Michael is an angel and a person, so also his opponent is a person. A battle can only happen between intelligent beings. It's clear, then, that the scriptural account assumes that Satan has a personality, that he is a person. Jesus also perceives His mission, His ministry, as a war waged against evil spirits, against Satan. He always uses this term in a concrete way, it always refers to a personal being. And so when addressing His opponents, He says:

> You are of your father the devil, and the desires of your father you will do. He was a murderer from the beginning, and he stood not in the truth; because truth is not in him. When he speaketh a lie, he speaketh of his own: for he is a liar, and the father thereof. (John 8:44)

Thus, Scripture shows in many places that Satan is a person who wishes to deceive the whole world. The Word of God tells us that he will eventually be cast down into Hell with his retinue — as portrayed in the Book of Revelation. There are no personifications involved here — how, may I ask, could personifications be cast down into Hell? How could a personification be judged? Also in another passage Jesus says to the damned, "Depart from me, you cursed, into everlasting fire which was prepared for the devil and his angels" (Matt. 25:41). How would this sound if we were to use the language of modern liberal theology? "Depart to the symbolic place prepared for the personification, where it resides with its personifications." This makes no sense at all. Those summoned to depart are *persons*. They are to remain in the eternal fire prepared for the devil and his angels. It's simply not possible to understand these statements as if they were referring to symbols, structures, or personifications.

We have already referred to this problem several times, but now let me ask you directly: do we still have orthodoxy and heresy in the Church? How is it possible that people with important positions in the hierarchy of the Church, such as generals of religious orders, bishops, or cardinals, can express views that are so diametrically incompatible with revelation, Tradition, and the teachings of the Church and still keep their positions and authority? Do questions of religious truth and fidelity to dogmas still have any relevance in the Church today?

This is precisely the crisis in the Church that has been happening since the Second Vatican Council. What the Jesuit general or certain Western bishops are saying is nothing new; after the Council, a range of claims, shocking to varying degrees, can be found in theology departments, in seminaries, in sermons to the faithful, and in books.

Hence my question. For years, Rome has also been acting as if the question of orthodoxy has lost its meaning.

Indeed, there have been interventions, but they are rare, only in really extreme cases. There seems to be no discernible plan or strategy to reverse the situation. There hasn't been a sufficiently effective strategy to reclaim the seminaries and to restore sound doctrine in them. From time to time a document is published, usually with generally correct assertions, but it's nothing more than words on a page. That which should have happened never did — that is, a strict investigation of heretical statements, a reaction to the spread of false teachings, and, when necessary, the expulsion of professors who spread them from departments and seminaries. None of this has been done. All along it has been the same disease of relativism that affects all spheres of the life of the Church: dogmatics, morality, and liturgy. Let me repeat, since the end of the Council there have been some papal interventions, and some good papal documents by Paul VI or John Paul II, but that was all. With few exceptions, such as the case of Professor Hans Küng, who incidentally rejected all truths of the Catholic faith, the Magisterium has limited itself to issuing documents.

In fact, this is happening everywhere. I know many priests from Poland and I know that exactly the same phenomenon is beginning to unfold there. More and more often they are complaining about the prevalence of teachings in certain seminaries that are openly heretical, or suspected of heresy, or unclear.

I think that in the future, when the present crisis has been successfully overcome, the Church will have to develop a formula of a profession of faith repudiating modern errors. A compilation of all the erroneous teachings that have become prevalent in the last fifty years will have to be prepared and then severely condemned. There is no other way. This is, after all, how the Church has always done it.

But who could actually do that in the future? After all, you yourself said that everyone has been infected by this relativistic way of thinking, that it has been spreading, that it has found no resistance. So where would the revival come from? Let's look at the situation realistically. If, as you yourself have pointed out, the liberal cardinals succeeded in securing the throne of Peter for their candidate in 2013, and that candidate has been filling the most important positions with his own people over the years and has been appointing and nominating candidates to the college of cardinals who think in a similar way, how could someone just appear and reverse the course of history?

I have proposed several times that theologians, along with well-educated laymen, should prepare a list of the most prevalent errors. Why not prepare something like this? Something that may be called *Professio fidei catholica*. In June 2019, for example, a group of several hierarchs, including me, prepared such a declaration. Among the signatories were Cardinal Raymond Burke, Archbishop Emeritus of Riga Cardinal Jānis

Pujats, Archbishop Tomash Peta of Astana, and Archbishop-Bishop Emeritus of Karaganda Jan Paweł Lenga.

The text had forty points. We began by emphasizing the fundamental truths of the Faith and wrote that "whatever new insights may be expressed regarding the deposit of faith, nevertheless they cannot be contrary to what the Church has always proposed in the same dogma, in the same sense, and in the same meaning."[37] We emphasized that the meaning of dogmatic formulas remains "ever true" even when "it is expressed with greater clarity or more developed." Additionally, we even explicitly told the faithful that they must avoid those expressions that "distort or alter" the truth. We decisively rejected "dogmatic relativism" that corrupts "the Church's infallibility relative to the truth."

The declaration maintains that "spiritualities and religions that promote any kind of idolatry or pantheism" are "deceptions" that "preclude eternal salvation." In my opinion, an important part of it was the statement that ecumenism is not intended to establish a Church that does not yet exist, but that it is based on the unity that the Catholic Church already has. The declaration affirmed the existence of Hell and stated that those eternally damned "will not be annihilated." Given the confusion today after Pope Francis signed the document in Abu Dhabi, we wrote that "the religion born of faith in Jesus Christ" is "the only religion positively willed by God."

This document, I believe, can serve as a preparation for a future great declaration, a *Professio fidei*, from a future pope. It's not a huge thing, but such small steps bring us closer and closer to our goal. In the end, we will surely see an orthodox pope, dedicated to defending the dogmas and the Tradition of the Church. Someone who will prepare and promulgate, and then be willing to implement, such a declaration of faith. I think that such a new profession of faith will be much more elaborate than our "declaration of truths," that it will, as I said, include a detailed index of the errors prevalent in the Church over the last five

[37] "Declaration of the Truths relating to some of the most common errors in the life of the Church in our time" (May 31, 2019), https://www.lifesitenews.com/images/local/Declaration_Truths_Errors.pdf.

decades, and that the future pope will present it to every bishop and cardinal. He will convene the entire college of cardinals in Rome, and all will solemnly pledge to uphold it and fight with all their might against the errors contained in this declaration. That is my expectation. Yes, I am waiting for a truly Catholic pope who will do this.

But this seems like a distant dream. If we just look at what the German bishops are doing these days, it seems that they have already completely abandoned the Faith in many respects.

Yes, some statements by the German bishops are shocking. I recently read that the bishop of the Diocese of Osnabrück, Franz-Josef Bode, Deputy Chairman of the German Bishops Conference, said that "Jesus became human, but not male."[38] That is absolute heresy and pure gnosis.

You can find countless examples of such "wisdom" from the German bishops.

Yet such heresy is precisely the perfect reason why the future declaration that I am talking about should include the statement that "Jesus became human and was born as a man." You see, this is specifically a response to heresy. After all, until now no one in his right mind would have thought to define it because it was obvious that Jesus was a man. But when, as a result of the pressure of the gender ideology, this too is called into question, conclusions must be drawn and clarifications made. Today, then, this needs to be done because such crazy theories are being propagated.

Going back to what I said about the need for a future declaration, I think that every cardinal should take a solemn vow before the pope in St. Peter's Basilica, swearing on the Gospel that he will defend the truths contained in such a declaration and condemn the errors described in it. Anyone who fails to do so should automatically lose his cardinal's hat. There is no other way. This is a must. It's no longer

---

[38] See "Bischof Bode: Christus ist 'Mensche, nicht Mann geworden,'" Katholisch. de (February 6, 2020), www.katholisch.de/artikel/24451-bischof-bode-christus -ist-mensch-nicht-mann-geworden.

possible to continue with the way things are now. The same should then apply to every bishop: each one of them should make a renewed profession of faith before the nuncio, before a papal legate. As in the case of the cardinals, here too anyone who would fail to do so would automatically lose his office.

I can only wish I myself had that kind of faith. I wish I could imagine it when you describe this potential future event so realistically. My reason, however, refuses to accept this vision as realistic.

But the Church has acted this way when confronted with error. And I am sure she will again. There is only one thing we don't know: when it will happen. Perhaps it will be after we are dead. But it will certainly happen.

6

The Leftist Face of the Church

The leftist ideologues claim that Pope Francis is now the world leader of the left. He supports a greater role of women in Church institutions and granting privileges to homosexuals. He is fighting for immigrant rights, and he believes in a new, culturally diverse society. He is open-minded, environmentally conscious, and progressive. He is also an outspoken supporter of a complete ban on the death penalty, and more recently, the life sentence. Many ask themselves: are we not dealing with an attempt to build a new, leftist Church?

Well, it seems that such a judgment could be justified. What comes to mind is *Amoris Laetitia* — and also the support given to Argentine bishops who decided that they would give Communion to divorced people in new relationships, the tolerance and even support of various ecclesiastical radicals, and the appointment of heretical bishops as cardinals. So it is no longer just about tolerance, but active support.

All these concrete actions, statements, and gestures seem to indicate that we are dealing with an attempt to build a church that is completely conformed to the world. This is not just a project of a church that is leftist, but of a church that is aligned with and adapted to the world. You could get the impression that the pope is pursuing an agenda similar to that of the United Nations and various masonic organizations, which are all about pure humanism. I am afraid that the papal office is being used to achieve objectives that have nothing to do with Catholicism:

for building an unbelieving, humanistic new world. On issues such as ecology, custody of the earth, mass immigration, the rise of a "multi-culti" society, the establishment of a new world government, a uniform global society, a uniform common mentality, a uniform progressive worldview in which there is no place for Jesus Christ, the incarnate God, Pope Francis seems to be siding with those forces and world powers that support all these ideas.

It saddens me to say that I am watching this papal involvement with growing concern. It's clearly a far-reaching abuse of papal authority. It's with great regret that I feel compelled to say this, but Pope Francis will have to answer to God for these actions. After all, he has accepted the most sacred office in the Church. He should be, according to the nature of the papal office, the most fervent promoter of the Catholic Faith, its staunchest defender and propagator. The most important task of the pope is to bring as many people as possible to Jesus, so that they will accept faith in Him and persevere in it. The pope should be the one most concerned with preserving the purity of the sacraments because the sacraments offer supernatural life. He should be the first to support the missions among non-Christians, the first to defend the purity of the holy Faith. This is his first and foremost task. Under no circumstances should the papal office serve to promote naturalism. What is the point of building up a world that is not rooted in the Gospel and the Faith?

What is your perception of the proceedings of the Amazon Synod that took place in October 2019 in Rome? What do you think of the synod itself, regardless of your opinion of the final papal document on the matter?

For me, it was one of the saddest events in the entire history of the Church. I cannot comprehend how a synod of bishops, a very respectable institution, could be used to support explicit worship of physical matter, of prosperity, of that which is natural. The Synod should always be concerned with supporting that which is most important in the Church: supernatural life, grace, and the Gospel. Instead, we witnessed a concern for pure naturalism.

What's even worse, in the context of the synod, acts of true idol worship took place. I am referring to everything that happened in connection with the Pachamama statue at the Vatican and in Rome. I consider these idolatrous acts one of the greatest tragedies in the entire history of the Church. A statue of a pagan goddess named Pachamama was being worshipped in the presence of the pope and the bishops. Both the native American participants in the ceremony and the pope were well aware that this is a pagan symbol. It was a truly pagan ritual: candles were lit, prostrations were made, true religious worship was being performed, and that goes against the first commandment of God. In my opinion, what happened at the Vatican was a repetition of the horror of the worship of the golden calf in Old Testament times. For the first time in the history of the Church, a pagan idol was publicly worshipped in Rome, at the tomb of St. Peter, on the ground soaked with the blood of the martyrs, in the presence of the pope. This was an expression of religious veneration directed at a statue worshipped by pagans as Pachamama, the Incan goddess of fertility. The video is available if you want to watch it. There can be no doubt about it. Never before in the history of the Church did such an act take place.

As far as the degree of absurdity, the veneration of Pachamama exceeds even the macabre story from the Middle Ages known as the Cadaver Synod. This was a synod convened by Pope Stephen VI in 897 in Rome. As you can see, this was a really long time ago. At that time, Pope Stephen VI came up with a bizarre, preposterous idea so that he could posthumously judge his predecessor, Formosus. We must remember that these were extremely difficult times for the papacy, when the occupancy of the See of Peter was decided by prominent families, and their rivalry involved changes on the throne of Peter. At that time, Arnulf, who had been crowned by Formosus in 896, and Lambert, his opponent, were rivals for the position of emperor. Probably under pressure from Lambert, Stephen convened a synod to posthumously disgrace and judge Formosus. During the synod, which was attended by bishops, the corpse of the dead pope was exhumed from his grave and dressed in pontifical robes. Then, as a sign of disgrace, three of his fingers that had been used to bless the people were cut off. Once the trial was completed, the body of the deceased was quartered and thrown into the Tiber River. However, justice came quickly. The same year that Pope Stephen carried out this macabre act of judgment, he was arrested and strangled. To date, this was perhaps the greatest horror in the history of the Church. I believe, however, that the veneration of the Pachamama statue was even worse than that Cadaver Synod from the time of Stephen VI.

You are very harsh in your assessment of the events that took place in October 2019 in Rome. Many commentators go as far as to say that the outbreak of Covid-19 is God's punishment for these acts of idolatry.

I don't have absolute certainty that the outbreak of the pandemic is God's punishment for the Pachamama events at the Vatican, but such a belief would not be far-fetched. Back in the early days of the Church, Christ already rebuked the bishops ("angels") of the churches in Pergamon and Thyatira because of their tolerance of idolatry and adultery. The figure of "Jezebel," who seduced the Church into idolatry and adultery (see Rev. 2:20), can also be interpreted as a symbol of the world of our time with which many of those in charge of the Church are flirting. The following words of Christ remain relevant even in our day:

> Behold, I will cast her into a bed: and they that commit adultery with her shall be in very great tribulation, except they do penance from their deeds. And I will kill her children with death, and all the churches shall know that I am he that searcheth the reins and hearts, and I will give to every one of you according to your works. (Rev. 2:22–23)

Christ threatened with punishment and called the churches to repentance:

> But I have against thee a few things ... because thou hast ... cast a stumblingblock before the children of Israel, to eat, and to commit fornication.... In like manner do penance: if not, I will come to thee quickly, and will fight against them with the sword of my mouth. (Rev. 2:14–16)

I am convinced that Christ would have spoken the same words to Pope Francis and other bishops who allowed the idolatrous worship of the Pachamama and implicitly accepted sexual relations outside of a valid marriage by allowing the so-called "divorced and remarried" who are sexually active to receive Holy Communion.

It could be suggested that the pope, along with the cardinals and bishops, should make a public act of reparation in Rome for the sins against the Most Holy Eucharist and for the sin of religious worship of Pachamama statues.

More and more often in today's Church we hear conversations about the new role of women, about the need to redefine it and determine it anew. The argument is that the social conditions are changing, that women are assuming increasingly important functions in political life and in business, and therefore their position in the Church should also change. The most radical proponents of change are talking about women priests, while others argue that they simply need to gain power equal to men in the Church. The Jesuit superior general whom I mentioned earlier has said, "The inclusion of women in the Church is a creative way to promote the necessary changes in it. A theology and an ecclesiology of women should change the image, the concept, and the structures of the Church. [It] should push the Church to become the People of God, as was proclaimed by the Second Vatican Council. Women's creativity can open new ways of being a Christian community of disciples, men and women together, witnesses and preachers of the Good News."[39] There is already a third commission at the Vatican investigating the possibility of admitting women to the diaconate. However, in 1994 John Paul II stated explicitly that the priesthood was instituted exclusively for men. After the release of the papal exhortation *Querida Amazonia* — in which Pope Francis writes with skepticism about the proposal to ordain women, pointing out that it would be a form of clericalism — we are still told that the issue is open and that change is a matter of time. A frequent argument in this debate is that the diaconate is not a degree of the sacrament of priesthood, but a separate sacrament, and therefore John Paul II's words did not apply to the diaconate. This claim, however, seems untenable: the

---

[39] Arturo Sosa, S.J., "Stirring the Water — Making the Impossible Possible" (March 8, 2017), http://www.sjweb.info/documents/assj/2017.03.08_Voices_of_Faith_2017_Fr_General's_speech.pdf.

diaconate, the presbyterate, and the episcopate are three degrees of a single sacrament of Holy Orders, otherwise known as the sacrament of priesthood.

Of course that's the case. We have seven sacraments, not nine or eight. If the diaconate were not a degree of the sacrament of Holy Orders, then logically we would have six sacraments plus the diaconate, plus the presbyterate, plus the episcopate — so nine total. Or if we consider that the presbyterate and the episcopate are one sacrament, and the diaconate is a separate sacrament, there would be eight sacraments altogether. But we have seven sacraments, and one of them is the sacrament of ordination, *sacramentum ordinis*. Since apostolic times it has been one sacrament that includes three degrees. Logically, then, we cannot admit women to the diaconate without admitting them to the presbyterate and to episcopal ordination. From this perspective, granting them access only to the diaconate would be, if we use the language of the proponents of this solution, a form of discrimination. After all, if women could be ordained as deacons, we would immediately hear: "How come, why only the first degree? This is clearly discrimination. After all, men can be ordained to the second and third degrees, and we can be ordained only to the first." By giving women the right to be ordained as deacons, we would have to give them the right to be ordained as presbyters and as bishops. This is logical. This is what the Anglican church did, following the same logic, by first allowing women to the diaconate, then to the presbyterate, and finally to episcopal ordination. Step by step, gradually.

I do, therefore, believe that if it were ever to happen that women were admitted to the diaconate, which for dogmatic reasons is absolutely out of the question, it would be the end of the Catholic Church in her present form. We wouldn't be able to maintain communion with the bishops who ordain women. They would no longer be Catholic. However, let me emphasize that I don't believe that this could happen. The Holy Spirit guides the Church and won't allow anything like this to happen. Instead, I expect to see attempts to create various new "women's" offices under new names. Formally, it would not be admitting women to the diaconate, but in fact there will be an attempt to create new offices in such a way that women holding them can do the same things as deacons. Besides, we must be aware that in many local churches, for decades now, women have been doing almost everything that belongs to the diaconate.

For example, they distribute Holy Communion. After all, this is an action that should be reserved exclusively for the priest or deacon, because only they have been ordained. Never before has the Church allowed women to be ministers of the sacrament of the Eucharist! In times of persecution, the Church has allowed lay people to bring Communion to prisoners or to those who are gravely ill. However, this was *after* Mass, never *at* Mass. At Mass, only the priest would distribute Communion — no matter how many faithful wanted to receive it, and no matter how long it would take. We don't offer a cafeteria service. I must say that I really like the fact that in the Orthodox Church even today the deacon is not allowed to distribute Holy Communion, regardless of how many people are in the church. People know that they must be patient, that the service of God takes time. I have a friend who is an Orthodox priest here in Kazakhstan. I have seen how even during solemn feasts, when there were a lot of people in the church, he distributed Communion by himself, even though the deacon was also there. This lasted half an hour. However, this is only a digression.

Going back to the involvement of women in the Church, I must say that in many Western countries they actually do what deacons do. They wear albs and something resembling a stole. In some Swiss dioceses they regularly baptize and assist at weddings. Of course, the marriage is conferred by the spouses, but women assist, that is, they act in a role that until now has been reserved for priests and deacons. In the same way, they preside over funeral services in Switzerland, Germany, the Netherlands, and other countries. You can see that they are performing all the duties of a deacon. Besides, in Germany there are already cases when female pastoral assistants, dressed in albs, with a sash resembling a stole or with some other sign, read the Gospel during Mass. There are Catholic communities in Germany and Switzerland in which women perform all, I repeat, all the duties reserved for deacons. The label of "deacon" is all that is missing. This is a very dangerous situation, and the Holy See should intervene. Unfortunately, this is all the result of a process that started long ago. Pope Paul VI tolerated it, and Pope John Paul II tolerated it. One by one, women started acting as lectors, ministers of Holy Communion, pastoral assistants, and altar servers ("altar girls"). Behind all this is a false understanding of service at the altar, which has been intended for priests and male servers since apostolic times. In Scripture, woman symbolizes the Church, which the nave also represents, and the sanctuary with the altar symbolizes Christ; therefore only a man should serve at the altar as a deacon, altar server, or lector. Even if he is not a priest, he performs a service that is oriented toward the priesthood. Thus we can see how contemporary secular, temporal, democratic thinking is replacing thinking in sacred and symbolic categories.

This new thinking permeated the practice of the Church after the Second Vatican Council. Since then, women have gradually taken over ministries at the altar in many Western countries. Given the current developments, we can expect that soon there will be voices demanding the right for women to read the Gospel even without sacramental ordination. Or some new, non-sacramental form of blessing will be introduced. This must be creating great confusion among the faithful, for it will be practically impossible — in fact, it already is impossible — to understand the difference between the diaconate and such a form of women's ministry.

You mentioned the changes that took place earlier in the Anglican church. Many commentators now are saying that the Roman Catholic Church is following down the path set by Anglicanism, that we are dealing with an "anglicanization" of Catholicism.

That is happening before our very eyes. This process is already underway. Actually, we can even say that in some respects the Catholic Church is already functioning like the Anglican church. What else can we call a situation in which there are bishops and cardinals within the Church who publicly preach heretical teachings? Earlier, I gave the example of a bishop who maintains that God became human but not male. And what can we say about bishops who declare homosexual intercourse acceptable? The cardinal of Brussels is the one who sees nothing wrong with the active erotic life of homosexuals. This is heresy. These people are tolerated and even supported by Pope Francis. Or what should we call a situation where, in defiance of currently binding Church laws, women are reading the Gospel at Mass and preaching? For several decades, the situation in the Catholic Church has been redolent of what we know from Anglicanism.

Recently, some theologians have been suggesting that women should be allowed to hold the position of cardinal. According to Fr. Federico Lombardi, the former Vatican spokesman, such a solution is "theoretically possible." Prominent theologians such as Fr. James Keenan, S.J., and Professor Karl Heinz Menke support this solution. They argue that unlike ordination, the cardinalate is not a degree of the priesthood, so it is not necessary for cardinals to be exclusively male. They also add that since laymen have been cardinals in the past, perhaps it is time for female cardinals. What do you think about this idea?

> This is unacceptable. Cardinals, as a general rule, are the clergy of the Roman dioceses. The college of cardinals is the college of the clergy of the Roman dioceses representing all three degrees of ordination, cardinal-deacons, cardinal-presbyters, and cardinal-bishops. So if women cannot be deacons, presbyters, or bishops, it is logical that they cannot be cardinals. If there was a desire to open the position of cardinal to women, then the college of cardinals would have to be redefined and recreated. Fulfilling such demands is incompatible with the essence of the college of cardinals.

Still other experts believe that women should be given more power in the Church in such a way that they have the right to vote in the synods.

> But this is impossible by its very definition. After all, a Roman synod is an assembly of bishops, of the episcopate. It's a way in which the pope seeks the advice of the college of bishops on specific matters. This is the purpose and significance of the synod. From this it follows that the right to vote may be exercised only by the participants in the synod, that is, by the bishops, and possibly by the heads of religious congregations, who have a special jurisdiction entrusted to them by

the pope. Women can appear at synods only as advisors, perhaps as experts.[40] If they are women who practice the Catholic faith and are faithful to the Tradition, why not? For example, if Mother Angelica, the founder of EWTN, had been an advisor at a synod, surely her input would have been very valuable for the deliberations.

Somehow, I don't think that the proponents of expanding women's rights in the Church had such women in mind.

If St. Catherine of Siena, St. Brigid of Sweden, or St. Hildegard of Bingen had appeared at a Roman synod, they would certainly have had a positive influence on the deliberations. Margaret, Queen of Scots in the eleventh century, is worth mentioning here. She came to Scotland from Hungary and married the Scottish ruler Malcolm. When the Hungarian princess came to Scotland, she was struck by how bad the morals were in the Church there. Priests had concubines, simony was ubiquitous, and purity was lacking in morals and faith. That is when she took action. She convened synods, forced the bishops to attend, and through her good advisors, the priests, introduced concrete reforms. This was the positive contribution of the holy Queen of Scotland to the work of the synod. At the same time she herself didn't vote; she knew that this was not her role, that she could only encourage, set an example, advise, and exhort. So I have nothing against women of faith contributing to the work of the synods.

But the best possible contribution of a woman of faith is to be involved in family life, to bear children and to raise them, especially if she raises her sons well in the Catholic faith so that they may later become good priests. And then these good priests can become good bishops who will participate in synods defending the Faith.

---

[40] After this passage was written, on February 6, 2021, Pope Francis appointed Nathalie Becquart an undersecretary of the Synod of Bishops, making her the first woman to have the right to vote in the Catholic Synod of Bishops. While His Excellency is correct that women can't be bishops and bishops can't be women, the real issue here is that Francis is giving a synodal vote to a non-bishop (a nun), which is certainly a novelty. — *Ed.*

This model you have mentioned, of a woman who is a mother, a woman raising children, is considered by many to be outdated and incompatible with modern times. It's a relic from the era of a patriarchal society, a society of domination and power of men. It's a relic that must be vanquished. Today the roles of men and women are different.

Nothing of the sort. Human nature doesn't change. The mother and the father — that cannot change. Perhaps in some cultures there has been a distorted understanding of what fatherhood and motherhood are, but these are only isolated cases. There may have been situations where because of shortages of men, for example when they were still fighting wars, all the power over the family belonged to the women. It can also be the other way around: there have been civilizations in which women were treated as slaves — as is still the case today in some regions governed by strict Islam following the Quran. But this doesn't change the basic fact that there is natural law that defines the relationship between the child, the mother, and the father, that defines motherhood and fatherhood.

Let's not forget that Christianity has purified and sanctified nature. Ultimately, God as the cause of human nature has in a way inscribed motherhood in women and fatherhood in men. Accordingly, Christianity has exalted and sanctified that which was already present in nature. That is why it's only in Christian cultures that the woman is accorded such great dignity as a mother. The woman can have a great influence, a good influence on society when she is a good mother. As a well-known adage goes, "The hand that rocks the cradle is the hand that rules the world." Therefore, the true model for a woman is to be a good mother and wife. By nature, men are in leadership roles, because by nature, the mother has to care for the children, to be directed toward them, which in practice means that she is at home with the children, that she is the source of warmth in the family. We must restore the value of motherhood, for only in this way will our society be reborn and our civilization become more humane. Then also the relations between the sexes in our society will be more beautiful.

After all, chivalry and respect for femininity have completely disappeared in our civilization. Often the woman in our day no longer

feels like a lady, and often the man has nothing of the knight in him.
The man doesn't feel that his role is to care for and protect the woman
on account of her being physically inherently weaker, and the woman
doesn't believe that she deserves special attention and respect because
she can be a mother. Similarly, the understanding of fatherhood as
solicitude for the woman and children is also fading. The man needs
the warmth that the woman gives, the warmth that a family brings.
When this is missing, social life suffers. Sexual promiscuity destroys
family life and social life. That is why it's so important to emphasize the
role and significance of motherhood. Societies from which it's missing
become inhuman and cruel. That's the only possible outcome whenever
the warmth of motherhood is missing. In such societies, everyone just
uses and abuses everyone else as objects of desire.

**In his recently published book *A Future of Faith: The Path of Change in Politics and
Society*, which is a transcript of a conversation with the French journalist Dominique
Wolton, Pope Francis says that while we cannot accept the recognition of same-sex
unions between two men or two women as marriages, such unions can be granted legal
status. The point, argues the pope as quoted by Wolton, is not to discriminate.[41] But
if this position has been accurately reported by the journalist, it's a radical departure
from all the previous teachings of his predecessors and from the guidelines of the
Congregation for the Doctrine of the Faith, according to which no support whatsoever can be given to those legal solutions that could be interpreted as an approval of
homosexuality. Experience as a whole clearly shows that granting homosexual unions
legal status and privileges that are equal to those of marriage has the effect of making
them legally equivalent to natural marriages.**

Precisely. Reality itself shows exactly this. First, the claim is made that
not having a separate status is a form of discrimination. Then, once that
status is granted, we are told that it should be equivalent to marriage.
The right to adopting children by homosexuals is introduced. Then the
criticism of homosexual relationships is forbidden. The next step in the

[41] See Pope Francis, *A Future of Faith: The Path of Change in Politics and Society*
(New York: St. Martin's Essentials, 2018).

fight against discrimination is abolishing the existence of fathers and mothers. It's a logical conclusion: since it was first accepted that a union between a man and a man, or a woman and a woman, is worth the same as a marriage between a man and a woman, it follows that it cannot be better for children to be raised within a natural union than for children to be raised by a homosexual couple; so if in the one case children are unable to address their parents using the terms "mom" and "dad," these terms must also be forbidden in the other case. That's why the Holy See has clearly taught from the beginning that even if the legal status granted to homosexual couples is not defined by the term "marriage," such a law is still morally unacceptable, under *any* label. This is what I would call "label fraud." Sexual intercourse between two women or two men is in itself an act against nature and a sin. It's a violation of natural law and God's law based on revelation. Ultimately, it's not about men and women living together as they do in a monastery or living as brothers and sisters, but about a relationship based on homoerotic gratification. In the case of granting legal status to homosexual couples, it's about the State declaring explicitly its full acceptance of homosexual eroticism. Two men or two women are, as it were, saying to the State and to society: "We are living together because we are bound by a mutual erotic desire, and we demand that this fact be accepted and recognized publicly by the State." In this way, the society indicates its acceptance of the sin against nature. The Church, therefore, cannot endorse this or condone it in any way. It's about the public recognition of evil. Besides, the vast majority of these relationships fall apart very quickly.

In any case, the legal recognition of homosexual relationships is an outright defiance of the natural law, which must lead to scandal in society. And the legal recognition of scandal ultimately destroys the principles by which society is governed. It's also a real, almost direct form of advocating homosexual relations as such, a promotion of homoeroticism.

But aren't we approaching a breakthrough when it comes to the Church's teaching on the harmfulness of homosexuality? According to the German bishops, homosexuality is "a normal form of sexual predisposition." The press office of the German Bishops'

Conference announced in December 2019 that this was the position taken by Bishops Heiner Koch of Berlin, Franz-Josef Bode of Osnabrück, Peter Kohlgraf of Mainz, and several other unnamed hierarchs representing the German Bishops' Marriage and Family Commission. In their opinion, people acquire a heterosexual or homosexual orientation during adolescence and this can no longer be changed, nor should it be attempted. The bishops have urged a ban on any form of discrimination against persons with homosexual tendencies. Based on that, it can be concluded that the Church's prohibition of the practice of homosexual acts appears to be erroneous. This should logically entail a change in the official Catholic teaching on the subject. Above all, it would mean no longer treating homosexual acts as sinful and accepting same-sex unions (including some form of blessing of such couples in Catholic churches, which is already happening in some places, without any objections from the local hierarchy). Are these bishops still members of the Church?

> Certainly these bishops are taking a relativistic stance. Their position rejects natural law and God's creation. It's a rejection of the fact that God actually created the world. I should add that the idea of exploiting homosexuality ideologically originated in the Gnostic circles. From the beginning it was the Gnostics who taught that the division of living creatures into the male and female sexes is evil, the work of an evil demiurge. The good God, whom they saw in Lucifer, doesn't recognize any sexual division, but his creation instead is a human including both sexes — an androgyne. Androgyny is the view that the human being is both male and female. This was a view represented by the Gnostics from the beginning, the main principle of gnosis. It was adopted by Freemasonry and has remained a constant part of their ideology ever since.
>
> As I said, the goal is to construct a whole new reality, different from the one created by God. This is what the satanic way is all about: seeking to subvert this fundamental division and rejecting the Creator who, according to revelation, created mankind male and female. God didn't create mankind as male, homosexual, lesbian, asexual, pansexual, and so on. Instead, He created mankind as male and female! This is a fact. This is part of our biological, animal nature. In the same way, among animals there are no homosexuals or lesbians. There are males and

females, that which is male and that which is female. The division into the two sexes is natural. This polarity can be observed everywhere, in flowers and trees. Without it, the world of living beings would cease to exist. Sexual differentiation ensures the transmission of life. If it were not for sexual differentiation between males and females, the human species would cease to exist. Even the smallest cell of the body has either female or male characteristics. There are no homosexual cells, no cells that are half male and half female. Science clearly says that a person's sex is biologically determined. A person with XX chromosomes is female, while an individual with one X chromosome and one Y chromosome is male.

Bishops who speak against this are speaking against the order of creation. Ultimately, they are taking a Gnostic or entirely relativistic position. Appealing to discrimination in this case is a sham. If I tell someone who they are, if I name the reality, that is not discrimination. Quite the opposite. Because of original sin, human nature has been wounded, deformed, and pathologies have emerged, also in the area of sexual life. I am referring not just to homosexuality, but also to other pathologies: masochism, sadomasochism, necrophilia, zoophilia, and such. Homosexuality is a form of sexual pathology. We must do our best to cure it. People with homosexual tendencies should be able to benefit from therapy and from the assistance that society can offer them. A man can be cured of any pathology. This is exactly how bishops should be helping such people, by showing them the path to healing. But they are doing exactly the opposite: by making homosexuality normal, they are confirming these people in sin. They are supporting them in their attitude against God. By doing so, these bishops are pushing these people — I am not talking about people with homosexual tendencies, but about active, practicing homosexuals — toward Hell. It's cruel. This is real discrimination. It perpetuates these people's inclinations against nature and reinforces their sexually pathological state. At the same time, they are not told about the terrible danger of eternal damnation they incur by engaging in such acts. I am convinced that these bishops will have to answer to God for these words and actions.

Another German leader, the Archbishop of Munich Cardinal Reinhard Marx, until recently chairman of the German Bishops' Conference, said that priests should bless homosexual couples. That would mean that the Church is blessing mortal sin, which is absurd. Of course, as usual, nothing has happened. There has been no reaction to this. The cardinal has been making these horrendous statements and there has been no resistance in the Church. The same archbishop has said that the Catholic Church should apologize to homosexuals for their treatment up until now and for discriminating against them in the past.

I am not aware of any official Church document that prescribes discriminating against them.

It all depends on what we regard as discrimination. If the lack of a blessing itself is discrimination, then in that sense the Church has certainly been discriminating against homosexuals.

It's exactly the opposite: if they are blessed and reinforced in sin — that is true discrimination. Not only are they left in an inner state of rupture, but they are actually being persuaded not to attempt to heal it. Instead of truth, they are being offered an illusion. These people find themselves in a state of inner rupture. They can see that biologically they are male or female, but they are acting against their biological constitution. Whenever a person goes against nature, it means that he is in a state of inner rupture. And this is a sign of an illness. I repeat, whoever confirms them in this commits mortal sin. He bears responsibility for their possible future damnation.

Society persecuted homosexuals in the past, and Church representatives also occasionally did so. However, this was not the official teaching of the Church. The point is not to despise these people or to demean them as persons. Today, however, we have gone from one extreme to the other. I don't think it's right to impose the death penalty on these people, as was once the case (and still is in some legislatures). Since it is a form of immaturity and disability, it must not be punishable by death. Another issue is the question of the criminalization of these acts in general. Historically, the homosexual subculture started spreading like wildfire after being decriminalized. It's not just about a private, individual sin, but about a lifestyle, a publicly promoted immorality that is being encouraged. This has a contagious effect on young people in particular. The State and society must defend themselves against this form of promotion. If we are confronted here with propagating or abetting vice, with breaking the rules of public order, then in such a case punishment is acceptable as a form of self-defense of the State against the propagation of attitudes contrary to nature. However, it must not be a harsh punishment. The purpose of the law should be, on the one hand, to provide protection for society, and on the other hand, to offer help to these people. If this is to be effective, discreet assistance should be available so that those who wish to avail themselves of it are not humiliated.

A radically different position from that of the German bishops was taken by Archbishop Marek Jędraszewski of Kraków, who called the LGBT ideology the "rainbow plague" and compared it to Bolshevism. He called on the Church to fight LGBT ideology. Do Cardinal Marx and Archbishop Jędraszewski still belong to the same Church?

If we were to judge by their actions, then definitely not. This is another proof that the Catholic Church has been anglicanized, that the Roman Catholic Church is becoming the Anglican-Catholic Church. Within a religious community that is nominally one and the same, different bishops and cardinals maintain conflicting positions on key, fundamental issues. We are not talking just about trifles, but about the substance of the moral law and about universal ethical rules. I fully support Archbishop Jędraszewski and I agree completely with his judgment. We saw how the Communist ideology spread almost all over the world. Now homosexuality has taken over the role of such a global ideology under the name of the "LGBT movement." As a result, attempts are being made, using the pseudo-science of gender ideology, to poison the minds and the emotional and moral lives of young people and children. In my opinion, this is one of the most dangerous spiritual pandemics to have befallen humanity. Gender ideology attacks the core, the very heart, of social life. The target of this attack is marriage and the family. It's also a direct attack on God the Creator. I would even say that from a certain point of view gender ideology is more dangerous than Communist ideology. Communism preached atheism, maintained that there was no God, and persecuted every form of religion. LGBT and gender ideology goes even further. It says: that which God created is false. It strikes at the basic cell thanks to which societies exist, it undermines the meaning of the union of the man and the woman, the meaning of marriage and the meaning of family. The destruction of the family results in a degradation of society. Researchers of morality clearly indicate that sexual promiscuity leads to a destruction of culture and civilization. As a result, man falls into animalism, returns to a state of animalism and barbarism. The more permissive a society and the more corrupt its customs, the lower its level of culture and the lower its level of civilizational development. There are sufficient studies to show this.

Today, sexual promiscuity in the West has reached such a level that it's difficult to find civilizations in the past to equal it. That is why our society is becoming more and more selfish. People are forgetting what sacrifice and devotion are. They are thinking only of themselves and about satisfying their desires. Only those who are strong, healthy, and conscious count. The unborn can be eliminated at will. The old and the sick are urged to part with their lives as quickly as possible. All limitations must be eliminated. I repeat, only strength counts. It's all about living physically to the fullest and finding gratification. So we are living in one of the most cruel societies, where only the strong have rights. The weak and the suffering have no rights. On the contrary, selfishness is constantly being cultivated.

In such a society, the Church must be the salt of the earth, even more so now than before. It must slowly and incessantly imbue society with a different way of thinking. It must shatter selfishness and point to loftier goals. Here is what I see as a mandate for true ecumenism: for all Christians to take the natural law and the order of creation seriously. It should be clear to all Christians that it's essential to defend the laws of nature, sound human reason, the rights of the family, and the right to life. We must build a coalition around these goals. The goal is not, let me say it clearly, preserving the traditional family, but the natural family. It's not about defending inherited customs, or tradition, but about that which is objective — about nature. It's about defending the natural marriage between a man and a woman. This is a challenge for all Christians, but also a task for all other religions. Defending the basic principles of natural law is simply man's duty in the face of the onslaught of this global gender ideology, LGBT ideology, the ideology of a new world order headed by one world government. We must pray for a pope who will clearly and explicitly summon all people of good will to build a coalition to defend unborn life, marriage, and the family. We must pray for someone who will not support people promoting gender ideology or LGBT ideology and who will not create global, worldwide pacts in favor of naturalism.

In the course of our conversation I have quoted multiple statements made by various bishops or cardinals. How is it that they meet with no condemnation from Rome? Why were the Ukrainian bishops the only ones to react to the new teachings of the German bishops?

This is indeed very tragic. For years, we have not had a sufficiently consistent plan to counter the progress of LGBT or gender ideology. Our tragedy is that both Pope Francis and the Vatican remain silent.[42] What's even worse, some of these "progressives" are subsequently rewarded with offices in the Curia. This is nothing else but a form of collaboration with those who are spreading corruption and error. If I am watching an arsonist start a fire in a house, and I am standing nearby and passively watching, then I am culpable. I am culpable for the fire in that house. This is happening right before our eyes. You could say that in a spiritual sense, fire after fire is breaking out before our very eyes. All this is happening in the Church because of these heretical bishops and cardinals.

[42] On February 22, 2021, a year after this interview was conducted, the Congregation for the Doctrine of the Faith published a *Responsum* to a *dubium* regarding the blessing of the unions of persons of the same sex. The document said the Church does not have the power to bless such unions. It was approved for publication by Pope Francis. Its release set off a firestorm of illicit blessings, especially in Germany. — *Ed.*

Why is it that the only ones protesting were the bishops from Ukraine or earlier the bishops from Kazakhstan, including you?

For sure, it would be better if more bishops were to speak out on this issue. There is no doubt that they can see what is happening; after all, we are now living in a global world where, through the Internet, everyone is interconnected. There are various reasons for this silence. Some bishops agree with these heretical claims and practices. For example, inviting LGBT activists to the cathedral in Vienna in Austria, so that they can propagate their ideology there, is a form of heretical practice. Other bishops, who oppose this ideology, assume that it does not affect them directly. "That's not my diocese, not my business," they are saying, "Leave me alone." Some others are simply afraid. They think that if they were to speak out, they would immediately be seen as traditionalists or as fanatics. They are concerned about their image. They would like to be perceived as moderate, open, and ready for dialogue. There are also those who remain silent for tactical reasons, because they want to make a career. They know that if they stand firm against such heretical statements, they cannot hope to be promoted in the Church. Finally, we must not forget those who, although they themselves would like to disagree, are afraid that they will be reprimanded by the Vatican, the nuncio, or their own bishops' conference. As you can see, we are talking about a whole range of possible motivations to explain the bishops' silence. Only a few have plucked up the courage to speak out clearly on this issue. Indeed, there are really only a few.

Keeping silent is much easier, and it's also easy to justify it. For example, some say, "I am only an auxiliary bishop," or, "I am very far away," or, "I am responsible for my diocese and not for another; God wanted to put me here and not anywhere else. This is the pope's business, not mine." Frankly speaking, I think that such explanations are just a cheap excuse. Ultimately, we are not a secular company or society, nor are we a government in which each minister can say that he has his own domain and cannot interfere with what the others are doing. No, we are not a corporation; we are not a government; we are a living family. All of us all over the world are one Catholic family. We are one

Body. As St. Paul says, if one member of the body suffers, all the others suffer with it. That is why I can't say that I don't care. Obviously, I can pray, do penance, make reparation for the sins committed by the bad shepherds. But the way I see it, a bishop must do even more. By his ordination, every bishop becomes a member of the worldwide college of bishops and a successor of the apostles. As the constitution *Lumen Gentium* says, every bishop should feel responsible for the good of the whole Church. Even if his jurisdiction is limited to his diocese, he must feel a solicitude for the whole Church. He must also help the whole Church. He must make his contribution.

So with this in mind, the considerations I mentioned earlier represent a cheap excuse. If I had remained silent, I would not have been able to handle the voice of my conscience. I could not stand before God. How could I say, "I know what the German bishops are doing, but I don't care, it's far away, and it should suffice that I pray for them"? I don't believe that God would accept such an explanation from me. That is why I am speaking out. I am speaking out because I am solicitous for the good of the whole Church. Since the current pope is not fulfilling his role in this regard and is keeping silent, the bishops must come to his assistance and do what is needed in his stead. This is exactly the form of collegiality that the Second Vatican Council so strongly emphasized. When we are speaking about collegiality, it's not about the relationship between an employee and the boss. It doesn't mean that the employee has to do what the boss says. That is how officials and employees working for companies can behave. But the pope is not the boss, and the bishops are not his employees. We are a college, we are bound to each other. The episcopate is a living body. This is the point of collegiality: if the head is showing weakness and failing to perform the task entrusted to him, then the other members of the body come to his aid. We say *corpus episcoporum*. They come to help and they defend the Faith. The pope should be grateful for this. Even if at the moment he is not showing gratitude to the bishops who are doing what he should be doing, even if today he cannot see this, or perhaps he is even angry and would like to punish such bishops, certainly when he stands before the judicial throne of God — after all, this will be the case with everyone, including Pope Francis — he will be grateful for the fact that some bishops spoke in his stead. I am absolutely convinced of this. At the judgment, God will show him this. He will point to those bishops whose actions, the fact that they spoke when he should have spoken, will help him at the judgment and thus they will be interceding for him.

Let me share an anecdote with you. A few years ago, in 2015, after the synod on the family in Rome, the final report was drafted. It contained highly ambiguous and dangerous statements and theories — first of all, very vague theories on marriage, openness and understanding for unions of same-sex couples. That's why I decided to criticize it. Let me emphasize that at that point the document didn't come from the pope, but from my fellow bishops. I posted my article online, and, as usual, various readers started commenting on it. One of them wrote, "Yes, I agree with this analysis by Bishop Schneider, but let me ask, how will the Vatican punish him for this?" To which the next person commenting responded as follows, "Well, Bishop Schneider is already in Kazakhstan."

More and more European countries are attempting to radically restrict freedom of speech and freedom of opinion. Fortunately, in Poland it's still possible to openly criticize the LGBT movement and its demands. In many other countries, however, this is either not possible at all, or such criticism is becoming increasingly risky. I am thinking of the United Kingdom, France, or the Netherlands, among others. In practically all countries that have introduced laws giving same-sex couples equal status to that of normal marriages, an attempt is being made to silence the critics of this solution as well as opponents of the homosexual lifestyle. Don't you think that these anti-discrimination laws are simply a form of democratic totalitarianism? This was the question I had prepared before my arrival in Kazakhstan. Yesterday, when we were talking, you called homosexuality a form of pathology, a form of disease. Almost at the same time as our conversation, a referendum was being held in Switzerland, in which 60 percent of the Swiss people voted in favor of sanctions against those who spread "homophobia" or "hate speech." There is no doubt in my mind that the statements you made about homosexuality would be regarded in those countries as a sign of "homophobia" or "hate speech," and you could be prosecuted for them. If you had said those things not here in Kazakhstan, nor in Poland, but in one of the supposedly

democratic countries of the West, it could have resulted in severe repercussions. You could be prosecuted immediately, either by one of the LGBT organizations, or by the prosecutors of the country in question. In fact, we can't rule out that even now, after our interview, an attempt will be made in one of these countries to arrest you and prosecute you. If you don't withdraw your opinion that homosexuality is pathological and should be treated, you are facing a prison sentence. Are you not afraid of that? That one day when you show up at an airport in Italy or Great Britain or some other place, you will be arrested?

> One thing is certain: if something like this were to happen, with the help of God's grace, I will definitely not retract any of my statements.

So you will not be asking for forgiveness, like so many other politicians or Church figures? You will not retract your opinions?

> With the help of God's grace, not under any circumstances.

Even if, as we can assume, you were to face imprisonment for it?

> Not even then. I will ask God's help to not retract anything I have said, even if that meant going to prison. When a man suffers for the truth, he suffers for Christ. And suffering for Christ should be our honor. Let me remind you that John the Baptist suffered martyrdom when he reproached King Herod, saying that he had no right to take his brother's wife. He was beheaded for this. He didn't die directly for Christ. He defended the value of marriage. But he is venerated as a martyr. It's a fact that homosexuality is against nature, and in this sense a pathology.

You are saying that it's a fact. However, in many European countries this would be considered "hate speech." The belief there is that homosexuality is normal, that it doesn't need to be treated, that, on the contrary, it's something to be happy about and proud of. Such words as yours are punishable by law.

> This is an abuse — an abuse of language and of law. It's also an attack on freedom. Why is it that when someone is blaspheming against Christ, it's not hate speech? Or when someone is attacking the Catholic Church or ridiculing Catholics? Why isn't that hate speech?

Because when Catholics are being attacked, that's freedom of opinion. But when you criticize LGBT ideology, that's hate. It's as simple as that.

This is purely arbitrary. The promotion of homosexuality runs against human dignity. Let me repeat: we must help these people overcome their inner rupture. When I see a sick person and I tell him that he is healthy, I am deceiving him. If I show him compassion, I am not discriminating against him. I am not, after all, addressing individual people here. I am not saying that Mr. Smith or Mr. Miller is a homosexual — that would be defamation. That would be naming a specific person. I am speaking generally about a type of behavior. People who have such inclinations suffer from a certain affliction. This is a fact, this is a diagnosis. This is what all scientists, psychiatrists, and psychologists have always believed until the 1970s. All international science until the 1970s represented this view. The change came about not through a discovery, but through political action, influenced by effective political pressure.

It was the same in the Nazi and the Communist regimes. There, too, certain opinions, absurd and ridiculous in themselves, were treated as scientific with all seriousness and could not be questioned for fear of severe penalties. In Germany, for example, after Hitler came to power in 1933, it was declared that the Aryan race was more valuable than other races, which is absurd. If I had said during the Third Reich that the Jewish race was of equal value to the Aryan race, I would have been imprisoned. My opinion would not have suited the ruling Nazi ideology at the time and would have been, in the eyes of the Nazis, a form of discrimination against the master race. Moreover, this ideology was supported by the scientists who used their academic credentials to justify the inhumane actions of the authorities. This had nothing to do with reality. As far as the ontological dignity of human beings is concerned, different races are completely equal. It doesn't matter whether a person is Jewish or German, whether his skin color is white or black — he has the same rights, he is equally human. This basic equality of people, so fiercely opposed by the ideology of racism in the Third Reich, is actually a fact.

Likewise, what I am currently saying about homosexuality is a fact. And if God were to allow me to go to prison for those words, I am willing to go. Because nothing happens without God's permission. But if that were to happen, then I think that the pope, in communion with the whole episcopate, would have to speak out forcefully in defense of human dignity. He would have to say clearly that defending dignity requires calling things by their proper names. For the good of man, we must say that homosexuality is not in accord with nature and that satisfying such desires is not proper. It's harmful to man. Man must be assisted in living a sexual life in accordance with the demands of nature. This alone can make him happy and complete. Supporting the state of rupture and sugarcoating reality can't lead to anything good.

It's currently very trendy to say that we live in harmony with nature. Everything has to be natural and organic: food, lifestyle, housing. Even the chickens can no longer be kept in cages, but must be kept free range — because this is in harmony with nature. Strangely enough, this love of nature doesn't manifest itself in judgments on sexual behavior. After all, there are organs in the human body that are naturally assigned to certain functions. The woman's body and the man's body have different organs. They perform physiologically important functions. This sexual differentiation manifests itself throughout the human organism — you can see it even in the genes and in the structure of the DNA. We can say that down to the smallest particle of the body, down to the smallest cell, the human being is either male or female. This is how the organism has been designed from the beginning. As you can see, I am not using religious argumentation here at all. An atheist, too, must recognize this difference of biological structures, the difference of functions and purposes of the human body depending on its natural sex. The male-female distinction is absolutely crucial. Whoever wishes to live in harmony with nature must not ignore it. At the level of biological life, human beings have a body that is subject to the same laws as animal bodies. If we are saying that animals should live according to nature, the same also pertains to human beings.

That is why it's so important to help these people. After all, there are proven methods, excellent therapy treatments, proper ways of treatment that bring excellent results. Thanks to them, the person will become much happier. The man must live in harmony with his male nature and the woman must live in harmony with her female nature.

Again, we are reaching the same point. What you are calling therapy or help, LGBT activists are calling an assault on their way of life. Their goal is to bring about a situation in which this way of life will be fully accepted, where it will not be subject to any judgment or criticism. In this sense, the Church and her teachings must be their main adversary. Year after year, activist groups are becoming more aggressive and gaining more influence. During the months of so-called gay pride, entire cities are covered with rainbow flags. Pedestrian crossings are painted rainbow colors, rainbow stickers are displayed in store windows. For several years now, the LGBT movement has been increasingly supported by large international corporations, which allocate more funds to promotional campaigns. At the same time, more countries are tightening their laws against gender critics. They are being expelled from universities, not allowed to meet with students, removed from public spaces. How can we defend ourselves against this? How can we win the war against homoterror?

We live in democratic societies, and we must take advantage of it and defend ourselves. The way of life of 1 percent of all citizens can't be imposed on everyone. We must not accept a situation in which criticism or calling things by their name is not allowed under threat of imprisonment or a fine. This is real discrimination — this is actually totalitarianism. We must exercise our civil rights and not surrender. These [LGBT] people have the same rights as everyone else. No one is discriminating against them. They have voting rights, they can form associations, they can express their opinions. They have the same rights as other citizens. They are, in the full sense of the word, human beings, and they are entitled to all the rights that human beings inherently possess. People are not defined by being a homosexual or a lesbian. The fact that people are always viewed through the prism of their sexual preferences and inclinations is a form of discrimination in itself. In this way, human dignity is reduced to just one dimension, as if nothing else mattered. As if the most important thing in a human being was his or her sexuality, or orientation, as it is called today by some ideologues.

I think that an international coalition should be formed, led by the Vatican, against these increasingly powerful totalitarian tendencies. In this sense our morality must become organic, to use a fashionable term. But as I understand it, it signifies a morality that is once again in harmony with nature and its principles.

We must not yield to those who accuse us of discrimination. If we were talking about the danger of alcoholism and the need for alcoholics to be treated, would that be discriminating against them? Alcoholism is a disease. If we were to use the logic of LGBT ideologues, we would say that we must not call alcoholics sick, or alcoholism a disease, because it is a form of discrimination against them. Similarly, there is a variety of phobias, of different persistent irrational forms of fear and anxiety. For example, claustrophobia is a disorder in which people experience a fear of confinement. It's said that claustrophobia is a form of pathology. But if I took at face value what gender activists are saying today, I would have to conclude that I am not allowed to call claustrophobia a pathology. Why? Because that would make claustrophobic people uncomfortable. In fact, alcoholics probably outnumber homosexuals, although it would depend on the country. Either way, they are a minority. According to this new approach, in which criticism is a form of discrimination, these people could not be regarded as sick.

The same applies to drug addicts. Any form of addiction is no longer considered a sickness or an abnormality. It turns out that no pathology, no affliction, no addiction should be judged in these terms — by asking whether it's healthy or not. Why would we want to treat people addicted to cocaine, hashish, or other drugs — why would we want to help them? After all, taking such substances gives these people satisfaction and pleasure. Many of them are unable to live without it. And yet we call it a disease and a pathology. So what if these people declare that they are healthy? And that anyone who calls them sick is discriminating against them? What if this minority of drug addicts organized itself — after all, they may be a few percent of the population — and started fighting against the alleged discrimination? They would declare that they are proud and happy, and that they should not in any way be judged and should be accepted. And under such pressure, a law would be passed prohibiting the claim that drug addiction or alcoholism is a disease.

In this way we have reached an absurdity. And these are the only logical consequences of the position that claims that calling homosexuality a disease should be forbidden because it is a form of discrimination. Another logical consequence would be the decriminalization and de-stigmatization of drug addicts, people addicted to cocaine, hashish, or heroin. Similarly, we should ban therapy for alcoholics and suppress Alcoholics Anonymous meetings. In this way, we would find ourselves in a society completely controlled by absurdity — a society based on the denial of reality, a rejection of facts, and of the basic distinction between what is healthy and what is diseased, between nature and anti-nature.

In the last few years, the number of attacks on Catholic places of worship has definitely increased. More and more often crosses are being desecrated, and symbols of the Faith are being destroyed. Sometimes the churches are targeted, sometimes Catholic cemeteries. What is the cause of this wave of anti-Christian actions? The pattern is the same, whether it takes place in Belgium, France, or Germany. Interestingly, it's rarely reported in the news; at best, it may get a passing mention.

Indeed, we are encountering a new phenomenon. It seems as if these activities were somehow organized. It seems — and this is merely conjecture on my part — as if someone behind the scenes were pulling the strings and executing a certain plan. Besides, we have to recognize the contemporary mentality, and the prevailing prejudices and stereotypes about the Church in our society. The hatred and hostility toward Christianity are becoming more and more pronounced. It's perfectly evident when we follow the reporting of the media and the messages of mass culture, films, and popular books. A huge segment of Western society has not only lost its faith and is no longer Christian, but they also hate Christianity. Even if these people are baptized — in some Western countries this is still the statistical majority — it doesn't mean anything. Or rather, hostility toward the Church ensues. There are also those who hate what the Church teaches, who reject the commandments of God and are rebelling against them. They don't want to hear anything about chastity, obedience, or renunciation.

So when they hear what the Church is teaching, it triggers their aggression. Since the cross is a symbol of Christianity, they try to defile it, degrade it, destroy it. In this way, they are clearly opposing the commandments of God: you shall not kill, you shall not steal, you shall not commit adultery, you shall not covet, you shall not lie, you shall not worship idols. While rejecting this internally, they want to express their opposition publicly. That is why acts of vandalism are a manifestation of this hostility toward the message of Christianity, toward revelation.

This confirms my conviction that we are living in a neo-pagan society, indeed, a completely pagan society. We can only expect that in such a society, outbursts of irrational hatred against Christians will become more and more common. After all, Christians, and I am referring here to true believers, are living witnesses whose very presence and life are unbearable to the new pagans. They are a living reproach to people who want to live without God, who want to manifest this lifestyle and take pride in it. That was the fate of Christians in the first centuries, under the rule of pagan Rome. Christians were a minority then, a foreign body in a pagan society. They refused to conform to the morality of the pagan majority and could not be persuaded to worship idols. This was the true source of the hatred against them: they refused to do what everyone else was doing, and consequently incurred wrath against themselves. While the hatred of the human race was literally attributed to the Christians (this was the original meaning of the term *odium humani generis*), later on Christianity was increasingly regarded as deserving of the hatred of the human race as its object. Being different was precisely the reason for this hatred.

In Europe and in the Western world, something very similar is happening today. Christianity, and especially the Catholic Church, is becoming the *odium*, an object of hatred. Acts of vandalism prove this.

Is there even such a thing as a morally neutral state? Can we conceive of legislation that would not be grounded in any higher law? You will often hear that Christian symbols

should disappear from public spaces because their presence favors Christians. Neutrality, in this view, would entail the removal of Christian signs and symbols because they are disturbing to followers of other faiths or non-believers.

> Such an approach is contrary to the nature of man as God created him. We have been created for God. We have been created first and foremost, like all of creation, for His glory and His honor. We, human beings, with our human nature, immortal souls, and reason, have one primary purpose: to worship God. And that's not just individually. It's not just about private adoration. As Aristotle said long ago, the human being is a *zoon politikon*, a social or political being. That implies that man has a duty to worship God together with others, in a community, in society. The ultimate form of the organization of society is the State, and so the State as such also has a duty to God, to the true God. The State by its very nature has a duty to worship the true God, not a false one, not an idol. The true God is the Holy Trinity, the Triune God. Thus, there can't be a religiously neutral society, for that would be contrary to man's purpose from the moment of creation. In other words, it would be an atheistic society. Complete neutrality is only possible in the case of an atheistic society. Such a perfectly atheistic society has never yet emerged. All societies in human history, even if they were savage, uncivilized peoples, have had their forms of religious expression.

Neo-Marxism is not only the origin of the LGBT ideology or gender ideology, it also manifests itself in other popular leftist movements today. Another form of such new radicalism is extreme veganism. Its proponents claim that humans must not be treated better than other animals, that inter-species equality must be restored. A consequence of this position is the cry for a complete renunciation of eating meat, a complete ban on livestock breeding, and such. Some radicals attack livestock farms and release animals into the wild. There are also those who attack people and claim that the value of an animal's life is greater than the life of an ill human being. Finally, environmentalism is becoming increasingly popular, and in its extreme version, which is also gaining popularity quickly, it assumes that the only way to save the allegedly endangered Earth is to significantly reduce procreation. Supporters of this movement claim that humanity should either disappear altogether, or at least the global population should be drastically reduced.

It's true, there is such a tendency. It can be spotted easily in the new Hollywood movies. They often portray animals as smarter and more valuable than humans. Animals talk, they are intelligent and happier than humans. This places animals above man in the hierarchy of creation. In God's order, the animal is lower than the man. In this way, that which is instinctive, animalistic, and irrational is being promoted. It's demonic, because it involves a distortion of the order of creation, an overturning of the hierarchy. The perverse reversal of God's order of things is ultimately satanic. Notably, in the biblical tradition Satan often appears in animal form. He is shown as a snake, a dragon, or a beast. Experienced exorcists also mention this. They say that when they cast out Satan, he often appears in the form of a disgusting, hideous animal.

But I hope that this radical environmentalism movement will not have such a broad impact.

In the UK or the Netherlands such attacks on farms are becoming more common. Radicals are beginning to prevail. Governments, under their pressure, are introducing higher taxes on meat.

Against such a radical environmentalism movement there is, after all, a self-preservation instinct in man, an instinct that tells him to defend himself. This instinct cannot be simply banned and destroyed.

And what do you think about the concept of "animal rights"? Many environmentalists readily mention such rights. Some are calling for an animal rights spokesperson. Governments are beginning to change laws and punish crimes against animals. Politicians are talking about the need to make our treatment of animals more humane.

Animals can't have rights. Only rational beings, only human beings, can have rights. By definition, rights belong only to those who have reason. The real problem today is that terms are being twisted or reversed quite arbitrarily. They no longer represent reality, but are products of human cognition. Those who believe this think language can be freely manipulated. This is also true of many other concepts. For example, the concept of "marriage" necessarily entails the union of a man and a woman, of two sexes. Marriage understood as the union of two persons of the same sex is a contradiction in itself. Such a contradiction is also inherent in the concept of "animal rights." "Flower rights" or "tree rights" would be equally illogical. The notion of a "right" is necessarily linked to the notion of a duty. A right to something corresponds to a duty. One doesn't exist without the other. Where there is a right, there is also a duty. It would follow that if animals have rights, they should also have duties. You can't be the subject of rights without being the subject of duties. If a person breaks the law, if he doesn't fulfill his duty, he should be punished. It follows that animals should also be punished. And so we are moving from one absurdity to another. Therefore, right, similarly to duty, refers only to man because only man has reason and only man can assume responsibility. By its very definition, the concept of animal rights is impossible. The fact that people have started using it is the result of increasing attempts to put man and other animals on the same level.

Why is it happening? What makes people today think that animals have the same value as they do?

Because in the end many want to reduce man to what is animalistic. They want to view man as a collection of instincts and to reduce his rights to a boundless, unbridled freedom to exploit himself and to satisfy his instincts. Man is supposed to be pure arbitrariness, unbridled, pure freedom, which is not bound by any moral law. If you look at man in this way, it is no wonder that you eventually lose the ability to distinguish him from an animal. If man is merely naked instinct, sheer debauchery and wantonness, then nothing actually distinguishes him from an animal. Implicit in this desire to equate man and animal is also a rejection of the order created by God.

During the Amazon Synod, much was said about the need for ecological conversion. It was also proposed that a new category of sin, ecological sin, be introduced into the

Catechism of the Catholic Church. What do you think about this? There are also cardinals who claim that environmentalism has a Christian aspect.

The current ideology of environmentalism is not Christian. It's an anti-Christian ideology. The whole of revelation clearly says that man is to be converted to God. Man is not to be converted to nature, but to God. Turning to nature would be a form of materialism. Turning away from the Creator and turning toward creation is the definition of sin given to us by St. Augustine: *Aversio a Deo* — turning away from God, and *conversio ad creaturam* — turning toward creation. This is a perversion. That's why we can firmly assert that there is something sinful in the concept of ecological conversion: man is turning to creation instead of turning to God.

Of course, God also said that man should use creation and care for it in accordance with God's will. Man may use nature, he may employ it for his needs, but never in contradiction to God's will. He shouldn't destroy nature or deliberately torment animals, for this goes against God's will. God is the God of beauty, order, wisdom, and life. But this is nothing new. Because of this, man has a responsibility to take care of his body. Man is to be the temple of the Holy Spirit. During each Mass, we sing the Sanctus with the following words, "Heaven and earth are full of your glory. Hosanna in the highest." The Church, of course, has always used created nature to express praise to God through it. Speaking of ecology, the first true ecologists in the proper sense of the word were Catholic monks. Let's look at the work and achievements of Cistercians in eastern Germany and western Poland. They cultivated the land, established magnificent gardens, and taught people about organic, healthy agriculture. They cultivated grapevines, from which wine was produced. The most beautiful gardens, the most magnificent flowers — all this was the work of the monks. In the monasteries the healthiest liqueurs were produced. Beer was also invented in monasteries. This is all the great work of the Church. So was the splendid architecture, art, painting, and sculpture. In this way, the Church used created things for worship, for glory, and for the praise of God. Look at the beautiful cathedrals, their ornaments, wall decorations, statues — we can see the extent to which the order of God's creation has been reflected in them.

We can speak of ecology in yet another sense. Let me mention the beautiful blessings, so many of which were familiar in the Church and have now become almost completely obsolete. In the traditional liturgical books, we find the Church's blessings of animals, bees, flowers, herbs, and fruits. These blessings are accompanied by beautiful prayers. The faithful would bring herbs and fruits with them, and the priests would bless these gifts of the earth and of nature. For Easter, eggs were blessed.

In Poland, this custom has been preserved to this day. On Holy Saturday, the faithful bring to church wicker baskets with foods to be blessed: eggs, bread, and cold cuts. Herbs, flowers, and harvest sheaves are also still blessed, even in big cities, on August 15, the Feast of the Assumption, which is called Our Lady of the Herbs.

Yes, there you can see most clearly how well the Church has been able to use creation for God's glory. So we don't need any ecological conversion. What we really need most is a conversion to God. That's true everywhere, including the Amazon region. There is nothing more urgent than turning to God, to His commandments, to His will. Jesus said clearly, "Repent and believe in the Gospel!" That call is always relevant. Perhaps even more so today than it was back then. But I'm afraid that those who talk about ecological conversion today really are referring to paganism, a typically pagan orientation toward matter and nature. At least that is how these radical calls for ecological conversion manifest themselves.

The biggest problem today is not ecology in the sense of preserving a healthy material environment, but ecology in the sense of the concern for a morally worthy and beautiful life. The truly dangerous pollution is not excessive carbon dioxide, but moral filth. There is nothing worse than the phenomenon of mass slaughter — and I am using such a strong word deliberately — of unborn children, which has never before occurred to such an extent and on such a scale. This is truly horrifying. Similarly horrific is the destruction of the family and marriage through LGBT ideology. That to me is the real pollution, the real filth. This is the real moral pollution of society. Today we need a

human, spiritual, moral ecology. Remarkable are the following words
of Pope Benedict XVI:

> In order to protect nature, it is not enough to intervene with
> economic incentives or deterrents; not even an apposite educa-
> tion is sufficient. These are important steps, but the decisive
> issue is the overall moral tenor of society. If there is a lack of
> respect for the right to life and to a natural death, if human
> conception, gestation and birth are made artificial, if human
> embryos are sacrificed to research, the conscience of society
> ends up losing the concept of human ecology and, along with
> it, that of environmental ecology. It is contradictory to insist
> that future generations respect the natural environment when
> our educational systems and laws do not help them to respect
> themselves. The book of nature is one and indivisible: it takes
> in not only the environment but also life, sexuality, marriage,
> the family, social relations: in a word, integral human develop-
> ment. Our duties toward the environment are linked to our
> duties toward the human person, considered in himself and
> in relation to others.[43]

You mentioned the mass killing of unborn children. It seems that when it comes to
abortion we are also dealing with a new phenomenon, with some significant radicalization of the pro-abortion movement. While earlier supporters of abortion talked
about the lesser evil, now more and more often we hear that abortion is good. In the
past, supporters of changes in the law argued that abortion is a necessary evil, that it is
inevitable, that such procedures are going to be performed anyway and therefore it's
better that, if they do have to take place, they be performed in civilized conditions in
compliance with the law. This has been the argumentation of supporters of abortion
until now. However, in recent years we have been witnessing a change in this regard.
For its supporters, abortion is no longer a lesser evil, a necessary evil — it has become
a good. It's presented as a fundamental right of the woman. We are told that there is
nothing wrong with it, that, on the contrary, it's a sign of the woman's dignity and

[43] Encyclical *Caritas in Veritate*, no. 51.

autonomy. Recently, the Polish newspaper *Gazeta Wyborcza* put on the front page of its women's supplement *Wysokie Obcasy* (*High Heels*) a photo of several women wearing T-shirts that read "Abortion is OK." Those smiling women were almost encouraging the killing of babies. Feminists have apparently decided to go the way of LGBT activists. In a similar fashion, they now want to show that abortion should be a cause for pride, joy, and dignity. Why has this happened? What do you see as the reason for this new approach?

Evil and wickedness have an inherent tendency to radicalization. If evil is not restrained, if it's not held in check, if it's not hindered but instead is tolerated or supported, then it reaches an extreme, an increasingly more terrifying form. Evil seeks to propagate itself. Let's not forget that ultimately we are dealing with personal evil, with Satan. Evil wants to conquer the entire created world, to completely negate and reject it, to wrench it out of God's hand. In this sense it tends toward some perverted form of infinity and eternity — and ultimately toward the reign of Hell. Satan is a personal being with an intelligence incomparably higher than human intelligence. He himself has chosen evil, with all its consequences. To a certain extent, evil has eternity and infinity in itself. That is what makes it radical. It seeks to transcend all boundaries, all the way to the end, down to the very bottom. It seeks to immortalize itself, to make itself eternal. Hell is immortalized evil. It is eternal.

We can see this dynamic of evil using the example of alcoholism. The beginning seems innocent, not perilous. People start drinking little by little. Without any boundaries, they drink more and more, and with increasing frequency. And then, years later, they hit rock bottom. This is how evil works. It strives to take control of man completely, to the point of his ultimate destruction. This is precisely what happens to alcoholics. If they are not stopped, they bring about their own physical and mental destruction. It quickly becomes apparent that one shot of vodka is not enough. It has to be a whole bottle. And then two bottles. They have to drink more and more, until they literally drink themselves to death. I know one dramatic case of a man who emptied his entire house and sold everything he had to buy alcohol. That is the logic of evil. It's the same with abortion. First, it was legalized. This demonstrated that a person is allowed to kill a child. This permission sets in motion a dynamic, a process. The will to kill increases. Why only during the first twelve weeks? Perhaps we could be allowed to kill until the fourth month? Yes, that's fine. Then until the fifth month. Now in the United States it has reached the point that you can kill a baby up to the ninth month, and it's been taken even further: you can kill the baby during labor — you can cut off the head. This is so horrendously brutal and barbaric, and yet it's happening.

You see exactly this logic of how evil operates. You can see the true passion of evil. You can see the hatred of life. And you can see one more thing: a desire to prove that man is the real master of life. Man can control life, can decide about it without any restrictions. In this way, we have suddenly found ourselves under the rule of a homicidal dictatorship. Both Hitler and Stalin found the mass murder of people enjoyable. This is exactly the direction taken by those people who want to make something enjoyable out of the killing of babies, who want to brag about it and show pride in it.

Another new tendency in Western societies is the attempt to eliminate the words "mother" and "father" from the language. Gender ideologues seek to replace these words with "neutral" terms. Instead of "mom and dad" we would have "parent 1 and parent 2" or "parent A and parent B." How are we to understand this tendency?

It has nothing to do with any development, progress, or civilization. It's a sign of an anti-civilization that is being established before our very eyes. In this way, the entire structure and purpose of the family are being destroyed, fatherhood and motherhood are being shattered. These examples illustrate perfectly what is at stake. Man wants to create himself anew. He is trying to replace the reality created by God, that which exists, with his own constructs. The mother and the father are an obstacle to these constructs. They are a sign of a reality given from above, of nature created by someone else. Man wants to replace God and create the world on his own, extracting it from his own thought. "Father" and "mother" are concepts that must be rejected. It's an attempt at rebellion against God, against *His* order and governance. But it's also a rebellion against the reality in which we live. It would mean that man would have to rewrite all the biology and anatomy textbooks. We would have to rename and reconstruct everything from scratch and bring to life abstract human beings who are neither women nor men — human beings without reproductive organs that are biologically different. Take, for example, the word "uterus": in German it is called *Gebärmutter* and in Russian *matka* — expressions derived from the word mother (in German *Mutter*, in Russian *mat*). We would have to cancel our anatomical knowledge, biological knowledge, all genetics. It is absurd and ridiculous.

In February 2020, two famous American biologists, professors Colin M. Wright and Emma N. Hilton, wrote something of a cautionary manifesto. Their article was published in the prestigious *Wall Street Journal*. In it, they stated that "in humans, reproductive anatomy is unambiguously male or female at birth more than 99.98% of the time. The evolutionary function of these two anatomies is to aid in reproduction via the fusion of sperm and ova." They went on to write that "no third type of sex cell exists in humans, and therefore there is no sex 'spectrum' or additional sexes beyond male and female. Sex *is* binary."[44] It's also worth noting that four years ago, the American College of Pediatricians agreed that extremely rare disorders of gender development "are all medically identifiable deviations from the human binary sexual norm.... Nevertheless, the 2006 consensus statement of the Intersex Society of North America did not endorse DSD as a third sex."[45] I am quoting these words because these scientists are saying exactly the same things as you, and they are speaking from the position of people who have nothing to do with religion. But how can that help, when gender ideologues, through massive media campaigns, are able to brainwash people and make them believe that there are other "genders"?

Consider the terrible harm that is being done to children in this way. Children say "mama" and "papa" from the very beginning. These are

---

[44] See Colin M. Wright and Emma N. Hilton, "The Dangerous Denial of Sex," *Wall Street Journal* (February 13, 2020), www.wsj.com/articles/the-dangerous -denial-of-sex-11581638089.

[45] See American College of Pediatricians, *Gender Dysphoria in Children* (2018), www.acpeds.org/position-statements/gender-dysphoria-in-children.

the first words they learn. They express the deepest need of every human being. Everyone wants to have a mom and a dad, and everyone longs for them. The greatest source of psychopathology are situations in which the mother or the father is absent in childhood. The absence of the mother or the father causes the greatest inner wound in a person, which often lasts a lifetime. Without the mother, without her warmth, her affection, and her presence, a person cannot fully develop emotionally. As a result, inhibitions are formed. The same is true about the absence of the father.

What a child must be going through in such a dramatic situation is depicted well in certain films. For example, I would recommend watching the World War II war-drama *Little Boy*, directed by Alejandro Gómez Monteverde. In a beautiful way, it shows the close bond between a son and his father, who had to go to war. Then we see what a terrible tragedy it was for the boy, how difficult the situation was for him; with the father gone, the son's life almost fell apart. The film shows how the boy goes looking for his father and how the boy does everything in his power to find his father. Catholic actors played in this production. There are so many examples of that need, evident in so many people's lives. It cannot be suppressed. Our very nature demands a mother and a father. A child only develops well and feels good when he or she has a mother and a father. Of course, in real life there are problems. Some children grew up with no father, no mother; there are also double orphans. But this doesn't change the standard.

The last few decades have seen a huge rise in the popularity of so-called feminist theology. We can see this both in the Catholic Church and, even more so, in Protestant communities. The Protestant Church in Sweden, for example, has decided to change the content of some prayers to emphasize the feminine features of God. Pastors claim that in this way the language has become more "inclusive." According to this approach, God should not be addressed as Father, because God has no gender, so He must be simultaneously Father and Mother. Can we change Our Father to Our Mother? Feminist theologians claim that the biblical language is metaphorical, and that God can therefore be addressed as both Father and Mother. In their view, these two words are synonymous. Similarly, other liturgical texts are being altered to emphasize the presence and importance of women. This approach is becoming more common among Catholic theologians, many of whom are following the Protestant lead.

Such things must not be done. Replacing God the Father with God the Mother would mean that this is no longer Christianity. It would be a different religion. Many such religions existed in the past. Just think of the various pagan beliefs that worshipped goddesses, Mother Earth, Mother Goddess, Venus, Astarte, and many other female figures. The Gnostics also invented various female figures, which were symbols of the divine. They created male gods and female goddesses. Their main god was Abyssus, the foundation of all things, who could not be named or defined in any way and who incorporated both masculine and feminine characteristics, a male-female dyad. He was a being, if that word is even applicable, who was unknown and unknowable. But this is gnosis, not Christianity. I have already mentioned these beliefs. One of the most famous teachers of gnosis was Valentinus, who lived in the second century after Christ and who attempted to popularize his teachings in Rome. From him comes a specific form of gnosis, "Christian" gnosis. St. Irenaeus of Lyon exposed it and showed its dangers. He did this at the end of the second century in his work *Adversus Haereses* (*Against Heresies*). In it he showed that gnosis contradicts God's revelation.

God Himself has revealed what we are allowed to call Him and in what way we should do that. So the fundamental problem with all these attempts at "new interpretations," as presented by feminists, for example, is that they overlook divine revelation. In this way a new version of gnosis is created, a new form of a man-made religion. It's a religion created in accordance with the rules of Gnostic feminism. The ideologues of this movement believe that there was no historical divine revelation at all and that whatever the Bible conveys to us is merely a record of the state of awareness of man at the time. Since the late eighteenth century, this has been the constant refrain of rationalists. If we accept this view, then the rules of faith and prayer can be freely changed as our state of awareness is changing.

But this is a complete misunderstanding. God has clearly instructed us on how to address Him. And He did that not only for people at some point in the past, but for all times and indeed for all eternity. Holy Scripture says that God called Himself Yahweh, "I am who I am," "I am the Being." This word, in Hebrew, also indicates that God is living. This clearly indicates that God is a personal being. We can say that in these designations we come to know the metaphysical essence of God. In Holy Scripture He also says: "I am the God of Abraham, Isaac, and Jacob." In the New Testament revelation received its fullness, given by Christ Himself. He told us how we should worship God and how to address Him. This is how you should pray, He said: "Our Father!" We must not address God in any way other than that which Jesus revealed to us. In the same way, Christ Himself said, "Go and make disciples of all nations, baptizing them in the name of the Father and of the Son and of the Holy Spirit." Therefore, when someone prays in a different way, it's no longer Christianity, but rather a thought-construct generated by man. From the very beginning, God condemned the worship of human creations: man is obliged to worship God as He Himself has commanded. Therefore, calling God our Mother, or our Mother and Father, as feminists insist, would be a kind of Gnostic paganism and idolatry.

It seems fair to say, then, that feminist theology is simply another form of modernism. Both talk about the development of awareness and about the fact that what a person believes is merely a development of a feeling or an expression of a longing.

Yes, feminism is a consequence of modernism. Pius X stated it with unparalleled precision: "Modernism is the collection of all heresies."

Another area where a change in the Church's moral teaching can be seen is the issue of the death penalty. According to Pope Francis, the Church's previous teaching that the death penalty is morally permissible must be changed. From now on, says the pope, the teaching must be an absolute prohibition of the death penalty, which is inadmissible under any circumstances. This new approach is to be included in the *Catechism*.

Certainly the pope has no right to change a teaching that is based on sources of divine revelation, the teaching that is present in Scripture itself, both the Old and the New Testaments, and that has been handed down for two thousand years in the Church. This is a revolution and a rupture. Introducing such a change exceeds the limits of papal authority. The First Vatican Council, which defined the doctrine of papal infallibility, declared that the Holy Spirit has not been given to the pope to introduce new teachings or to institute them, but to faithfully guard the deposit of divine revelation. A change in the stance on the permissibility of the death penalty is an abuse of papal authority. Let me repeat, the pope doesn't have the power to change the permanent doctrine of the Church. He has no such authority. For two thousand years the Church has taught that capital punishment is legitimate, of course when certain clearly defined conditions are met. This is also what God taught us in Holy Scripture. How then could Pope Francis change this? He exceeded his authority here. There is no doubt in my mind that after his death, his successors will reverse this modification. We are temporarily in a situation of some darkness. History has seen examples of popes who have abused their power. This is also the case now. This abuse will certainly be recognized and the error on the death penalty will be corrected by future popes.

What is at stake here is the basic *principle* of capital punishment, not the manner in which it is implemented, which may change. It's also conceivable that the death penalty is administered only in a very limited way, which is the case today. However, it's not about how, or how frequently, the punishment is administered, but about the basic principle. We must remember that the first time the death penalty was pronounced on man — on Adam and Eve — was by God Himself. He was the first to issue the death sentence after man disobeyed and sinned in Eden. As a result, every person, every one of us, has been sentenced to death. Everyone will have to die. It was God who said to Adam, "You will have to die." This punishment now affects all people. You must die because you have done this, God said to Adam. And He said the same thing to Eve. We are all descendants of Adam; in him, as it were, we are all enclosed. In this sense, God's judgment affects everyone — me, you, and everyone else.

So when someone says that the principle on which the death penalty is based is false, he is actually accusing God. By rejecting the principle of capital punishment, you are ultimately telling God that He has acted unjustly. In my opinion, the rejection of the principle of the moral permissibility of capital punishment ultimately leads to a denial of God's justice. He was the first to sentence each of us to death; after all, from the beginning, He saw each of us in His infinite wisdom and knowledge. And to each He said, you will die — "remember you are dust, and to dust you shall return" — because each one of us inherits original sin. You could say that the radical opposition to the principle of the permissibility of capital punishment stems from a conviction that accuses God of being unjust.

The second reason is a dramatic reversal of the hierarchy of values. What has become most important is this earthly, temporal, contingent, and finite life. Much more weight is given to it than to the life of the soul. That which is mortal and transient is treated as more important than that which is immortal and eternal. Compared to eternity, this life is so fleeting. If a criminal is pardoned, he gets an extra twenty, maybe thirty years of life. After all, he has been sentenced to death, and that by God Himself — he will have to die anyway!

The death penalty is not administered for trifles or minor offenses. People are sentenced to death for committing grave crimes, for heinous murders, for the worst and most despicable homicides. Man must answer to God for committing such crimes. He must atone for them. So when such a person, after committing a crime, is punished with death, God counts this punishment as a penance and reparation for the evil and wickedness for which he must pay in eternity anyway. In this violent death, God sees atonement for sin, for the crime. Depending on the attitude of that criminal — on whether he has remorse or regret, on whether he desires reparation — the death penalty may even reduce his sufferings in Purgatory. There exists an opinion that says that the death suffered by an unrepentant criminal would reduce his punishments in Hell, taking into account the possibility of different degrees of punishments in Hell, as there are also different degrees of eternal beatitude in Heaven. This is the greatness of God's mercy, that He will accept the criminal's death penalty also as an atonement.

We must never consider justice as a contradiction of mercy. For this reason, in the past, priests accompanied convicts until the end, until the sentence was carried out. Until the very end, they would say: accept this punishment as just and fitting, and then it will become a reparation for sin. And often convicts accepted the punishment in this spirit. The attitude of penance and contrition protected them from Hell and shortened their due suffering in Purgatory. After all, a murderer, if pardoned by the secular power, may not have opportunity to do reparation for his monstrous sin. In any case, after some time in this world he would have to appear before God's throne of judgment. Then his situation might be worse than that of a person who had at least partially atoned for his crimes through capital punishment. A person who has not had the opportunity to atone for his crime will find himself in a dramatically difficult position — he may have to suffer punishment until the end of time, or forever. Many saints have spoken about the suffering souls in Purgatory, about their yearning and regret that they had not done their penance and reparation on earth. We must not look at the question of death penalty solely from a secular, temporal perspective, as if the questions of condemnation, repentance, reparation, and eternal salvation didn't matter at all.

How, then, am I to interpret the words of the Prefect of the Congregation for the Doctrine of the Faith, Cardinal Ladaria, who claims that the change made by the pope regarding the doctrine on the admissibility of the death penalty is a development of the previous doctrine of the Church? According to the cardinal, the new teaching doesn't contradict previous teachings, but is a proper development of what was previously taught. Ultimately, these words are unacceptable.

These words are an example of denying reality. It's simply a denial of facts. Such claims can only be made by someone who is essentially a Hegelian. It's like saying that two plus two used to equal four and now it's five and it's the same result, only there has been an organic development. This would mean that today we have a new mathematics in which all the results are different than in the old mathematics. Let's imagine a dialogue between a student and a teacher of the new mathematics. During class, the student says that two plus two equals four, to which the teacher replies, "No, it's five." The puzzled student says, "But how can that be, it's impossible." And the teacher replies, "No, you don't understand anything, it's an organic development." This is exactly what Cardinal Ladaria is doing when he claims that the rupture is a continuation. This is spinning reality. I don't know how else to define it. It looks like a blatant lie. In fact, this is also the ultimate consequence of using the so-called hermeneutic of continuity in relation to some problematic affirmations of the Second Vatican Council. They try to tell us that we are dealing with a harmonious unity, a harmonious continuity, even if in fact we are dealing with ruptures.

In this way human language loses all meaning. Everything can be named and associated arbitrarily. Reality is no longer the measure of language. You can utter any sentence or any judgment, regardless of whether one is compatible with another or not. It's purely arbitrary.

Precisely, human language would lose all meaning altogether. Logic would also be gone. In fact, no single sentence could affirm anything or refute anything. Everything would be open to doubt. As a matter of fact, I can also doubt Cardinal Ladaria and the pope's statements. Since they are passing judgment on the principle of non-contradiction when it comes to the doctrine of capital punishment, their judgments can be reversed at will.

Perhaps at the bottom of this apparent ease of moving from contradiction to contradiction lies the conviction that human reason can no longer reach God and can no longer determine whether God exists. According to this logic, revelation would be merely a historical form of self-awareness achieved by humanity at different historical moments. Can man today still be convinced that his reason is capable of discovering objective laws of existence? Based on an examination of the phenomena in the world, can reason clearly discover the existence of God?

The first and foremost thing is the certainty with which we can assert that man is a rational being. No one denies this. We are rational beings. Reasoning distinguishes us from animals. Animals are guided by instinct, whereas humans have reason. The very definition of man suggests this fundamental difference: *animal rationale*, or rational animal,

animal equipped with reason. This is how God created us, this is our nature. So we can know God according to our nature. Of course, man also has a will, he has feelings. We are not machines. It's true that the will directs man, but reason enlightens it. When God created Adam, He told him to name all the animals — naming is an act of intelligence. Thus, Adam gave each animal its proper name.

We must also remember that the Word, the Logos, is the name of God, the Second Person of the Holy Trinity. God revealed Himself to us in this way, as the Logos. It was the Word, not the feeling, that became flesh. God thus showed us that He is an intellectual nature. The second divine Person, the Son, is the Logos. God in Himself is intellect. And since God created us in His image, reason is that very image of God in us. The Trinity is reflected in man in general: just as the Holy Spirit, the Spirit of love, proceeds from the Father and the Son, so in man we have reason and will, in which is included love. The image of God in the human soul is manifested in reason and will, in thinking and loving. We can therefore truly reach God only when we employ thinking. God has revealed Himself to us through the Word, and we can reach Him through thinking. That's how it is in this life.

Again, Jesus said, "I am the Truth." And that means you can reach Him through thinking, through reason. How else would we come to Christ without the knowledge of reason if we are to discover the truth? Reason and thinking are contained in our very souls; without them there is no human being. And there is no knowledge of God. Similarly, it's impossible to imagine a human being without free will and, consequently, without love.

To verify the legitimacy of her mission, the Church has usually referred to prophecies and miracles. The teachers and Doctors of the Church have always tried to show that the prophecies contained in the Old Testament were fulfilled in Christ. This was a way to prove that God is the Lord of time and history and that Christ was foretold from all eternity. In the same way, the importance and authenticity of the miracles performed by Christ were emphasized, as a way of showing that He was truly sent by God. A classic example of such an approach can be found in Pascal's *Pensées*. This is why he devotes so much attention to collecting Old Testament prophecies and demonstrating that they are all referring to Christ. Similarly, he shows that the miracles performed by Christ pointed to His supernatural power and authority. Is such argumentation still possible today, after the victory of the historical-critical method? Or perhaps today we can talk only about probabilities? Is it possible to have certainty based on the authenticity of historical events?

These are the challenges that apologetics, above all, has to face. It's a question about ways in which we can demonstrate the divinity of Christ and the truth of the stories described in the Gospels. We must rediscover the meaning of apologetics, support it in new ways, and learn to use it anew. The prophecies of the Old Testament clearly point to the figure of Christ. Let's take the prophet Isaiah and his song of the suffering servant:

> Who hath believed our report? and to whom is the arm of the Lord revealed? And he shall grow up as a tender plant before him, and as a root out of a thirsty ground: there is no beauty in him, nor comeliness: and we have seen him, and there was no sightliness, that we should be desirous of him. Despised, and the most abject of men, a man of sorrows, and acquainted with infirmity: and his look was as it were hidden and despised, whereupon we esteemed him not. Surely he hath borne our infirmities and carried our sorrows: and we have thought him as it were a leper, and as one struck by God and afflicted. But he was wounded for our iniquities, he was bruised for our sins: the chastisement of our peace was upon him, and by his bruises we are healed. All we like sheep have gone astray, every one hath turned aside into his own way: and the Lord hath laid on him the iniquity of us all. He was offered because it was his own will, and he opened not his mouth: he shall be led as a sheep to the slaughter, and shall be dumb as a lamb before his shearer, and he shall not open his mouth. He was taken away from distress, and from judgment: who shall declare his generation? because he is cut off out of the land of the living: for the wickedness of my people have I struck him. (Isa. 53:1–8)

This prophecy is so obvious, so clearly referring to Christ, that Talmudic Jews will not read this chapter. And if they do, they attempt to apply the story to the people of Israel alone — contrary to its very content, which clearly shows that it's not about a nation, but about a particular person. But it takes faith to interpret prophecies in this way, as referring to the foretold Messiah.

Similarly, faith is needed to accept the authenticity of the miracles described in the Gospels: without faith, it will always be possible to look for another explanation. We must have faith that we are encountering the Word of God and that what the apostles communicated to us is credible. In other words, events in themselves, even if they are unmistakably supernatural, are not enough, unless we look at them through the eyes of faith. Man has the ability to twist their meaning, to turn them around, to distort their significance. Let's take the story of the resurrection of Lazarus, described in the Gospel of St. John. Lazarus was in the tomb for four days. There were already signs of decay on his body. When Jesus raised him, everyone could see him alive again. And yet the Pharisees and chief priests decided to kill Jesus, out of hatred! Hatred of the truth can be so irrational that it disregards facts and perverts the meaning of events. Let's note that Jesus' opponents knew that Lazarus had died. They were at the tomb and saw that he had been lying dead for four days. And then they saw that at the words of Jesus, Lazarus came to life and came out of the tomb. What other miracle would have been more remarkable? What could have been a better proof of Jesus' divinity? Who, if not God, could command a dead man to come back to life? And yet the Pharisees reject the truth. They refuse to accept it. Ultimately, it's their will that decides. It turns out that man may not want to obey God. He wants his own freedom. Therefore, he may reinterpret the signs and wonders in such a way as to take away their meaning.

The same hatred of Christ was evident when the news of the empty tomb and the Resurrection reached the Pharisees. This is described by St. Matthew. He shows that the news, instead of generating conversion, led to a false rumor about the disciples stealing the body.

Who when they were departed, behold some of the guards came into the city, and told the chief priests all things that had been done. And they being assembled together with the ancients, taking counsel, gave a great sum of money to the soldiers, saying: Say you, His disciples came by night, and stole him away when we were asleep. And if the governor shall hear this, we will persuade him, and secure you. (Matt. 28:11–14)

In his commentary on this passage, St. Augustine pointed out that the witnesses who report on what happened while they were asleep are not very trustworthy. "Sleeping witnesses" — that doesn't sound very convincing.[46] What can a sleeping witness possibly testify about? What is his knowledge of things? It's simply preposterous. Except that reason doesn't decide here, the will does. Someone who doesn't want to believe, who rejects God's revelation, will sooner accept that the truth is being told by sleeping witnesses than by those who saw the Risen One with their own eyes.

For me, for instance, one of the most significant proofs of the authenticity of the Resurrection is the Shroud of Turin. A detailed examination of the research conducted by a number of renowned, eminent scientists will suffice. The evidence gathered by them doesn't leave the slightest doubt. Thanks to special microscopes, the imprints of a coin issued by Pilate could even be detected on Christ's eyelids. It was possible to detect plant pollen from Palestine and to trace in detail the wounds and afflictions that Jesus endured. If we bring all the data together, there is no doubt that the Shroud could not have been the work of a medieval forger. If we are using reason and appealing to common sense, no explanation for all these findings is possible other than the fact that the Shroud is an authentic proof of Christ's death and Resurrection. And yet there are people who can reject all this. Simply put, hatred for God and for His Son can prevent or derail any quest for truth.

---

[46] See *Enarrationes in Ps.* 59:3.

7

How Many Religions Are True?

Let's now turn to the question of the plurality of religions and the relationship between them and Christianity, between them and the Church. More and more modern theologians claim that all religions are at least partially true and that Catholicism is just the shortest path to God. It's also argued that there are seeds of truth in different religions and that man can be saved through them while remaining faithful to other religions. Therefore, there is no need to convert to Catholicism.

Let me answer as simply as possible: such a position contradicts God's revelation and the words of Christ. Jesus said, "No man cometh to the Father, but by me" (John 14:6). There is no other way. Jesus also said, "Amen, amen I say to you, I am the door of the sheep. All others, as many as have come, are thieves and robbers: and the sheep heard them not. I am the door. By me, if any man enter in, he shall be saved: and he shall go in, and go out, and shall find pastures" (John 10:7–9). Whoever rejects me, rejects also the Father, said Jesus (Luke 10:16). This is quite clear. Perhaps one more quote will be helpful:

And the Father himself who hath sent me, hath given testimony of me: neither have you heard his voice at any time, nor seen his shape. And you have not his word abiding in you: for whom he hath sent, him you believe not. Search the scriptures, for you think in them to have life everlasting; and the same are they that give testimony of me. And you will not come to me that you may have life. I receive glory not from men. But I know

167

you, that you have not the love of God in you. I am come in the name of my Father, and you receive me not: if another shall come in his own name, him you will receive. How can you believe, who receive glory one from another: and the glory which is from God alone, you do not seek? Think not that I will accuse you to the Father. There is one that accuseth you, Moses, in whom you trust. For if you did believe Moses, you would perhaps believe me also; for he wrote of me. (John 5:37–46)

Therefore, Jews and Muslims who reject Jesus as the incarnate God and Savior are also rejecting God's revelation. St. Paul writes the same thing: "When the Lord Jesus shall be revealed from heaven, with the angels of his power: In a flame of fire, giving vengeance to them who know not God, and who obey not the gospel of our Lord Jesus Christ. Who shall suffer eternal punishment in destruction, [away] from the face of the Lord, and from the glory of his power" (2 Thess. 1: 7–9).

It's absolutely certain that God forbids — precisely, *forbids* — any other way than the one He Himself has shown, which is His Son. "In him I am well pleased," says the voice of God from Heaven. That is why St. Peter in his first speech says to the Jews:

Do penance, and be baptized every one of you in the name of Jesus Christ, for the remission of your sins: and you shall receive the gift of the Holy Ghost. For the promise is to you, and to your children, and to all that are far off, whomsoever the Lord our God shall call. And with very many other words did he testify and exhort them, saying: Save yourselves from this perverse generation. (Acts 2:38–40)

In Mark's Gospel, we read: "This is my most beloved son; hear ye him" (Mark 9:6) — these are words spoken by God. And then we hear, "He that believeth and is baptized, shall be saved: but he that believeth not shall be condemned" (Mark 16:16). That is the case, of course, as long as one is not in a state of invincible ignorance.

I have quoted all these passages from the Bible here, and I could go on and on. It's clear that God doesn't want any other ways to Him, any other ways of worshiping Him, than the one and only way that He has revealed. That is evident already in the first commandment, "I am the Lord thy God, who brought thee out of the land of Egypt, out of the house of bondage. Thou shalt not have strange gods in my sight" (Deut. 5:6–7). The God who has revealed Himself is, after all, the divine Trinity, the Triune God. The same God who commanded obedience to His incarnate Son. The whole teaching is already contained in this first commandment: God forbids man to follow any other way to Him than the way He Himself has indicated, which is His only Son who became man, Jesus Christ. Other ways are other religions and other beliefs. Jesus Christ alone is the way that God wills and commands us to choose. Man has no natural right to choose otherwise. Not only are other religions forbidden by God, but the punishments that fall on those who choose them, rejecting Jesus Christ, are clearly stated. The Gospel clearly mentions the threat of eternal damnation for those who don't accept the one Truth, revealed by God in Jesus Christ. Let me remind you that we are speaking here about an objective command of God and the ordinary way. This excludes situations of invincible ignorance through no fault of one's own. But in principle the issue is clear: there is only one way that God wanted for mankind and for man, and that is Jesus Christ.

You mentioned the doctrine that talks about the seeds of truth. This is an old teaching, dating back to the time of St. Justin the Martyr. Yes, we can speak of the seeds, because although man was born in original sin, his mind, his reason, was not destroyed. It has only been dimmed and obfuscated. The ability to reason, though impaired, remains in man after original sin. That is why we have a natural ability to know God. This is a dogma of the Faith: with the natural light of his reason man can know the existence of God, as well as some truths about Him: that He is the Creator, that He is infinite and eternal — these are truths man can know without supernatural divine revelation. Human reason can also discover natural law. St. Paul writes about it clearly in his Epistle to the Romans:

> Because that which is known of God is manifest in them. For God hath manifested it unto them. For the invisible things of him, from the creation of the world, are clearly seen, being

understood by the things that are made; his eternal power also, and divinity: so that they are inexcusable. Because that, when they knew God, they have not glorified him as God, or given thanks; but became vain in their thoughts, and their foolish heart was darkened. For professing themselves to be wise, they became fools. And they changed the glory of the incorruptible God into the likeness of the image of a corruptible man, and of birds, and of four-footed beasts, and of creeping things. (1:19–23)

The Book of Wisdom tells us the same thing: "For by the greatness of the beauty, and of the creature, the creator of them may be seen, so as to be known thereby" (Wisd. 13:5).

This natural ability to know has been written in the heart of every man; the ability to distinguish between truth and falsehood, the conviction that good must be chosen and evil rejected, that what is true must be accepted, that the structure and order of the world lead to God the Creator. In this sense, we can say that there are grains of truth in different human doctrines. Every human being has been created in the image of God. The likeness of God, as the Church teaches, was lost through original sin, and man can regain it through faith, through participation in the life of God, through the supernatural, sacramental life. The likeness can be restored by becoming like Christ. However, man has the image of God in his nature — his natural reason, prudence, and intellectual powers of cognition testify to this. It may be distorted, diluted, obscured, but it's there. It follows that if there are true elements in other religions, they are there not because of the message of a given religion as such, but because of true discoveries and intuitions of natural human reason. Therefore, it would be wrong to claim that since grains of truth are found in other religions, those religions are paths to God. That is an erroneous conclusion. Let me repeat: it stands in direct contradiction to God's first commandment and to the divine revelation of Jesus Christ.

How, then, can we understand the position of those theologians who claim that today we are dealing with a dialogue among various "faiths"? Or how is it possible that many statements from the Church's hierarchy speak of "believers" of various religions? The term "believer" in reference to the followers of other religions has also been used by recent popes, especially in their messages for the Day of Peace.

> There is only one faith. We cannot speak of faith in the case of any other religion. We must use the word "faith" very strictly. There are not many "faiths" as some statements might imply. In English, for example, the term "interfaith dialogue" has been accepted. But there is no dialogue between faiths. This term is wrong. There is only one faith. One faith, one Baptism, one Lord, as St. Paul says (see Eph. 4:5). In the proper sense, only those who confess the Triune God and the revelation of God in Jesus Christ have faith. Even the Jews, the Pharisees and their successors, who rejected the Son of God, don't have supernatural faith. That is what St. Paul says. Jesus Himself says to them: "Unless you believe that I am he you will die in your sins" (John 8:24). They replied, "Abraham is our father." To which Jesus answers them, "If you were Abraham's children, you would be doing the works Abraham did.... Your father Abraham rejoiced that he would see my day. He saw it and was glad" (John 8:39, 56). Only those who profess Jesus Christ the Son of God and the Holy Trinity have faith. This is faith in the proper sense, supernatural faith.

However, the term "the faithful of all religions" has entered church vocabulary. It is ubiquitous.

> Let me reiterate that this is a false expression. There is no such thing as "the faithful of all religions." We can talk about faith — this is what Jesus and the apostles taught — only when a person receives the supernatural light of faith as a gift, a grace from God to believe in His Son and thus believe in the Holy Trinity. As St. John says in the prologue, "But as many as received him, he gave them power to be made the sons of God, to them that believe in his name" (John 1:12). These are those who "are born, not of blood, nor of the will of the flesh, nor of the will of man, but of God" (John 1:13), those who believe in the Son. In the same way, St. Paul writes in his Epistle to the Galatians that only those who believe in Jesus Christ are children of Abraham. "Know ye therefore, that they who are of faith, the same are the children

of Abraham" (3:7). And to clear up any further doubt, he adds, "For you are all the children of God by faith, in Christ Jesus.... And if you be Christ's, then are you the seed of Abraham, heirs according to the promise" (Gal. 3:26, 3:29). Only those who believe in Jesus Christ are children of Abraham. All those who don't believe in Jesus Christ are not true children of Abraham. They may be his children according to the flesh, but they are not true children of Abraham. Just read the third chapter of the Epistle to the Galatians carefully — I have given only a few quotations here. Neither should we call Christianity, Judaism, and Islam "the Abrahamic religions." There is no such thing as Abrahamic *religions*. The only true Abrahamic religion is the Catholic Church and the Catholic Faith. The Judaism of today, Talmudic or Rabbinic Judaism, and similarly Islam, are not Abrahamic religions. Jesus clearly said, Abraham saw me. "Abraham your father rejoiced that he might see my day: he saw it, and was glad" (John 8:56).

Many modern theologians claim that the Holy Spirit is present in other religions. Some of them maintain that other religions have emerged as a result of man's longing for God. In their view, the Holy Spirit sustains this longing and works through other religions. Some also maintain that the Holy Spirit works outside the boundaries of the Church, that He works throughout human history, that this perspective is broader than the old, traditional one, according to which the Spirit led people into the Church.

But these opinions stand in stark contradiction to the first commandment of God! Moreover, Jesus clearly said that He is the only gate. And He said about the Holy Spirit that

> he shall not speak of himself; but what things soever he shall hear, he shall speak; and the things that are to come, he shall shew you. He shall glorify me; because he shall receive of mine, and shall shew it to you. All things whatsoever the Father hath, are mine. Therefore I said, that he shall receive of mine, and shew it to you. (John 16:13–15)

The Spirit does not speak of Himself! He shall speak everything that He hears from Christ. Such is the mission, such is the message of the

Holy Spirit. The Holy Spirit proceeds from the Father and the Son, from the Father through the Son. Everything that Jesus Christ said, the Holy Spirit continues to proclaim to all people through the perennial Magisterium of the Church. How, then, could we reconcile the claims that the Holy Spirit supposedly works in other religions and at the same time that God didn't want those religions to exist? This would mean that the Holy Spirit is working against God's will. And that would lead us to a contradiction, to an absurdity. God, after all, is unity, is one will. God has only one will, not three wills that would be in opposition to each other. The three divine Persons have one and only one will.

Besides, the Holy Spirit is the soul of the Church, the soul of the Mystical Body of Christ. God can't contradict Himself. Therefore, these claims you have cited are false, they contradict God's revelation and speak of a self-contradictory God.

The only true thing is that the longing for God is written in the nature of man. But the *expression* of this longing, which can be found in various religions, is something else. God permits them to exist, He tolerates their existence. Other religions are various kinds of false paths — God doesn't want them, He only permits them. And if man finds himself on them through no fault of his own, if he is caught in invincible ignorance, he will certainly not be condemned by God for that reason alone.

Let me use an analogy. It's somewhat similar to the situation of someone who has a servant to whom he gives a gift and asks him to carry that gift to a given address. And he says to him, "This is my will." But the servant misheard and misunderstood the name of the person to whom he was to bring the gift. This was not his fault and so he goes with the gift, convinced that he is doing the will of his master. So he goes to the wrong address and brings the gift to the wrong person. He makes a mistake, but through no fault of his own — he simply misheard what was said. Of course, we are not in a position to judge the extent of this man's culpability. Perhaps his fault is slight, perhaps not. Perhaps he hadn't been listening carefully, which led to the mistake, or perhaps he was in a situation where it was difficult to hear the master's voice. Either way, he is not doing the will of the Lord. So it is with the followers of other religions. They are not doing the will of God.

Let's take this analogy further. Let's imagine that the person sending the gift is a fiancé who is sending his fiancée an engagement ring. The servant sent with the ring gets her name and address wrong and so he goes to another house where he gives the engagement ring to another girl. Clearly this is happening against the will of the fiancé! Under no circumstances did he want his engagement ring to go to another woman. He would never consent to it because he loves only the one. This is the case with God and religions: He loves only the one way, the way of His Son, Jesus Christ, and His Bride, the Catholic Church. A fiancé will never consent to his engagement ring going to one he doesn't love. He wants no other woman but his fiancée. Objectively, that is the situation. However, when it comes to the messenger who made a mistake, and went to the wrong address and to the wrong woman, the master will probably not punish such a person severely. This man did it unknowingly, probably through no fault of his own in the case of invincible ignorance.

Going back to other religions: God definitely doesn't want them. However, He tolerates their existence. Why exactly that is, we don't know, just as we don't know exactly why God allowed the sin of Adam and Eve. I think the real reason was God's respect for freedom. God respects freedom, even if that freedom brings bad consequences.

All religions that don't accept Christ are false. The situation is different if we are not talking about other religions, but about other Christian denominations. All who have been baptized belong to the Body of Christ. True Baptism grafts a man onto the Body of Christ. The Orthodox have valid sacraments, they venerate the Mother of God, and therefore we have such essential things that unite us with them. Protestants, on the other hand, are united with us only by a valid Baptism. It's the most important sacrament, through which we become children of God. Some promoters of ecumenism say to us that we should follow the example of the Protestant devotion to the Word of God and their knowledge of it. Others point to the free churches, Baptists, Evangelicals, to the fact that they live simply, don't drink or smoke, and that their women are modest — which is supposed to be a model for us Catholics. Such things are good, but they are not sufficient for a life in the truth. For example, the fact that the Orthodox have the priesthood, the Holy Mass, the sacrifice of Christ, the sacraments — all this they got from the one Catholic Church. They took it with them when they separated from the Catholic Church. Likewise, Protestants have a valid Baptism and they love the Word of God because they took that with them when they separated from us. St. Augustine makes this clear: if Christians who have separated from the Church keep something true, it is not theirs, it doesn't belong to them.[47] It's similar to a situation where a son leaves his father's house, takes something from that house with him, and places it in his new home. This, however, belongs to the father's house all the time. Therefore, those authentic Catholic truths that other Christians hold and revere are the property of the Catholic Church. There is only one true Church of God, not two, three, or four churches, not the Orthodox Church or the Protestant Church. No, there is only one holy, apostolic, and catholic Church, headed by the pope as the visible vicar of Christ on earth.

You have said that although there are three divine Persons, there is only one divine will. The Spirit cannot will something other than the Son, and the Father cannot will something other than the Spirit. How, then, are we to understand the words of Pope Francis, who said that inside the Holy Trinity they're all arguing behind closed doors, but on the outside they give the picture of unity? Is the inner unity of the Trinity just an appearance? These words were supposedly said by Pope Francis on March 17, 2017, at a meeting with participants in the International Cultural Conference "Catholic Theological Ethics in the World Church."

Such a claim is blasphemous. The greatest possible unity of intellect, will, and love exists in the life of the Triune God. This is a truth of the Catholic faith: God is one being, He has one will. There can be no contradiction in Him, no duality, no division, no quarrel, no dispute. This alleged statement of Pope Francis is more reminiscent of the claims of pagans with polytheistic beliefs. It was in a pagan religion that Zeus argued with Apollo, Hera with Aphrodite, and so on. The vision of

[47] See *Sermo* 97, 2.

an internal feud within the divinity comes from pagan depictions. The word "blasphemy" is therefore most fitting here. I think, if Pope Francis really made such an affirmation, he must certainly retract and regret this statement because through it he offended God, the Most Holy Trinity. No greater unity can be conceived than that which exists in the Holy Trinity.

After Pope Francis signed the document on human fraternity with the Grand Imam of Al-Azhar in Abu Dhabi, you asked him in Rome to elaborate on the following passage: "The pluralism and the diversity of religions, color, sex, race and language are willed by God in His wisdom."[48] In what way, you were asking, is it to be understood that God wills the diversity of religions? The pope, as he said himself, meant that God permits the diversity of religions. Pope Francis also acknowledged that juxtaposing diversity of religions with sexual diversity in one sentence can lead to misinterpretations because it's clear that God positively willed sexual diversity and did not merely permit it. With this in mind, the pope authorized the Central Asian bishops to make this clarification public. However, it may be difficult to take these clarifications at face value. First, they contradict the content of the document itself. Secondly, in none of the subsequent speeches relating to the Abu Dhabi Declaration did the pope rectify his statement. Finally, no official documents of the Holy See reflected such a correction. So what do you think about this document now, more than a year after it was signed?

Well, let me start by saying that, as you yourself rightly pointed out, this explanation contradicts the letter of the declaration itself. I must also clarify that in his conversation with me, the pope did not use the term "positive will" as you have now quoted it. He only mentioned the "permissive will of God." Here is what happened. I quoted this sentence from the declaration, "The pluralism and the diversity of religions, color, sex, race and language are willed by God in His wisdom," and I said: "Holy Father, I implore you to retract this sentence because it

48 Pope Francis and Ahmad al-Tayyeb, "A Document on Human Fraternity for World Peace and Living Together," www.vatican.va/content/francesco/en/travels/2019/outside/documents/papa-francesco_20190204_documento-fratellanza-umana.html.

relativizes the exclusivity of Jesus Christ as the unique Savior." I didn't ask the pope how that sentence should be understood. I didn't ask such a question. Let me reiterate so that there is no ambiguity here: I quoted the sentence above and said, "In the name of Jesus Christ, I beseech you, Holy Father, to retract this sentence."

So it wasn't a question, but a request to retract that sentence?

That is exactly what happened. I did it in the presence of other bishops from Central Asia. Then I repeated this request in writing. I asked the Holy Father to proclaim to the world again today, as St. Peter did, that there is no other name that gives salvation but the name of Jesus Christ. "Neither is there salvation in any other. For there is no other name under heaven given to men, whereby we must be saved" (Acts 4:12). Pope Francis responded immediately to my first request, "The phrase should be understood to mean 'the permissive will of God.'" Then I replied, "But, Holy Father, the distinction between the male and female sexes is not the result of the permissive will of God." At these words the pope seemed somewhat perplexed, and after a while he said, "Yes, perhaps that sentence is misleading."

The pope said these words?

Yes. His exact words were, "Yes, perhaps this sentence may be misleading." And immediately he added, "But you bishops can explain that this is about the permissive will of God." Then I spoke out once more and said, "Holy Father, it is important that *you* should say this." But he didn't respond. He fell silent. A few weeks later, in a written reply to me, the pope mentioned that the point of this sentence was to emphasize human freedom. But I don't see any direct connection between human freedom and the meaning of this sentence. I am certainly not denying human freedom. If I argue that God wants positively only Christianity, only the Catholic Church, then I am in no way denying the existence of free will and man's free choice. I don't understand this implication. Perhaps the pope meant to say that different religions flow from human freedom. This, however, is just my speculation.

On April 3, 2019, during the General Audience, the pope used the phrase I asked for, thank God. He mentioned "the permissive will of God" when he talked about different religions. However, it was a brief mention, without an in-depth explanation. But regular people don't understand the term "God's permissive will." So I think it was insufficient. Especially seeing that when the Vatican later sent the text of the declaration to various universities and institutions, it was not accompanied by any explanation of these words. So my request to the pope proved ultimately futile.

Several months later, the Vatican is presenting this document as a great success of the pope, as a milestone on the road to a united humanity, a sign of universal brotherhood. No mention is made of any doubts, nor is there a single clarification.

This is very sad. The text is being disseminated without any qualification, without any attempt to correct this false statement.

A year later, on February 4, 2020, Pope Francis said, "Today we celebrate the first anniversary of this great humanitarian event, as we hope for a better future for humanity, a future free from hatred, rancor, extremism, and terrorism, in which the values of peace, love and fraternity prevail. Today, on this first anniversary, I express my appreciation for the support offered by the United Arab Emirates for the work of the Higher Committee for Human Fraternity. I thank you for the initiative led by the Abrahamic House, and for the presentation of the Human Fraternity Award. I am therefore pleased to be able to participate in the presentation to the world of the International Human Fraternity Award, in hopes of encouraging all virtuous exemplars of men and women who in this world embody love through actions and sacrifices made for the good of others, no matter how different they may be in religion, or ethnic and cultural affiliation. And I ask Almighty God to bless every effort that benefits the good of humanity and helps us to move forward in fraternity."[49] The authorities of the United Arab Emirates have announced the construction of a center for interreligious dialogue on Saadiyat Island

---

[49] Pope Francis, Video Message to the Participants in the Arab Media Convention for Human Fraternity, www.vaticannews.va/en/pope/news/2020-02/pope-francis-human-fraternity-convention-message-uae.html.

near the capital. As part of the Abrahamic Family House project, a church, a mosque, and a synagogue will be built next to each other. According to the visualization which was presented, all the buildings will have a similar structure and will be devoid of any distinctive religious symbols. That is, there will be no cross, no sign of Christianity. The temples are to be connected by a common square, large enough to host future conferences on dialogue. It's supposed to be a meeting point for followers of the three religions. The Abrahamic Family House was designed by the Ghanaian-British architect Sir David Adjaye, who commented, "I believe architecture should work to enshrine the kind of world we want to live in: a world of tolerance, openness, and constant advancement."[50] These are the fruits of this document signed by the pope. The anticipated completion date for the house is 2022.

> Yes, these are the fruits. What we see here is a complete relativization of the belief in the uniqueness of our Lord Jesus Christ. In fact, it amounts to challenging God's first commandment, "You shall have no other gods before me." The existence of Islam and Judaism, which reject Jesus Christ as the incarnate God and Savior, contradicts God's will. The fact that these religions continue to exist is against the will of God. Also, the expression "Abrahamic religions" is false and misleading, because, as I said earlier, Christians are the only true children of Abraham. St. Paul is perfectly clear:
>
>> Know ye therefore, that they who are of faith, the same are the children of Abraham. And the scripture, foreseeing that God justifieth the Gentiles by faith, told unto Abraham before: in thee shall all nations be blessed. Therefore they that are of faith, shall be blessed with faithful Abraham. (Gal. 3:7–9)
>
> And he goes on to explain exactly what kind of faith he means:
>
>> For as many of you as have been baptized in Christ, have put on Christ. There is neither Jew nor Greek: there is neither bond

---

[50] See Elizabeth Fazzare, "AD100 Architect David Adjaye to Design Three Houses of Worship Alongside One Another," *Architecture and Design* (October 15, 2019), www.architecturaldigest.com/story/ad100-architect-david-adjaye-to-design -three-houses-of-worship-next-to-each-other.

> nor free: there is neither male nor female. For you are all one
> in Christ Jesus. And if you be Christ's, then are you the seed
> of Abraham, heirs according to the promise. (Gal. 3:27–29)

Others may be descendants of Abraham according to the flesh, but his spiritual descendants are only those who believe in Christ. We Christians are the spiritual descendants of Abraham, as it was formulated by Pope Pius XI: "through Christ and in Christ we are the spiritual progeny of Abraham. Spiritually we are all Semites."[51]

Again we come up against the real source of the crisis in the Church: the conflation of the natural with the supernatural. Since the Second Vatican Council, as a result of modernism, the supernatural has practically dissolved into the natural. Thus it turns out that one can profess an "Abrahamic religion" regardless of whether one believes in Christ or denies Him as the incarnate God and Savior, as the Talmudic Jews and the Muslims do. To place Christianity alongside Islam and Judaism as if equating "the three Abrahamic religions" is, in my opinion, actually a form of heresy. I am saying that this is the case in practice, because those who do so will look for theoretical justifications and will attempt to show that we are not in a situation of a departure from the Faith here.

Regarding the new approach to religion, I will quote Pope Francis again: "God wanted to allow this: . . . there are many religions. Some are born from culture, but they always look to heaven; they look to God."[52] The pope said this after his apostolic journey to Morocco. What God wants is fraternity among them. In Egypt, in April 2017, Pope Francis said, "In facing this great cultural challenge, one that is both urgent and exciting, we, Christians, Muslims and all believers, are called to offer our specific contribution: 'We live under the sun of the one merciful God. . . . Thus, in a true sense, we can call one another brothers and sisters'" — he was quoting John Paul II here. "God, the lover of life, never ceases to love man, and so he exhorts us to reject the way of violence as the necessary condition for every earthly 'covenant.' Above all and especially in our day, the

---

[51] Allocution to the Belgian Pilgrims, September 16, 1938.

[52] Pope Francis, General Audience (April 3, 2019), www.vatican.va/content /francesco/en/audiences/2019/documents/papa-francesco_20190403 _udienza-generale.html.

religions are called to respect this imperative, since, for all our need of the Absolute, it is essential that we reject any 'absolutizing' that would justify violence."[53] In Abu Dhabi, he taught that religions should promote "a fraternal living together, founded on education and justice; a human development built upon a welcoming inclusion and on the rights of all."[54] He also stated that the main task of religion is fighting violence and building peace. We can get the impression that the main focus of papal thought is building brotherhood and fighting violence. What does this actually have to do with revelation? I could quote many more such statements. The same spirit of syncretism is present in all of them.

> We can clearly detect syncretism and Masonic ideas here. For Freemasons, all religions are equal. There are no significant differences between them. In these words, you can see Christianity being reduced to the level of other religions. The first sentence that you quoted is simply not true. It's not true that religions "always look to heaven, they look to God." If someone worships an idol in Hinduism, he is not looking to God, but looking at the idol. Jesus said clearly, "He that is not with me, is against me; and he that gathereth not with me, scattereth" (Luke 11:23). I already quoted this verse from the Gospel of Mark, "He that believeth not shall be condemned" (Mark 16:16). Whoever is not doing the will of God is not looking to God. And the will of God is that everyone believe in Christ, and give Him honor and glory.

So far I have focused on describing Pope Francis's new approach to religion. But shouldn't we go much deeper? Are the statements made by Pope Francis really all that new? I believe that the Abu Dhabi declaration and other statements by the pope are a consistent and logical development of the teachings of Pope John Paul II. In particular, I am thinking of the World Day of Prayer for Peace he organized in Assisi in 1986. According to John Paul II, Assisi was "an expression of theological openness."

---

[53] Pope Francis, Address to the Participants in the International Peace Conference, Cairo (April 28, 2017), www.vatican.va/content/francesco/en/speeches/2017/april/documents/papa-francesco_20170428_egitto-conferenza-pace.html.

[54] Pope Francis, Address at Interreligious Meeting in Abu Dhabi (February 4, 2019), www.vatican.va/content/francesco/en/speeches/2019/february/documents/papa-francesco_20190204_emiratiarabi-incontrointerreligioso.html.

That meeting could have been understood as a recognition of different religions as different ways of salvation, a recognition of their essential equality. How else could we understand the papal invitation to pray to the various deities? He said, "This Day is, therefore, a day for prayer and for what goes together with prayer: silence, pilgrimage and fasting."[55] And at the end, he added, "We have prayed, each in his own way, we have fasted, we have marched together."[56] The conclusion is self-evident: religions are equal in principle, and the prayers of non-Christians can be effective.

> Well, I agree with your conclusion here. Anyone who follows logic would have to agree. The sentence I mentioned above from Pope Francis's Abu Dhabi declaration, just like other similar-sounding claims, is a necessary consequence of the 1986 Assisi event. The very sight of religious leaders standing side by side, the pope in the midst of them, was very telling. It was a clear sign: they were all on the same level. The pope, however, is the representative, the vicar of Christ on earth. Of course, as a private person he is equal to all other men, he has the same dignity, rights, and duties. But in Assisi he was not a private person. He was representing Christ. He was there as the successor of Peter, the visible head of the Church. And he appeared alongside idol worshipers as if an equal. In Assisi, John Paul II was the sign of what Pope Francis put into words: God positively wants other religions.
>
> The very invitation that Pope John Paul II extended to each individual religious leader also demonstrated this. He invited each of them to pray in his own way. This is unacceptable. How could it be acceptable for a pope to call on everyone to pray in their own way if it meant also praying to idols? How were the Hindus or the Buddhists supposed to pray there otherwise? As a rule, they address idols in their prayers. God forbids worshiping idols and praying to them. He forbids it always and under all circumstances. Exhorting someone to pray according to his own religion, therefore, means being complicit

---

[55] John Paul II, Address to the Representatives of the Christian Churches and Ecclesial Communities and of the World Religions (October 27, 1986), www.vatican.va/content/john-paul-ii/en/speeches/1986/october/documents/hf_jp-ii_spe_19861027_prayer-peace-assisi.html.

[56] Ibid.

in this idolatrous worship and supporting it. In other words, it means exhorting someone to do that which God has absolutely forbidden. Let me emphasize: it's not a temporary and changeable prohibition, but an absolute one. In Assisi there were also shamans and voodoo followers who worship demons. Inviting them all and having them present in Assisi was an extremely grave error on the part of John Paul II, which in principle was not different from the wording of the declaration signed by Francis in Abu Dhabi. Drawing on logic, it's impossible to see any essential difference between the two acts — the meeting in Assisi and the Abu Dhabi declaration.

Both John Paul II and Francis refer to the texts of the Second Vatican Council in order to justify their new approach to other religions. But could a council change the Church's perennial, immutable teaching? Back in 1870, at the First Vatican Council, the Church taught: "Therefore, We reject and detest that irreverent and irrational doctrine of religious indifferentism by which the children of this world, failing to distinguish between truth and error, say that the gate of eternal life is open to anyone, no matter what his religion. Or else they say that, with regard to religious truth, only opinion in varying degrees of probability is possible and certainty cannot be had."[57] Although this text was not included in the final documents, it was ready to be voted on — it was the draft of the decree on the Church of Christ, chapter seven. This text expresses accurately the faith of the Council Fathers at the time. In the following section, the Council Fathers explicitly refute the objections of those who claim that the Church should not demand conversion to Catholicism from those who "grew up, were raised, or born" in false religions. How can we reconcile such radically different positions?

This is a very important quotation, well worth publicizing. The text is similar to what Pius IX put in his *Syllabus*. It's not well known, because this fragment was ultimately not included in the official texts for political reasons — the Council was interrupted due to the threat of war. But these words clearly show the Church's understanding of the Faith at the time, the common conviction of all the bishops, and you could

---

[57] Jesuit Fathers of Saint Mary's College, *The Church Teaches: Documents of the Church in the English Translation* (Saint Mary's, KS: TAN Books, 1973), 91.

even say the ordinary universal teaching of the Church. Yes, there is undoubtedly a direct contradiction between this and the new approach after the Second Vatican Council.

I will say it again: what is at stake here is not the understanding of the Church's faith, but the words of the Savior Himself and the apostles, Church Fathers, and all the popes up to the middle of the twentieth century. The primary source of both the meeting in Assisi and the Abu Dhabi declaration is, as I mentioned earlier, the declaration *Dignitatis Humanae* and those key words that recognize the natural right of the human person to choose and to spread a religion, or, in other words, not to be impeded in doing so. This natural right is understood as something positive, as the freedom to choose a religion and the right to propagate it freely without any hindrance.

Freedom belongs to the very nature of man, it's not a right but a faculty or capacity that everyone has. It's a gift that God has given to everyone. The freedom to make decisions belongs to human nature. But God gave it to man — and this is extremely important — for one purpose only, namely, to choose good and truth. Just because man by nature has the ability to choose between good and evil, as we see from the example of Adam and Eve, does not mean that this choice is his natural, positive right. A clear distinction must be made between the *right* to something (which presupposes on the other hand an obligation to recognize and respect that right) and the capacity to do something. Adam had no right to disobey God. He had no right to transgress God's command. And God had no obligation to respect or accept disobedience. Adam only had the ability to choose, not the right to choose evil. Adam and his descendants do not have a natural right of not being impeded in spreading a moral, spiritual, or intellectual evil (whether sin or a false religion).

That is the case with every human being. Everyone has the ability, the power to choose. He can accept or reject Christ, he can worship God or not, he can sin or not sin, but there is no natural right that entitles man to make false, erroneous choices or to worship idols or Lucifer and not be impeded in spreading such an evil. The only natural right of not being impeded in choosing and spreading a religion refers to the Christian religion and concretely to the Catholic religion.

Several times already you have pointed out a major error in a text of the Council itself. How was it possible for the entire text, including this error, to gain the approval of over two thousand bishops in 1965?

First of all, this document had the highest number of votes against it.

Two thousand bishops led by the pope, however, were in favor.

Still, around 250 bishops voted against it. That is a significant number. However, we know that when it comes to truth, the majority is not what matters. During the Arian crisis, St. Gregory of Nazianzus coined the phrase "God does not delight in numbers."[58] In this particular case [of *Dignitatis Humanae*], propaganda was employed on a massive scale. The media and proponents of change focused on showing only one part of the true affirmation of the Council, namely, "No merely human power can either command or prohibit acts of this kind."[59] Yes, no one should be forced to accept the Faith, no one should be forced to embrace it, no one should be forced to convert through violence. All attention was directed to this first part of the sentence. This is probably why bishops from countries ruled by communism, such as Poland, voted for the document. They thought that the assertion that everyone had the right to seek religion and to profess it freely — something that was forbidden by the Communists — would increase the freedom of the Church in Communist countries. The following argument was made: how can we say that Christians have the right to freedom of religious choice if the same right is not granted to every citizen?

And how would you respond to such an objection? At first glance, it sounds reasonable.

I would say this: what is being proposed in this document is a false conclusion. Instead, it should state that every human being, as a citizen of the State, has a right to the freedom of religion, but that it is by

[58] *Oration* 42:7.
[59] *Dignitatis Humanae*, 3.

no means acceptable to ground this civil right in the law of nature. Concluding that a State, which proclaims its neutrality, should grant its citizens an equal civil right to profess religion is one thing. But from this statement one must not conclude that man, therefore, has a natural right — and thus a right positively willed by God — of choosing any religion and spreading it.

During the Amazon Synod, in October 2019 in Rome, there was a dispute over a statue of Pachamama. As we know, it was placed in one of the Roman churches during the deliberations and was eventually taken from there and thrown into the Tiber River by a twenty-six-year-old Austrian Catholic, Alexander Tschugguel. After the incident, Pope Francis apologized for the goddess statue being thrown into the river. In doing so, the pope himself referred to the statue as "Pachamama." As we know, this is the name of the Incan goddess of fertility, who incidentally married her son. It can be regarded as a symbol of Mother Earth or Mother Cosmos. At the same time, the pope stated that the Pachamama statue was displayed in the church "without idolatrous intentions." I cannot fathom this. How is it possible to put a statue of a pagan goddess in a church and at the same time claim that it has nothing to do with idolatry?

It's always about the same thing — the denial of facts. It's about the unscrupulous, unprecedented denial of reality. All this has one purpose: to support an ideology that preaches the equality of religions. After all, the beliefs of Pachamama followers are religious. So if God in His wisdom wills the existence of different religions, He also wills positively the worship of Pachamama. Consequently, there is nothing wrong with worshipping it. However, it's not acknowledged explicitly, hence the formulation that the statue was placed in the church without idolatrous intentions.

Let's make a comparison with the behavior of Christians in the first three centuries after Christ's death. How many Christians died at that time — adults as well as children and young people — simply because they refused to burn even a pinch of incense in front of a statue of the emperor, presented as the father of the homeland, or in front of a statue of a pagan god? After all, if we were to adopt the logic of the defenders of Pachamama, we would have to consider the refusal of these Christians indefensible. They too could have considered Venus to be a symbol of life and love. They too could have said that emperors represent the order of law and the stability of the State. And yet they refused to burn the tiniest pinch of incense. After all, they could just as easily have said that they were burning incense "without idolatrous intentions." So many easy and rational-sounding explanations! However, the Church strictly forbade any such acts because she believed that only God should be worshipped and glorified. Burning the incense, bowing the head — these gestures carry an objective meaning. They indicate that such a person, to some extent at least, is worshipping an idol. How, then, can someone claim that placing the Pachamama in a church has no religious significance, has nothing to do with idolatry? That those who did it had no intention of supporting the worship of a pagan goddess?

Or another, similar example. Imagine that upon coming down from Mount Sinai, Moses sees Aaron pointing to the image of the golden calf and saying, "We built it not with idolatrous intentions, but because we wanted to comfort and amuse ourselves." And let's imagine that Moses accepts this. But something entirely different happened. God rejected these explanations and commanded Moses to destroy the golden calf. The statue was thrown into the water, almost in the same way as the Pachamama statue was thrown into the Tiber. When I heard about what young Alexander [Tschugguel] did, this image of Moses throwing out the golden calf immediately came to mind.

True Israelites reacted in this way to any threat of idolatry. Why are there two books of Maccabees in the canon of the Scripture? Why do they show, as a model worthy of emulation, those Jews who rejected eating pork? Because eating this kind of meat would make them look like Gentiles. Since God was positively forbidding it at that time, before the coming of the Messiah, those who wanted to remain faithful to the Law rejected eating pork. For the followers of the one true God, the One who made the covenant with the people of Israel, rejecting pork was precisely an outward, visible, universally recognized sign of piety and faithfulness. The Second Book of Maccabees talks about this (see 2 Macc. 7). There, we can read that not long before the revolt led by

Judah Maccabee, the Syrian ruler Antiochus arrested a certain mother and her seven sons. He then decided to force all eight of them to eat pork. The Scripture describes how one by one the brothers went to their deaths, for this reason alone. One of them spoke up for all and said that they would sooner die than renounce allegiance to the Law of God. The enraged king ordered the pans and cauldrons to be heated red hot and ordered his men to cut off this brother's tongue, to scalp him and cut off the extremities of his members. All this was done in front of the rest of the brothers and the mother, who meanwhile encouraged each other to passively resist the demands of their tormentors. The book describes the gruesome, horrible torments to which the brothers were subjected. Pan-frying, scalping, torture, and torment were inflicted on everyone. The mother, who died at the end, was forced to watch it all. By the way, the commemoration of the seven Maccabean martyrs was included in the liturgical calendar in the traditional Roman Rite; the Church venerated them as saints. It's a pity that this has been abandoned in the new Rite, when such attitudes are so greatly needed. We must bring back the feast of the holy Maccabean martyrs, a feast celebrated since the fifth century on the first of August.

According to *Evangelii Gaudium*, "due to the sacramental dimension of sanctifying grace, God's working in them [non-Christians] tends to produce signs and rites, sacred expressions which in turn bring others to a communitarian experience of journeying toward God. While these lack the meaning and efficacy of the sacraments instituted by Christ, they can be channels which the Holy Spirit raises up in order to liberate non-Christians from atheistic immanentism or from purely individual religious experiences. The same Spirit everywhere brings forth various forms of practical wisdom which help people to bear suffering and to live in greater peace and harmony. As Christians, we can also benefit from these treasures built up over many centuries, which can help us better to live our own beliefs."[60] These words grant sacramental power to pagan rituals and non-Christian ceremonies since they are "channels which the Holy Spirit raises up." What is your take on such statements?

---

[60] Pope Francis, *Evangelii Gaudium:* On the Proclamation of the Gospel in Today's World, no. 254.

Again, I must say that I am sorry, but this claim is false and contradicts divine revelation. What does "sacramental" mean? It refers to the sign given to us by God. We didn't dream it up ourselves. God gave us seven sacraments, seven efficacious signs of grace that can be received in the one true Church, the Catholic Church (these sacraments are valid in the Orthodox churches as well). The Church didn't invent them. Nor does the Church have any authority over them. The proper sign of God's presence and grace is the holy humanity of Jesus Christ. God who became man: this is really the only true holy sign we have. "In him dwelleth all the fulness of the Godhead," says the Epistle of St. Paul to the Colossians (2:9). The seven sacraments are seven channels through which God's grace, as from an immense ocean of God's infinite holiness, flows to men through the holy humanity of Jesus Christ. Only these seven sacramental signs were instituted by God Himself. Apart from them there are no sacred signs, no sacramental signs, no ways that please God, that are holy and efficacious and lead to God. All other non-Christian rites and rituals are human inventions. That is why the Church has never recognized them. We must remember that God has forbidden adhering to rituals that He has not established or permitted.

8

Between Heaven and Hell

In recent years, one of the subjects most often ignored, or discussed only with reluctance, is the existence of Hell. While in the mentality of Catholics of yore Hell was real and tangible, an actual threat to man, in contemporary theology Hell is not mentioned at all as a place of suffering eternal punishment. Occasionally, someone will allude to this danger, but usually with such caution and so many reservations that it's difficult to take those references seriously. A simple question arises: should modern man still believe that such a place or state of eternal damnation exists? Can we today conceive of a God who, as a just judge, imposes eternal punishment and torments on souls in the state of mortal sin as retribution for the evil and wickedness committed during their earthly lives? Some theologians — such as Hans Urs von Balthasar, the Swiss theologian made cardinal by John Paul II, who died some years ago — argue that Hell, if it exists at all, may be empty. Von Balthasar presented his views most clearly in two books he wrote toward the end of his life, *Dare We Hope "That All Men Be Saved"?* and *A Short Discourse on Hell.* In both books, he describes a vision of Christian hope that virtually excludes the belief in eternal punishment. In his view, if God were to consent to even one soul being damned after death, He would not be worthy of our love, He would not be a good God. Balthasar even contended that it's the moral duty of every Christian to hope that Hell is empty. If this opinion is correct, it follows that almost all Catholics who lived earlier must have sinned against such hope. The Church has never understood hope in this way, nor has she made the hope of an empty Hell a precept of faith.

This would naturally follow from such a theory. But we are not only *permitted* to believe in Hell, we are *obliged* to believe in it. It is, after all, a statement contained directly in divine revelation. We mustn't choose from revelation whatever we please. Catholicism is not an à la carte religion. Either we accept the whole revelation — all the dogmas of faith, including the truth about eternal damnation in Hell — or we reject the whole thing. As far as the existence of Hell is concerned, Jesus Himself speaks clearly about it in the twenty-fifth chapter of the Gospel of St. Matthew, which I have already quoted: "Depart from me, you cursed, into everlasting fire which was prepared for the devil and his angels" (Matt. 25:41). From the very beginning, the Fathers of the Church preached that some face eternal damnation, and the Magisterium of the Church has clearly taught this. If we deny this, we are no longer Christians or Catholics. Let me remind you that at the Second Council of Constantinople, in 553, the Church solemnly condemned the theory of apocatastasis[61] derived from Origen, which in fact corresponds to what Hans Urs von Balthasar preached.

I must admit that someone who talks about an empty Hell, who rejects the Church's constant teaching on this subject, who downplays it, displays an extreme lack of responsibility. After all, such a person is exposing people to horrific, real danger, almost pushing them toward eternal perdition. He is implicitly telling people that they can sin against God because in the end no eternal punishment will await them. It gives them a sense of impunity and convinces them that they can continue to live as they please. Ultimately, the conviction that there is no need to fear Hell — because God will save everyone anyway — amounts to just that. Such a person is assuming an enormous burden. He bears the responsibility for all those people who, following his theory, sin boldly and are heading for perdition. Thus, not only does this theory not protect man from condemnation, but on the contrary, it contributes to an increase in sins and to a situation in which offenses against God are multiplied.

---

[61] The word *apocatastasis* is typically used to refer to the belief that everyone — including the damned in Hell and the devil and his angels — will ultimately be saved.

Another consequence of this theory is that it practically undermines the point of Christ's sacrifice. For if there is no Hell and no perdition, Christ's propitiatory sacrifice on the Cross, the precious Blood He shed on Calvary, the drama of suffering, rejection, and humiliation — all this was merely a show, a performance. For why did Christ take our sins upon Himself? Why did He suffer for them? If His Passion were not so serious, if it were not about that which is so important — redemption from eternal death and perdition — the whole Christian story would resemble a theater play. Such behavior of God toward us, based on acting and pretense, would be unworthy of God.

Other theologians, in turn, argue that God should not be described as a judge. It's ultimately man who makes the decision about his fate, and God just passively acknowledges it. If it even exists at all, Hell is understood as a state of man shutting himself off from God, of being enclosed in his own egoism, and in any case it excludes the existence of external, objective punishments and torments imposed on the soul after death. The role of God nowadays is somewhat akin to that of a notary who merely certifies the choice made by man. There are also those who argue that the existence of eternal punishment cannot be reconciled with God's mercy. A god who would condemn anyone would prove to be a merciless god, a god unworthy of honor and devotion.

When God cast Adam and Eve out of Paradise, He judged them. It was not Adam who judged himself, but, as Scripture shows, it was God who passed the judgment and inflicted the punishment.

> To the woman also he said: I will multiply thy sorrows, and thy conceptions: in sorrow shalt thou bring forth children, and thou shalt be under thy husband's power, and he shall have dominion over thee. And to Adam he said: Because thou hast hearkened to the voice of thy wife, and hast eaten of the tree, whereof I commanded thee that thou shouldst not eat, cursed is the earth in thy work; with labour and toil shalt thou eat thereof all the days of thy life. Thorns and thistles shall it bring forth to thee; and thou shalt eat the herbs of the earth. In the sweat of thy face shalt thou eat bread till thou return to the earth, out of which thou wast taken: for dust thou art, and

into dust thou shalt return.... And the Lord God sent him out
of the paradise of pleasure, to till the earth from which he was
taken. And he cast out Adam; and placed before the paradise of
pleasure Cherubims, and a flaming sword, turning every way,
to keep the way of the tree of life. (Gen. 3:16–19, 3:23–24)

All that, handed down to us in Holy Scripture, describes God's punishment. It's the judgment of the Judge. In no way does God act like a
notary who merely acknowledges other people's decisions and verifies
the data provided. Adam didn't condemn himself — God condemned
him. That is the message in the story of the deluge, which describes
mankind's punishment. Similarly, God passed judgment on Sodom and
Gomorrah — both cities were destroyed. This is evidence from history
showing that God really does act as a judge. The New Testament also
makes it clear that Jesus is the judge:

For neither doth the Father judge any man, but hath given
all judgment to the Son. That all men may honor the Son, as
they honor the Father.... Amen, amen I say unto you, that the
hour cometh, and now is, when the dead shall hear the voice
of the Son of God, and they that hear shall live.... And he hath
given him power to do judgment, because he is the Son of man.
Wonder not at this; for the hour cometh, wherein all that are in
the graves shall hear the voice of the Son of God. And they that
have done good things, shall come forth unto the resurrection
of life; but they that have done evil, unto the resurrection of
judgment. (John 5:22–23, 5:25, 5:27–29)

God has passed the authority to execute judgment to Jesus; there is no
doubt about that. The "resurrection to judgment" is mentioned just as
clearly. That Jesus will judge the souls of men is also explicitly shown
in the Gospel of St. Matthew:

And Jesus said to them: Amen, I say to you, that you, who have
followed me, in the regeneration, when the Son of man shall
sit on the seat of his majesty, you also shall sit on twelve seats
judging the twelve tribes of Israel. (19:28)

The apostles will judge along with Jesus. It's a dogma of the Faith that God will judge the living and the dead. Every Catholic affirms this truth, whether by reciting the Niceno-Constantinopolitan Creed or the Apostles' Creed. The passage I quoted earlier from the description of the judgment in the Gospel of St. Matthew shows that Christ will not just passively accept what people will be saying, but will put them to the test. He will examine their hearts and will verify whether what they have for their justification matches reality or not. If found guilty, He will send them into eternal fire.

Could these be just metaphors? Or rhetorical devices typical of those times?

If we were to follow this way of thinking, we could completely erase most of Scripture. It may turn out that everything we don't like is a metaphor. We are simply introducing our own subjective interpretation here and rejecting the clear teaching of Holy Scripture. Our own invention is supposed to be more important than the Word of God.

Similarly, it is impossible to defend the claim that the existence of Hell is incompatible with God's mercy. God is not only infinitely merciful but also infinitely just. There is no contradiction in this. In one of the psalms we read, "Mercy and truth have met each other: justice and peace have kissed" (Ps. 84:11). Mercy and justice are one in God. No contradiction can be introduced here. God must not be divided into the merciful and the just. He is both. Opposing mercy and justice to each other is false and has no foundation in Holy Scripture. A god who would only be merciful and not just is a god of another religion, not the God of Christianity.

Another peculiarity of the contemporary debate is that even those theologians who speak of the real possibility of the existence of Hell do so in such a way that this reality seems quite nebulous. It's possible that the worst criminals in history, such as Stalin or Hitler, the monsters and brutes, could go to Hell, but never an ordinary human being. These theologians believe that man is essentially good and has a right to salvation. You get the impression that they are unable to imagine either a situation in which a person dies in mortal sin, or just mortal sin in general, which would condemn a person to eternal damnation.

No one has a right to salvation. Nor do we have a right to exist. Adam had no right to be created at all. The creation of man was a pure act of God's wisdom and love. If we had a right to exist, it would mean that we must necessarily exist, and that would mean that we are gods. In the same way, we have no right to eternal life, no right to Heaven. This is a pure gift from God. Both are gifts: our existence, the gift of natural life on one hand, and the Beatific Vision, participation in God's eternal, supernatural life, on the other. This latter gift is even greater, even more wonderful, even more difficult to envision, than the former. We have no right to demand natural or supernatural life. Humility is most important in God's eyes. Not insisting on our alleged rights, not placing demands, but humility is the highest, and it opens us to God's grace. It was Lucifer in his pride who claimed to have the right to participate in the eternal life of God, in the supernatural. That is why God cast him down into the abyss — clear proof that no creature has a right to participate in the supernatural divine life. Pride is a kind of virus that is present within creation and was also partially present in Adam. He thought he had a right to the tree of knowledge. But God forbade him access to the tree of life. This demonstrates clearly what a great sin disobedience was, appealing to one's own right, claiming for oneself that to which the creature is not entitled. Only the coming of Jesus Christ, the true Son of God, only His obedience unto death on the Cross, opened man's access to the tree of life anew. There is no other way.

What is sin, actually? In what does it consist? Does sin offend God? Is punishment the recompense for sin? Or does sin exist only in relation to our neighbor — the harm we do to him, the pain we cause him? Is sin a revolt against God or only a lack of love for our neighbor and a kind of selfishness?

All sin, obviously, is fundamentally a rebellion against God. God commands us to love our neighbor. Whoever doesn't obey this commandment disregards God's will. So when man sins against his neighbor, by hurting him, causing him suffering or pain, he is ultimately rebelling against God. In the final analysis, sin is a turning away from God and from His will, a rebellion against God. This must be emphasized again and again. Therefore, we should show contrition for every sin precisely for the sake of love for God.

Of course, we cannot offend God in the literal sense, otherwise He would be like man and would be dependent on us. God in Himself is not acted upon by our sins. However, we can speak of offending God in this way: our sins are a form of despising Him. God sees that we are disrespecting Him. This is the greatest possible injustice. How can anyone disregard and despise the greatest, most holy Love? Insulting God is therefore disregarding God. In Himself, God is fully self-sufficient, perfectly blessed and happy. Our sins don't diminish Him. But our sins diminish *us*. More importantly, our sins make us despise God, and that is the greatest possible injustice. God responds to repentant sinners with forgiveness; He gives us a chance to repent and sends His Son to us. Until the very last breath, every person can still repent, through God's mercy. Even at the last moment of life, he can still benefit from God's mercy. On his deathbed, he can accept Jesus Christ, God's only beloved Son.

Jesus Christ suffered and died on the Cross to appease God's wrath and atone for the sins of mankind; this claim can be found in all Catholic catechisms, including the most recent one, first published in 1992. Is this statement still true? We may get the impression that the understanding of Christ's Passion has changed in recent years. From the beginning, the Church has taught that Christ's sacrifice is propitiatory in nature. Many contemporary theologians think that the vision of a God who would await propitiatory sacrifice, the atonement offered to Him by His Son on the Cross, would be cruel, that it would evoke horror, fear, and anxiety. The image of such a God who can be propitiated by sacrifice and the obedience of His Son to the point of death doesn't correspond to the moral sensitivity of modern man. What do you think about this criticism of the traditional teaching of the Church?

I use the term "traditional" with reluctance. It's a conventional phrase to show that some truth has been accepted for a long time. But truth is truth, no matter how long people have been embracing it. That's why I'm so eager to emphasize that this is not about "traditional" truth in the sense of something that has been accepted by people for a long time (although that may be one of its accidental qualities), but about the truth of *divine revelation*, authentic truth, given to us by God.

Jesus says that He gives Himself as a sacrifice for sins, as the propitiation, the atonement. "And he that will be first among you, shall be your servant. Even as the Son of man is not come to be ministered unto, but to minister, and to give his life a redemption for many" (Matt. 20:27–28). The Gospel of St. Mark also conveys this: "For the Son of man also is not come to be ministered unto, but to minister, and to give his life a redemption for many" (10:45). In both cases, the Gospels are using the Greek term *lytron*. It's a translation of a Hebrew word meaning "propitiatory sacrifice," "ransom for sins." God's direct revelation can be seen in these words. This is not about any human tradition, any invention of the Church, any theological theory. It's a direct message from God Himself.

Christ also repeats this during the Last Supper. "And taking the chalice, he gave thanks, and gave to them, saying: Drink ye all of this. For this is my blood of the new testament, which shall be shed for many unto remission of sins" (Matt. 26:27–28). The "blood of the covenant" (or "blood of the testament," as some translations have it) is a technical phrase used in Old Testament theology to refer to an atoning sacrifice. That sacrifice was the lamb slaughtered in the temple in an act of atonement. These were the words used by Jesus when He instituted the sacrament of the Eucharist at the Last Supper, and that was exactly what the apostles continued to preach. For example, St. John wrote in his First Epistle, "And he is the propitiation for our sins: and not for ours only, but also for those of the whole world" (2:2). Here we come across the Greek term *hilasmos*, or *propitiatio* in Latin — again, a technical term for a propitiatory sacrifice, referencing the sacrificial theology of the Temple in Jerusalem.

As we can see, the doctrine of the propitiatory sacrifice of the crucified Christ is not an addition to early Christianity, but rather the very essence of it. The one who most emphasized the importance of this atoning sacrifice was St. Paul. Let's take, for example, this passage from the Epistle to the Romans: "For all have sinned, and do need the glory of God. Being justified freely by his grace, through the redemption, that is in Christ Jesus, whom God hath proposed to be a propitiation, through faith in his blood" (3:23–25). Here on the other hand we have the term *hilasterion*, once again denoting a propitiatory, atoning sacrifice. The whole New Testament explicitly says that Christ's sacrifice is a propitiatory sacrifice, an atonement. We find this teaching in the Epistles to the Galatians, Ephesians, Colossians, and Hebrews, in the Epistle of St. Peter, and, finally, in the Book of Revelation. This doctrine was accepted by the Apostolic Fathers and then by the Church Fathers. Hence, under no circumstances can anyone claim that it is a time-specific teaching that can be changed at will.

Critics claim that the father of the theology that saw Christ's death on the Cross as a sacrifice to propitiate God was St. Anselm.

But I have just quoted the words of Jesus Himself and the apostles, who clearly indicated the propitiatory nature of the sacrifice. In this context, there is no doubt that the One who is being propitiated is God. St. Anselm expounded it, but this teaching didn't come from him. He wanted to show that the sacrifice was necessary — an opinion that was qualified by St. Thomas Aquinas. But both of them faithfully adhered to the transmitted deposit of faith. St. Anselm presented this teaching in a coherent and systematic way, emphasizing the substitutionary death of Jesus in our stead.

And how would you respond to the accusation, increasingly common among contemporary theologians, that the image of a God demanding propitiation or reparation from His Son reveals Him as someone cruel and terrible?

But we must not reinvent God, or fashion Him according to our own perceptions. A Catholic theologian doesn't construct God according to his own views, but describes and explains what God has revealed about Himself — at least that's what he should be doing. And God Himself has revealed that Jesus Christ's death on the Cross had the character of a sacrifice for sins, a sacrifice that propitiated God. Propitiation, sacrifice — these terms presuppose atonement.

This is also logical. If someone has broken something, and someone else wants to help him, it's much wiser to let the one who broke it fix the problem. This is what taking a person seriously is all about. It doesn't mean correcting the problem yourself or ignoring it. That would not be pedagogical. But God takes us seriously as persons. That is why He Himself was willing to suffer in our flesh, in our nature, in order to correct the wickedness committed by man. God came to our aid in such a way as to elevate our dignity, to heal us. He became a human being. When the first human beings, Adam and Eve, disobeyed and offended God, scorned His word, and defiled His infinite holiness, the whole order of justice was violated. A great, immense, infinite injustice was perpetrated against God. God didn't fix it with a magic trick, but gave us His Son, who in our stead showed perfect obedience. This is what atonement was all about: a perfect sacrifice made by the one who is infinitely holy. This restored order and corrected the error. God took on our true nature, so that as a true human being — with soul and body, with reason and will, with affection, though without sin — He could correct the injustice done to God. Atonement or propitiation means just that: correcting, reconciling, restoring order, regaining the original state.

God has arranged everything in such a way that it would take place with our participation. He waited for that famous *fiat* uttered by the Blessed Virgin Mary. Let me emphasize it again, God takes man seriously. In this sense, we can say that Mary contributed to our redemption, that her "yes" was essential to God's plan. God accepted the sacrifice of His Son not because He wanted to satiate His anger, but because sin was something so serious, so infinitely serious, that only the God-Man could have borne it and made everything right. Nothing shows this great love of God for us better than the fact that He took upon Himself our sins, that He went to suffer on our behalf, that He took it upon Himself to serve the sentence that we humans deserved. It's as if a convict on his way to the execution was told that someone has decided to take his place — this is what God did for us. We deserved to die. In Adam, God condemned us to death and to being excluded from fellowship with Him — that is spiritual death. Jesus took it all upon Himself.

> For God so loved the world, as to give his only begotten Son;
> that whosoever believeth in him, may not perish, but may

have life everlasting. For God sent not his Son into the world, to judge the world, but that the world may be saved by him. (John 3:16–17)

This is exactly what St. Paul is describing in his Epistle to the Romans:

For why did Christ, when as yet we were weak, according to the time, die for the ungodly? For scarce for a just man will one die; yet perhaps for a good man some one would dare to die. But God commendeth his charity toward us; because when as yet we were sinners, according to the time, Christ died for us; much more therefore, being now justified by his blood, shall we be saved from wrath through him. (5:6–9)

We must, therefore, understand well what Scripture says about God's wrath. Unlike with human beings, it's not about anger, irritation, a thirst for revenge. Human anger always indicates limitations and helplessness. God's wrath, on the other hand, is His absolute will directed against evil. Wrath is the rejection of evil, the absolute rejection of wickedness. So in order for us to approach God, the God who rejects evil, someone had to arrange reconciliation on our behalf. Someone had to repair what had been corrupted. That someone could only be God, who assumed human nature. Jesus Himself emphasizes the fact that He acted out of love when He says that He gave His life for us as His friends:

Greater love than this no man hath, that a man lay down his life for his friends. You are my friends, if you do the things that I command you. I will not now call you servants: for the servant knoweth not what his lord doth. But I have called you friends: because all things whatsoever I have heard of my Father, I have made known to you. (John 15:13–15)

As a consequence of original sin, man was in a state of misery and abasement, a state from which only God Himself could deliver him. And this is exactly what happened.

We must remember that although Jesus Christ died once on the Cross, His sacrifice is made present and renewed in the Church through the sacrament of the Eucharist. Again we can see clearly that this teaching about the propitiatory character of Jesus' death is contained in the New Testament itself. In the same way, later the Council of Trent, when explaining the meaning of the Mass, pointed out that it is the propitiatory sacrifice of the New Covenant and invoked precisely the whole theology of sacrifice that we have briefly discussed here. That the Holy Mass is a propitiatory sacrifice is therefore a dogma of faith, not a theological theory of St. Anselm or any other theologian.

According to the classic teaching of the Church, Jesus died for us because without His sacrificial death, we would remain children of wrath. You have shown that this teaching is present from the very beginning in Scripture. We can add here another important quotation from the Epistle to the Ephesians, in which St. Paul writes, "We all ... were by nature children of wrath, even as the rest" (2:3). Today it seems that this understanding — that man without participation in Christ's sacrifice is a child of wrath — has practically disappeared from theology. And yet, as you just mentioned, this conviction also lies at the heart of the Catholic understanding of the Mass: one of its four ends is propitiatory. The post-conciliar theology instead explains the meaning of Christ's sacrifice as an act of solidarity with people, an act of love for people, but there is no mention of the payment for Adam's sin and the need to make reparation to God. Death on the Cross is explained as a sign of brotherhood with man, a way of showing solidarity with them. In that context, a simple question arises: why does anyone need such a sign?

In this approach, there is clearly a reduction of the teachings given to us in the Gospels and by the apostles. That passage from Paul's epistle that you just quoted is the Word of God, and we can't change it. I spoke about it a moment ago: the wrath of God is not a passion, as it is in man, but an absolute will to oppose evil, a total and unconditional rejection of evil by God. After Adam's sin, after he chose evil, we all found ourselves in the same situation, rejected by this will of God, by His wrath. We deserved to be excluded from fellowship with God. This is what the wrath of God means: excluding us from fellowship of life with Him because of the evil we committed in Adam. Thus we were by nature children of wrath until Christ set us free and restored us to divine sonship. Through His precious Blood we have gained access to the kingdom of God. Jesus Himself said this during the Last Supper, and these words are repeated in His name by every priest acting in the person of Christ during the celebration of the Holy Mass.

Why is it practically impossible to learn about this from the teaching of the Church today? Why is it that instead of reminding us that "by nature we are children of wrath," we are still being told about dignity? Why is it that instead of being reminded that sacrifice propitiated God and was due payment for sin, we are still being told about solidarity? Several times I have even read statements by important Church leaders who said that if someone innocent were to die for the guilty, it would be an injustice.

The main reason is that nowadays people don't want to take sin seriously. Sin is trivialized, dismissed, treated as a trifle or an insignificant scratch. If that's the case, then why would Jesus die on the Cross for such an insignificant reason? For such trifles? How could it be so? This is how we get the narrative that the death on the Cross was meant to show Jesus' love and solidarity with us. You can clearly see a Pelagian influence here. Pelagius also taught that the death on the Cross didn't save us from sin, because by nature, by birth, as God's creatures, we were almost good, we didn't need such redemption. So the reason for this change is a false understanding of sin, a general trivialization of sin, a reluctance to take sin seriously.

Archbishop Vincenzo Paglia, president of the Pontifical Academy for Life, during the interreligious International Symposium "Religion and Medical Ethics: Palliative Care and the Mental Health of the Elderly" in Rome, stated on December 11, 2019, that it is heretical to claim that Judas is in Hell. He said, "I always celebrate funerals for those who commit suicide, because suicide is always a question of unfulfilled love. We must also remember that, for the Catholic Church, if someone says that Judas is in hell, he is a heretic."[62] This is another example of where the theory of universal salvation can lead.

---

[62] See Diane Montagna, "Vatican Archbishop: Those Who Say Judas Is in Hell Are 'Heretics' and Priests May 'Accompany' Assisted Suicides," *LifeSiteNews* (December 11, 2019), www.lifesitenews.com/news/abp-paglia-on-judas.

The tendency to justify Judas, the urge to rehabilitate him, seems unchristian to me. The betrayal of the Son of God cannot be considered an insignificant trifle! Jesus Himself said to Judas, "It would have been better for you if you had not been born" (Matt. 26:24). These are the words of God Himself. It is difficult to imagine that God spoke such words and yet the man to whom they were addressed is now enjoying eternal happiness in Heaven. St. Peter said that Judas "hath by transgression fallen" from "this ministry and apostleship," "that he might go to his own place" (Acts 1:25), the place of one who committed suicide. We don't, of course, have certain knowledge that Judas is in Hell. God has not explicitly revealed this to us, and neither has the Church taught it solemnly, although her ancient liturgical texts bear witness to a belief commonly accepted. But to say that someone who thinks Judas is in Hell is preaching heresy is preposterous.

I have the impression that the new Judases among the high clergy are looking for a new patron saint, hence the tendency to justify him.

For centuries, many devout Catholics have been concerned about the fate of the souls in Purgatory. They believed that this was, we could say, the almost universal fate of ordinary mortals. The bond between the living and the dead was manifested precisely through such reasoning. Therefore, Masses were offered for the souls in Purgatory, services were organized on their behalf, and prayers were offered for them. Today, it seems that Purgatory has practically disappeared from Catholic consciousness. There is no mention at all of the so-called expiatory punishments that were supposed to cleanse souls from the evil accumulated on earth and not expiated. As I said, the common belief is that practically everyone is going to Heaven after death, while Hell, if it exists at all, is reserved for the greatest criminals of history. So is Purgatory real? Or is it just a legend, a myth?

The belief in the existence of Purgatory is based on the constant and immutable teaching of the Church. It appears clearly in the teachings of the councils and in the catechisms. It was first dogmatically pronounced at the Second Council of Lyon in 1274. It was reiterated by the subsequent Councils of Florence and Trent, and by the teachers and Doctors of the Church.

That's right, but I'm not asking a historical question about doctrine, it's clear where things stand there. I'm asking about the popular mentality, about the practical disappearance of the idea of Purgatory as an important reference point of the Faith. Concern for the fate of one's own soul, for the shortest possible stay in Purgatory, was the reason for the establishment of many churches and church foundations. The conviction that these souls can and must be helped has been the source of many prayers. Take St. Padre Pio, for example, and the amount of attention he paid to the souls in Purgatory. Today Purgatory has disappeared from the consciousness of Catholics. It's gone.

That's true. I think this is another consequence of an erroneous understanding of sin. People think that if someone's sin is forgiven, there are no consequences. But Scripture clearly teaches us that sin has consequences. The consequence of sin is punishment. Therefore, man, even if his sin has already been forgiven, must make atonement for it. This is the point of the punishment for sin, which he must suffer in order to be completely purified. In fact, this belief has often, in recent decades, disappeared from catechesis and from sermons. People must be told again and again that every evil act has consequences for eternity. By God's grace and with man's cooperation, this sin can be conquered and its debt of temporal punishments can be paid in Purgatory. Thus, there is no doubt that Catholics should continue to pray for our brothers and sisters, for the poor souls who are in Purgatory; we should offer the graces that God gives us for these souls so that they may expiate their sins and the punishments in the fires of Purgatory may come to an end for them as quickly as possible. Prayers and devotions are necessary; the Holy Mass is especially important from this point of view. We are all one great Church — we here on earth and they there in Purgatory, as well as the saints in Heaven. The *Catechism* makes it clear that here on earth we are the Church Militant, the saints in Heaven are the Church Triumphant, and finally the souls in Purgatory are the Church Suffering, or, as we might call it, the Church Penitent. Together we all constitute one great family. That is why we should help the souls suffering in Purgatory.

This assistance to the poor souls also comes from a natural human need. Look at people who visit cemeteries: they often stop at the graves of their loved ones and say prayers there. Some sprinkle holy water over the graves. There is something natural and spontaneous about this. It's the basic moral obligation that the living have toward the dead. I'm convinced that most don't view their departed loved ones already as saints. No, they ask the saints for intercession, for help, just as they probably generally ask God for mercy, for Him to somehow relieve the plight of the poor souls in Purgatory. If we are convinced that there is no Purgatory, what would happen to a person after death? Would his soul go immediately to Heaven?

Exactly. But this is what's believed nowadays. That's why priests at funerals generally say that the deceased has gone to the Father's house.

That's true, which is why at funerals you increasingly get the impression that we bury only saints; the tributes sound as if the deceased were already in Heaven. Of course, in a wide sense, we could say that Purgatory is the Father's house, but I agree that this is not what those who use the term most often have in mind. Heaven is the Beatific Vision, it's seeing God face to face, truly dwelling in the Father's house. Meanwhile, Purgatory could be called, at best, a dark part of that house. Perhaps a cellar, from which you will have to climb up to a higher floor? Purgatory isn't eternal; after the final judgment, it will be no more.

The regular faithful, however, still have not embraced this belief in the universality of immediate salvation. They don't write in their obituaries "St. John Smith" or "St. Joe Brown." Usually they go to the graves to pray *for* their loved ones who have died, not *to* them. A person visiting a cemetery, a person who is praying, who is saying the Our Father for the soul of the deceased, is actually showing that the deceased one needs help, that he is begging for it. In a certain way, we can say that this is also a proof for the existence of Purgatory, this petition for the deceased, this cry for help, this conviction that the deceased is not yet in Heaven but in a place and in a state where such a prayer will help him. I'm not talking about proof in the strict sense of the word, but about a certain sign, a hint. Besides, many saints have shared their encounters with the souls in Purgatory, their requests for help and for prayer. It's enough to read, for example, St. Catherine of Genoa's *Treatise on Purgatory*, or the writings of St. Padre Pio or the Curé of Ars.

In any case, I must confess to you that I also once received a sign from one of the souls in Purgatory. I was staying in a monastery — I cannot reveal the name because I have pledged myself to secrecy. Well, in this monastery, a soul from Purgatory was appearing for a year. It was the soul of a priest who came to the sisters. The soul was deep in Purgatory. At one point, Mother Superior discovered in her cell, in a drawer, a text written on a piece of paper. There were also traces of fire, and the handwriting pointed to a man. It's important to note that this was a cloistered community, strictly separated from the world. No one had access to the sisters. Mother Superior began to inquire as to who might have put the note in her drawer. Of course, no one would confess. Humanly speaking, it was quite impossible. The message was simple, "Pray for me, I am suffering greatly." After a few days, Mother Superior found another similar card in the same place, this time signed, "Your spiritual father." This was the phrase the sisters always used to refer to their chaplain. There was no chaplain at the time this happened, so it must have been a priest from the past. At least that's what the Superior concluded, and wrote to him, "If you were a spiritual father in our monastery, and now you are in Purgatory, then where is it?" And she received the answer, "I am deep in Purgatory, I need your help." Then the Superior promised that they would have Holy Masses said for his soul, that they would pray, and that they would hold devotions for the same intention. And she asked this soul if she could ask questions — dictated not by curiosity, but by concern for souls and the Faith, and for the development of spiritual life. And she received the answer, "Yes, for that I have permission." Then she left a note in that drawer with the question, "What is prayer?" And two days later, in the same place she found the answer, written in the same handwriting, by hand, on a piece of paper with traces of fire. I have read it, and it's one of the most beautiful definitions of prayer I know. Theologically perfect, not exaggerated, just right. Then the Sister Superior put new, clean sheets of paper in the drawer and wrote to the soul, "Use the clean, unstained ones." This dialogue continued for a year.

What was this definition of prayer?

It said that prayer must be an offering, that it must flow from humility. Clear, wise, and simple. Altogether, the Superior asked this soul over a hundred questions and received as many answers. The result was a record of a beautiful spiritual conversation. I saw it and read it. It can't be published now; the bishop of the diocese to which this monastery belongs doesn't want that. Perhaps he is afraid that it has all been fabricated, that it's a product of fantasy, that it's made up. He is guided primarily by caution. But I'm absolutely convinced that the record of this conversation is true. I saw it with my own eyes. I saw the envelope with the writing, the stains, fire marks — and my name was on one of the pages. Inside was a piece of paper with a text, also handwritten. After what I have read, I have no doubt whatsoever. It could not have been a forgery. I'm relating this story to show that not only saints but many people have had the experience of contact with the souls in Purgatory who turned to them for help, for prayer, for Holy Masses. As I mentioned earlier, the living and the dead, members of the Church Militant and Church Penitent, are all one family and can support each other in a spiritual way.

9

Automatism and Anthropocentrism

Now I would like to talk about another problem related to the question of the last things, although from a slightly different perspective. The issue is whether, as it seems, post-conciliar theology, or at least a significant portion of it, proclaims the automatism and universality of salvation. When reading various modern theologians who are considered authorities in the field, one can arrive at the conclusion that accepting and professing the Catholic Faith is no longer necessary for salvation. It doesn't matter what you believe; the important thing is to be a "good person." It doesn't matter if you are an atheist, if you believe in God or not — seeking the good is enough. This belief can be found almost everywhere. But the Church has clearly taught that faith is necessary for salvation: "without faith it is impossible to please God. For he that cometh to God, must believe that he is, and is a rewarder to them that seek him" (Heb. 11:6).

> This is the teaching of the entire New Testament. When addressing the Jews, Jesus said, "you shall die in your sins. For if you believe not that I am he, you shall die in your sin" (John 8:24). We are dealing here with the explicit words of the Savior. Jesus constantly demanded faith: "he that believeth not shall be condemned" (Mark 16:16). These are the words of God.

However, many theologians now argue that a particular person's faith is not necessary. They invoke God's general will for salvation and claim that the actual salvation of every person follows from it. They quote a passage from St. Paul's Epistle to Timothy, "[God]

... will have all men to be saved" (1 Tim. 2:4), and argue that since this is what God wants, it must happen.

> However, it would follow from this interpretation that the Savior's words I just quoted are redundant. God doesn't want any automatism. He doesn't want to give a share in His life automatically. We are confronted here with the great mystery of the freedom with which God has equipped every human person, every spiritual person. God doesn't want us to be with Him for all eternity as puppets. How could we love Him without being free? How could He enjoy the glory we give Him if we didn't have freedom? The free choice to love God, the freedom to choose the truth: that is true freedom, rather than an alleged right to offend God, or to reject Him, or to chose a false religion. The great mystery of God's love is that God allows us to love Him in freedom.
>
> Alas, it is true that widespread among theologians today is the idea of "anonymous Christianity," according to which a person, whether he knows it or not, is a Christian anyway. From this proposition it follows that there is no need to be baptized, to believe, or to belong to a church. Everyone is automatically already saved through Christ's death on the Cross. If this claim, if this doctrine of "anonymous Christianity" were true, then Jesus' words about the necessity of faith would prove to be absurd. Jesus also said, "Amen, amen I say to thee, unless a man be born again of water and the Holy Ghost, he cannot enter into the kingdom of God" (John 3:5). This necessity of faith, contrasted with its lack, is also perfectly demonstrated in these words, "He that believeth in him is not judged. But he that doth not believe, is already judged: because he believeth not in the name of the only begotten Son of God" (John 3:18). Freedom is mentioned in all these passages. Nowhere is there a hint of automatism. The claim of automatic salvation is erroneous, heretical doctrine that contradicts God's revelation.

The Church has clearly taught that someone who sins with insolence, presuming upon God's mercy, commits a sin against the Holy Spirit. But theologians today would argue that God accepts me as I am, that He loves me always, regardless of my actions, that He always affirms me wholly, with everything I do. On December 25, 2019, during the midnight Mass at the Vatican, Pope Francis said, "God continues to love us all, even the worst of us. To me, to you, to each of us, he says today: 'I love you and I will always love you, for you are precious in my eyes.'"[63] If God always accepts me, if He loves me constantly and always, even if I am the worst villain and criminal, it means that I can sin freely, trusting in God's mercy. And in *Amoris Laetitia* (no. 297) we read, "No one can be condemned for ever, because that is not the logic of the Gospel!" How are we to understand all these statements?

> The scene presented in the twenty-fifth chapter of the Gospel of St. Matthew, which describes the Last Judgment, reveals something very significant. The wicked are judged, condemned, and rejected through an assessment of their specific free actions. God doesn't condemn human beings through an arbitrary, whimsical, random judgment. He passes judgment on human actions. In the same way, when He demands faith, He demands an act of will from man.
>
> Naturally, God loves us always, even the greatest sinners, but He doesn't condone or accept our evil deeds. He definitely doesn't accept us "just the way we are." If we don't persevere in the Faith, if we don't perform good deeds, if we commit iniquities and do not repent, we will be condemned. The words of Pope Francis would be correct in the sense that God loves us always, just as a good father loves a prodigal son, or as a good shepherd follows the lost sheep. God waits for our repentance. He waits for us to be converted until the very end.

But the words that I quoted say nothing about the necessity of conversion. Quite the opposite.

> God loves me, for sure, but He wants me to become better. If God loves the worst man, it's only in the sense that He demands of him that he should cease to be the worst and become good. He certainly doesn't love the worst as the worst, but He loves the worst as the one who is supposed to become good.

[63] See Pope Francis, Homily (December 24, 2019), www.vatican.va/content/ francesco/en/homilies/2019/documents/papa-francesco_20191224_omelia-natale.html.

Then it should be mentioned. Otherwise, it may look as if God's love were confirming man in evil.

> God loves me not the way I am, but the way I am to become. A father awaits his son.

In the hope that the son should convert.

> That's why the correct way to understand it is as follows: the statement "God always loves man" means that God constantly expects the sinner to repent and always gives him sufficient graces for this to happen. Furthermore, the New Testament implies that some people will be condemned, which contradicts the sentence from *Amoris Laetitia*. If "no one can be condemned for ever," then the doctrine of God as judge is erased. In the same way, sin and responsibility are erased. What emerges is a very comfortable Christianity, behind which ultimately selfishness is concealed. If sin is not taken seriously, then selfishness wins. It turns out that God is reconciled to sin. It's impossible to say that God will never reject me because of my sin, no matter what I do. Such a belief would be nothing more than cultivating my selfishness. It would turn out that what matters is what I want, not what God wants.

Should man still believe that it's necessary to belong to the Catholic Church in order to be saved? What do the words "outside the Church there is no salvation" — *extra ecclesiam nulla salus* — mean today? According to Jean-Jacques Rousseau, the father of the French Revolution, whoever maintains that there is no salvation outside the Church should be banished from the State. Does the contemporary Church continue to recognize this principle, so adamantly rejected by the Enlightenment?

> This dogma is still relevant. Let's inquire into what the Church is. The Church is Christ, the Mystical Body of Christ. Ultimately, then, we could say: outside of Christ there is no salvation. This is the meaning of the phrase "outside the Church there is no salvation." Christ is the only Savior; no one can be saved without Him. He is the only and necessary way to salvation. Whoever consciously departs from it, whoever consciously either leaves the Church or refuses to join it, will

not be saved. Such a person will be condemned. Let me remind you
one more time: a person can be saved if through no fault of his own
he is in a state of invincible ignorance. God will ultimately determine
this, for He alone knows the secrets of the human heart. However, it's
not God's will for these people to be outside the Church. There is only
one ark, as shown in the story of Noah when the flood was coming
and there was a need for shelter from death. Noah's ark is a type of the
Church. Jesus said, "without me you can do nothing" (John 15:5).
That means you can do nothing without Christ.

Hasn't there been what could be called an anthropocentric breakthrough in the theology and thinking of the Church since the last Council? In the Pastoral Constitution *Gaudium et Spes,* **we read, "According to the almost unanimous opinion of believers and unbelievers alike, all things on earth should be related to man as their center and crown."[64] But from the perspective of believers, shouldn't all things on earth be directed toward God? Isn't there a serious error in this conciliar statement of the Council? Is it not precisely anthropocentrism, that is, the subordination of everything to man?**

This statement of *Gaudium et Spes* is very problematic. Indeed, it very
clearly manifests an anthropocentric tendency. This, in principle, contradicts the main message of divine revelation. From the very beginning, the Fathers of the Church as well as later theology emphasized
the Christocentrism of revelation. Already Adam was created for the
sake of Christ, for the sake of God who became man, as we can read it
in the following explanation of Tertullian:

Whatever was the form and expression which was then given
to the clay [by the Creator] Christ was in His thoughts as one
day to become man, because the Word, too, was to be both
clay and flesh, even as the earth was then. For so did the Father
previously say to the Son: "Let us make man in our own image,
after our likeness" (Genesis 1:26). And *God made man,* that
is to say, the creature which He moulded and fashioned; *after*

---

[64] Second Vatican Council, Pastoral Constitution on the Church in the Modern
World *Gaudium et Spes*, 12.

the image of God (in other words, of Christ) *did He make him.*
And the Word was God also, "who being in the image of God,
thought it not robbery to be equal to God" (Philippians 2:6).
Thus, that clay which was even then putting on the image of
Christ, who was to come in the flesh, was not only the work,
but also the pledge and surety, of God.[65]

I also doubt that there is such a thing as "the almost unanimous opinion of believers and unbelievers alike." Fortunately, not all believers
embrace anthropocentrism. Further, what are "all things on earth?"
If we are talking about the totality of creation, then, after all, man is
also part of creation. The whole of creation must be "related to man as
center and crown"? This is explicit anthropocentrism. All things must
be directed toward Christ! The following passage from the Epistle to
the Colossians perfectly illustrates this point: "who is the image of the
invisible God, the firstborn of every creature: for in him were all things
created in heaven and on earth, visible and invisible, whether thrones, or
dominations, or principalities, or powers: all things were created by him
and in him" (1:15–16). Thus we can see that the claim of the conciliar
constitution that "all things on earth should be related to man as their
center and crown" stands in stark contrast to St. Paul's teaching that all
things have been created for Christ! The whole of creation should be
directed toward Christ as its true center, and not toward man. Another
passage from the Scripture, from the Epistle to the Romans, says that
"of him, and by him, and in him, are all things" (11:36).

The statement itself is open to an anthropocentric interpretation
and should not have appeared in that form in a text of an ecumenical council. It should have been accompanied by an explanation to
prevent misinterpretation. In order to understand the quoted sentence in a proper sense, a long explanatory note would be necessary.
St. Thomas Aquinas admittedly said that all material creatures — as
far as their being is concerned — are below man and are ordered to
man as their proximate end, since man, having a soul, is also a spiritual

---

[65] *De resurrectione carnis*, 6.

creature. Individual earthly creatures exist for the betterment of the whole creation. The whole creation with all its parts is directed toward God as the goal [of its existence] so that they give honor to God in this way. Therefore, the proper end of every single material creature is to represent the goodness of God and to proclaim His perfection.[66] Although the authors of *Gaudium et Spes* go on to say that God has made man lord over all creatures of the earth in order that he may use them to glorify God, this reference is too weak to properly understand the excessively anthropocentric statement that man is the summit and center of all that exists on earth.

I believe that along with the passage from *Dignitatis Humanae* that speaks of the natural right to freedom of religion and the passage from *Lumen Gentium* that speaks of the common worship of God by Christians and Muslims, this statement in *Gaudium et Spes* is one of the most dangerous statements in the conciliar texts. They are classic examples of what one might call time bombs concealed in documents that may seem harmless at first, but over time can cause great damage.

Perhaps this anthropocentrism can be seen even more clearly in another passage from the document, which states that man is "the only creature on earth which God willed for itself" (GS 24). The significance of this sentence can be shown by the simple fact of how many times it has been quoted and extolled by conciliar theologians and later popes. However, as Romano Amerio carefully demonstrated in his book *Iota Unum*, all of creation, including man, was created for the sake of God, not man. If man were the only creature willed for its own sake and not for God's, man would be God.

But after all, everything, along with man, was created for God's sake and His glory. We spoke about this a moment ago. Man occupies the highest place, but only in the hierarchy of created *visible* beings — angels are invisible. This does not mean that everything else was created for his sake. On the contrary, man must always emphasize that he is not the center, but only a servant of God. Heaven and earth proclaim the glory of God, not the glory of man. In a historical sense, anthropocentrism

---

[66] See *Summa Theologiae* I, Q. 65, art. 2.

became especially strong in the philosophy of Kant, who tried to ground both all cognition and ethics exclusively in man. Later it was present in naturalism and rationalism.

Going back to the sentence quoted above, it could be defended by claiming that what is meant here is the natural order: man is the crown of the earthly creation, and what is on earth is subject to his authority. Commentators, including many conservatives, who acknowledge the truth of this claim, invoke St. Thomas Aquinas here. However, this defense is unconvincing. The entire order, both natural and supernatural, is directed completely toward God as its true summit and center. Man was created for the glory of God. The Book of Proverbs states, "The Lord hath made all things for himself" (16:4). The same thing can be found in the *Catechism of the Catholic Church* (no. 293): "Scripture and Tradition never cease to teach and celebrate this fundamental truth: 'The world was made for the glory of God.'" And it goes on to explain:

> St. Bonaventure explains that God created all things "not to increase his glory, but to show it forth and to communicate it," for God has no other reason for creating than his love and goodness: "Creatures came into existence when the key of love opened his hand." The First Vatican Council explains: this one, true God, of his own goodness and "almighty power," not for increasing his own beatitude, nor for attaining his perfection, but in order to manifest this perfection through the benefits which he bestows on creatures, with absolute freedom of counsel "and from the beginning of time, made out of nothing both orders of creatures, the spiritual and the corporeal."

It's clear that the statement quoted here from *Gaudium et Spes* is ambiguous, at the very least. In order to understand it in keeping with the Tradition of the Church, at least several interpretative steps must be taken. For example, one could cite the explanation of St. Thomas Aquinas, who said that within all visible creation, the more noble creatures are beings equipped with reason (intellectual beings), that is, human beings, because they are closer in their likeness to God. Therefore, intellectual beings equipped with reason, that is, human beings, are governed by Divine Providence for their own sake, while all the other non-rational creatures exist for the sake of human beings.[67] However, St. Thomas Aquinas is not saying here that man was created for his own sake, but that God governs him for his own sake, since, unlike other material beings, man bears God's likeness. Unfortunately, the authors of *Gaudium et Spes* are too direct when talking about man's existence and beings created for his sake. A sufficiently clear and direct affirmation of the truth that all creatures, including man, were created and intended for God alone is missing here. The passage (*GS* 24) should also mention that God is the only being who exists for His own sake. He is the being who exists in Himself and of Himself (*ipsum esse per se subsistens*). If this paragraph of *Gaudium et Spes* had included such necessary theological additions in the immediate context, it would not have been possible to use the passage for anthropocentric interpretations, and it would not have been necessary to write a short Thomistic treatise to understand the proper meaning of these teachings.

Thus, it requires some real mental gymnastics and balancing. As found in the conciliar document, this sentence is open to anthropocentric interpretations. It should have been written differently: man was created for God's sake. No creature, including man, is necessary. If man existed for his own sake, then he would not be a created and contingent being, but a necessary one, because that which exists for itself is necessary. The only absolutely necessary being is God, for He alone exists for His own sake. The quoted sentence from *Gaudium et Spes* certainly contributed to the development of this anthropocentrism that has infected the Church since the Council.

Another example of such an anthropocentric breakthrough, which many believe occurred at the Council, is the understanding of revelation in *Gaudium et Spes*. Paragraph 22 says that "Christ, the final Adam, by the revelation of the mystery of the Father and His love, fully reveals man to man himself and makes his supreme calling clear." Does this not bring us to the conclusion that the goal of revelation is not God but man himself?

---

[67] *Summa contra Gentiles* III, chap. 12, no. 4.

This statement of the Council refers to the goal of divine revelation, which is to reveal the mystery of the Father, that is, the Triune God and His love for mankind, as well as man's highest calling or destiny. It then goes on to speak of man's full participation in the Paschal mystery of Christ, that is, that man should be conformed to the image of Christ and thus become a son in the Son of God (*filius in Filio*). Revealing God's glory and goodness is the first and highest end of the whole of creation, revelation, and redemption. The second, subordinate end is that creatures may benefit from this glory and goodness. From that, the following conclusion could be drawn for our deliberations: this subordinate end is man's redemption and eternal happiness. The First Vatican Council teaches that God brought all creation into existence "not for the increase or acquirement of his own happiness, but to manifest his perfection by the blessings which he bestows on creatures."[68] Creatures, on the other hand, show and represent the perfection of God to the extent to which they truly know God in faith, adore Him, and love Him. Human beings can properly know, adore, and love God only in Jesus Christ, the God-man. People attain their perfection and eternal happiness through supernatural faith, adoration, and love.

God obliges people to accept His revelation. The First Vatican Council also taught this. "Since man is wholly dependent on God as his Creator and Lord, and since created reason is completely subject to uncreated truth, we are bound by faith to give full obedience of intellect and will to God who reveals" (*DF* 28). This passage is also quoted in the Second Vatican Council's Dogmatic Constitution on Divine Revelation *Dei Verbum* (no. 5).

Even though the same document *Gaudium et Spes* (no. 41) speaks of God as the final end of man, it would be helpful if in its statement on Christ as the new man (*GS* 22) the Council also explicitly mentioned the first and highest end of all creation, which is the revelation of the glory and goodness of God. Scripture says, "For of him, and by him, and in him, are all things: to him be glory for ever" (Rom. 11:36). Man

---

[68] First Vatican Council, Dogmatic Constitution on the Catholic Faith *Dei Filius* [henceforth *DF*], 18, www.ccel.org/ccel/schaff/creeds2.v.ii.i.html.

will be elevated to glory if he first gives God the honor due Him and
shows obedience to Him.

You have said that the claim of automatic salvation is incompatible with revelation.
How, then, am I to understand some of Pope John Paul II's words that seem to espouse
the doctrine of universal salvation? When he was still a cardinal, in a retreat for Paul VI,
which was later published as the book *Sign of Contradiction*, he wrote that "all men, from
the beginning of the world until its end, have been redeemed and justified by Christ
and his cross."[69] In the same book, the future pope wrote, "thus the birth of the Church,
at the time of the messianic and redemptive death of Christ, coincided with the birth
of 'the new man' — whether or not man was aware of such a rebirth and whether or
not he accepted it. At that moment, man's existence acquired a new dimension, very
simply expressed by St. Paul as 'in Christ.'"[70] Those statements seem to contain the
doctrine of anonymous Christianity.

> The first statement is ambiguous. All have been redeemed, but not all
> have been justified. The claim that all have been justified is contrary to
> the Church's teaching. Accepting it would mean that all people auto-
> matically go to Heaven, and so it's a proposition that claims universal
> salvation. It also contradicts the definitions of the Council of Trent and
> the teaching of the *Catechism of the Catholic Church*.
>
> We read, "The grace of the Holy Spirit has the power to justify
> us, that is, to cleanse us from our sins and to communicate to us 'the
> righteousness of God through faith in Jesus Christ' (Rom. 3:22) and
> through Baptism (see Rom. 6:3–4)" (*CCC* 1987). Here, the conditions
> for justification by grace are clearly faith and Baptism. Another article
> of the *Catechism* states this very clearly:
>
>> Justification establishes cooperation between God's grace and
>> man's freedom. On man's part it is expressed by the assent of

---

[69] Karol Wojtyła (Pope John Paul II), *Sign of Contradiction* (New York: Seabury
Press, 1979), 87. [The English text here says only "redeemed," whereas the Italian original, as well as the Polish and German editions, all say "redeemed and
justified." Evidently the English translator saw the need to correct the erroneous
theology. — *Ed.*]

[70] Ibid., 91.

faith to the Word of God, which invites him to conversion, and in the cooperation of charity with the prompting of the Holy Spirit who precedes and preserves his assent: "when God touches man's heart through the illumination of the Holy Spirit, man himself is not inactive while receiving that inspiration, since he could reject it; and yet, without God's grace, he cannot by his own free will move himself toward justice in God's sight" (Council of Trent, DS 1525). (CCC 1993)

Under no circumstances, then, can we speak of automaticity and of all men being justified. For justification, "the assent of faith to the Word of God" is necessary. Since justification entails sanctification, there can be no automaticity here as implied in the statement "all men, from the beginning of the world until its end, have been redeemed and justified." Man doesn't remain passive and indifferent. Thus this sentence by Cardinal Wojtyła should be corrected.

The real issue is that the same doctrine can be found in other texts, written already when he was pope. For example, in the encyclical *Redemptor Hominis*, which we could call a program for the pontificate, the pope states in reference to redemption, "We are not dealing with the 'abstract' man, but the real, 'concrete,' 'historical' man. We are dealing with 'each' man, for each one is included in the mystery of the Redemption and with each one Christ has united himself for ever through this mystery.... Her solicitude is about the whole man and is focused on him in an altogether special manner. The object of her care is man in his unique unrepeatable human reality, which keeps intact the image and likeness of God himself (see Gen. 1:27)."[71] It's clear that, in the pope's view, every single human being that has been conceived "keeps intact the image and likeness of God himself." However, the Church has always applied this phrase to Adam's situation before original sin (Gen. 1:27), while the pope seems to apply it to every human being already tainted by original sin. How are we to understand these statements? At first glance, they seem to speak of a universal and automatic salvation, exactly as Karl Rahner assumed.

As for the assertions in *Redemptor Hominis*, we must study them very carefully. Allow me to quote them once again: "We are dealing with

---

[71] John Paul II, *Redemptor Hominis*, no. 13.

'each' man, for each one is included in the mystery of the Redemption and with each one Christ has united himself for ever through this mystery." The first part of the sentence is correct, yes, everyone is embraced by the Mystery of Redemption. However, the part saying "with each one Christ has united himself for ever through this mystery" — this cannot be stated in such a manner. After all, Christ didn't unite Himself for ever with every human being, since a spiritual and supernatural union demands reciprocity, and there are human beings who freely reject a union with Christ.

Exactly. If Christ were forever united with every man, it would either mean that Christ is in Hell, or that there is no Hell.

It is true that Christ shed His Blood for everyone. Yet the statement from the encyclical can be misunderstood and misleading. And indeed that is the case: it has been misunderstood. A serious problem is posed by the next statement, which says each human being "keeps intact the image and likeness of God himself." The Church has always taught that "likeness" should be understood as salvation, as union with God. The image refers to that which man has by nature, and the likeness refers to that which man receives by supernatural grace. This is what the Fathers of the Church taught from the beginning. The likeness is restored through Baptism. The likeness makes man capable of communion with God.

Precisely. If, in the language of the Church, likeness means supernatural life, and if it can be gained only through cooperation with supernatural grace, then how can one claim that it abides intact in every human being? Doesn't this mean that man has inherent supernatural grace that can't be lost, that is: life with God and eternal life?

A pope's text should not be so unclear that it forces us to engage in arduous intellectual exercises. This sentence is ambiguous. According to the traditional language of the Church, as a result of original sin, the image has been distorted and weakened in man, and the likeness has been lost. God's image refers to that which man has by nature: his reason, his intellect. St. Thomas Aquinas, for example, distinguishes between God's image and God's likeness.[72] Let's consult the *Catechism of the Catholic Church* here. Article 2566 states, "Even after losing through his sin his likeness to God, man remains an image of his Creator, and retains the desire for the one who calls him into existence."

This sentence from the *Catechism* stands in stark contrast to the teaching of the encyclical, which maintains that this likeness is never lost.

I would say that the statement from the *Catechism* isn't fully compatible with what the encyclical says. According to the former, *similitudo*, that is, likeness, is lost as a result of sin, while the encyclical claims that the likeness to God abides intact in every human being. That is, indeed, a certain contradiction. It seems worthwhile to appeal to the Fathers of the Church here. St. Irenaeus of Lyon, in his work *Adversus Haereses* (see 4, 37 and 5, 16), says that by his sin man loses his likeness to God. Irenaeus makes a clear distinction between these concepts many times. He writes that God raises man to likeness. Man must mature, grow into likeness (see 4, 38). It's been a constant teaching of the Church, confirmed by the Fathers and Doctors, that as a result of original sin man has lost his likeness to God. Similarly, St. Clement of Alexandria in his work *Paedagogus* (*The Instructor*) wrote that likeness is to be understood as God's plan for man, which hasn't yet been realized (see 1, 98). Moreover, Clement writes in the same chapter that the perfect man is the man in whom both the image and the likeness of God abide, and that man is Jesus Christ. Only in Christ do the image and likeness continue unchanged. It is so because Christ is the new Adam.

That is why the likeness can be restored only by being born again of the Holy Spirit, so that man may attain perfection through grace and through the sacraments. Likeness, then, is perfection modeled after the Father in Heaven, which can be attained only by grace. We have the image of God in us by reason and other powers by nature, but we have the *likeness* of God in regard to His holiness. This distinction is perfectly expressed by the Church's liturgical prayer during the Offertory of the

---

[72] See *Summa Theologiae* I, Q. 93, art. 9, ad 4.

Mass, present since time immemorial in the Roman Missal: "O God, who didst wondrously create (*condidisti*) the dignity of human nature, and still more wonderfully hast repaired it (*reformasti*) ..." The first part of this sentence refers to the image, and the second to the likeness.

In conclusion, we can say that the claim found in *Redemptor Hominis* that the image and likeness of God abide intact in every human being is itself ambiguous, for in this form it contradicts the teaching of the *Catechism* and the Fathers of the Church, who explicitly said that original sin caused the loss of likeness, which can be regained only through grace and the sacraments of the Church.

Such ambiguities are quite numerous, and there is clearly a continuity between the ambiguous texts of the Council and their later interpretations. How should we understand this statement, "For by His Incarnation the Son of God has united Himself in some fashion with every man" (*GS* 22)? In his encyclical *Redemptor Hominis*, as I mentioned before, John Paul II interpreted it as follows: "We are dealing with 'each' man, for each one is included in the mystery of the Redemption and with each one Christ has united himself for ever through this mystery [of Redemption]" (no. 13). But if this understanding is correct, how can one still believe in Hell and eternal damnation? Can Christ be in Hell? Don't these words of the pope consistently point to the belief that every man is automatically saved?

The claim that "the Son of God has united Himself in some fashion with every man" can be understood appropriately, for it doesn't say that the Son of God has actually united himself with every human being. There is something that in a certain way unites the Son of God and every human being, namely, that the Son of God assumed a true and perfect human nature. The unity of the Son of God with all men, however, is only objective, not subjective — it concerns universal nature. It's not about unity with an individual person, with each particular person. Precisely such clarification should appear in a text of the Magisterium in order to avoid misunderstandings. The Fathers of the Church saw in the Incarnation of God a nuptial union, a union of the Son of God with the whole of humanity. St. Thomas Aquinas clarified this idea in an even more concrete way when he said that Christ married the Church as His Bride through the Incarnation and through His suffering.[73] The notion of the nuptial union, or the union with Christ, doesn't apply to every human being, but to those who are actually members of His Mystical Body, the Church, who is His Bride.

Pope John Paul II's statement that "with each [man] Christ has united himself for ever" is therefore a source of misunderstanding and can be understood in the sense of an automatic salvation of man, or as an example of the theory of "anonymous Christianity" propagated particularly by Karl Rahner. The statement can rightly be understood to signify that Christ deliberately died and shed His Blood for each human being, and that His salvific sacrifice, which involves all humanity, has an eternal significance. This is what is meant by the aforementioned statement of John Paul II, that every human being is included in the mystery of salvation. However, man's relationship to the mystery of salvation is only objective, not subjective and individual. Man can be truly united personally and individually with Christ, the Savior, only by supernatural faith in Him and by Baptism, or at least by the desire to be baptized. The Scripture teaches it as follows:

> For God so loved the world, as to give his only begotten Son; that whosoever believeth in him, may not perish, but may have life everlasting.... He that believeth in him is not judged. But he that doth not believe, is already judged: because he believeth not in the name of the only begotten Son of God. (John 3:16–18)

"But without faith it is impossible to please God" (Heb. 11:6). The claim that "with each [man] Christ has united himself for ever" also contradicts the words of Jesus, who described His unity with men by invoking the image of a vine and branches:

> Every branch in me that beareth not fruit, he will take away: and every one that beareth fruit, he will purge it, that it may bring forth more fruit.... If any one abide not in me, he shall

---

[73] *Summa Theologiae, Supplementum*, Q. 95, art. 4, ad 2.

be cast forth as a branch, and shall wither, and they shall gather him up, and cast him into the fire, and he burneth. (John 15:2–6)

Christ, therefore, is not united for ever with all men. God the Father gives Christ "ownership" of those people who accept and keep His word (see John 17:6).

In the same paragraph of *Redemptor Hominis*, Pope John Paul II says that every single person, from the moment of conception, shares in the mystery of Christ's salvation. This is a true statement in an objective sense, but not in an individual sense, not with respect to every single person. Personal participation in the mystery of salvation requires a voluntary acceptance of Christ in faith. Unfortunately, the paragraph in question lacks this distinction, which has been a source of misinterpretations and mistaken conclusions.

You have spoken about the danger of anthropocentrism. How then should we understand the new definition of the Gospel given by John Paul II in *Redemptor Hominis*? The pope said there that "the name for that deep amazement at man's worth and dignity is the Gospel, that is to say: the Good News. It is also called Christianity" (no. 10). How does this definition relate to the Faith, which always puts God first?

Reducing the meaning of the Gospel to "deep amazement at man's worth and dignity" is certainly a one-sided, reductive, anthropocentric view of both creation and the mystery of salvation. Christ is central to both the work of creation and the work of redemption. The Good News is amazement at the glory of God and the greatness of the love of Jesus Christ, the Redeemer. The first word of the Good News proclaimed at the birth of the Son of God into this world was the exhortation, "Glory to God in the highest" (Luke 2:14). Only after that is peace for people mentioned. The whole life of Christ, that is, the essence of the Good News, consists in the glorification of God through Jesus Christ, and in the glorification of Jesus Christ in men. Thus the Lord teaches us:

I have glorified thee on the earth; I have finished the work which thou gavest me to do.... I pray for them: I pray not for

the world, but for them whom thou hast given me: because
they are thine: and all my things are thine, and thine are mine;
and I am glorified in them. (John 17:4, 17:9–10)

The Paschal liturgy, which is the summit of the entire liturgical year,
has at its center a hymn of praise extolling salvation, the *Exsultet*. The
main message of this proclamation is not amazement at man's worth,
but amazement at God's mercy and the greatness of the Savior. The
fault of men has found so great a Savior (*O felix culpa, quae talem et
tantum meruit habere Redemptorem*). Instead of saying, as in *Redemptor
Hominis* (no. 10), that "the name for that deep amazement at man's
worth and dignity is the Gospel, that is to say: the Good News," we
should say, "the name for that deep amazement at *Christ's* worth and
dignity…," or, to use St. Paul's pithy statement, "Christ is all, and in all"
(Col. 3:11) — *that* is the Gospel or the Good News.

It seems that the passage in *Redemptor Hominis* quoted earlier takes
for granted that the readers should have knowledge of the theological presuppositions underlying the statement about human dignity.
However, without an explicit affirmation of the primacy of Jesus Christ
over creation, these words of the encyclical open the door to anthropocentrism or to a humanistic understanding. Since the objective always
takes precedence over the subjective, the essence of the gospel message
is not the created and saved dignity of man, but God's will and action
that saves man through Christ. Therefore, the essence of the gospel
message refers to the loving grace of God. Without emphasizing the
objective, that is, without emphasizing the primacy of Jesus Christ, the
statements in *Redemptor Hominis* can easily lead to an anthropocentric
reductionism of the gospel message.

Now I would like to ask about another matter that raises so many doubts, namely the
relationship between the Christians and the Jews, or between the Church and Judaism.
Many Catholic theologians now claim that in principle Jews and Christians belong
to one people of God, that in terms of salvation Jews follow their own parallel path
to God. They maintain that Jews don't need faith in Jesus as the Christ because they
are already with the Father. They also claim that the covenant with the Jewish people

that God made with Moses was never rejected and fulfilled, that it's still in effect, and therefore that the Jews don't need a new covenant in the Blood of Christ.

The claim that there are two parallel roads to God and that there are two parallel covenants side by side contradicts all of Holy Scripture and everything that Jesus Christ and the apostles taught. The first covenant, the Old Testament covenant, had only a temporary significance: it was a preparation for the final New Covenant. In God's covenant with the Jewish people, the new and final covenant in Christ, God's beloved and only Son, was already present in a hidden way. Only in this sense can it be said that the Old Covenant was not terminated: it led to the New Covenant, in which it's contained. In other words, God remained faithful to the covenant he made with Israel, but the Jews didn't keep it. There is only one path to God, there are no parallel paths. The Old Covenant led to the New Covenant and was fulfilled by it. By its very nature, the Old Covenant has a merely temporary, transitional character. St. Paul says, "For they, not knowing the justice of God, and seeking to establish their own, have not submitted themselves to the justice of God. For the end of the law is Christ, unto justice to every one that believeth." (Rom. 10:3–4). *Finis enim legis est Christus.*

The same claim is found in the Epistle to the Hebrews, where the Old Covenant is referred to as obsolete, outdated (see Heb. 8:13).

Yes, and earlier in the Epistle we can read, "There is indeed a setting aside of the former commandment, because of the weakness and unprofitableness thereof: (for the law brought nothing to perfection,) but a bringing in of a better hope, by which we draw nigh to God" (Heb. 7:18–19). So here we have explicit statements, and many similar ones can be found throughout the New Testament. The prologue of the Gospel of St. John reads, "For the law was given by Moses; grace and truth came by Jesus Christ" (1:17). Equally explicit are the words of Jesus Himself in this Gospel, addressed to the Jews, "Think not that I will accuse you to the Father. There is one that accuseth you, Moses, in whom you trust. For if you did believe Moses, you would perhaps believe me also; for he wrote of me" (John 5:45–46).

St. Augustine, whose words were quoted in the Constitution *Dei Verbum* of the Second Vatican Council, wrote about all this: "God, the inspirer and author of both Testaments, wisely arranged that the New Testament be hidden in the Old and the Old be made manifest in the New."[74] The Fathers used the following analogy to describe the relationship of the two covenants or testaments: it's like a woman who carries a child in her womb so that when it is born it can live freely on its own. Once it has been born, it's there forever. The Old Testament is like a child in the womb. It's still imperfect, immature, and incomplete. The New Covenant is eternal and permanent, not temporary or transient. That is why Jesus speaks so clearly about the New Covenant, which, according to the predictions of the prophets, is an eternal covenant. "This is the chalice, the new testament in my blood" (Luke 22:20). That it was meant to be eternal is shown in the text of Isaiah, when the prophet recalls God's words, "I will make an everlasting covenant with you" (Isa. 55:3). Let me quote once again a passage from Paul's Second Epistle to the Thessalonians:

> And to you who are troubled, rest with us when the Lord Jesus
> shall be revealed from heaven, with the angels of his power: in
> a flame of fire, giving vengeance to them who know not God,
> and who obey not the gospel of our Lord Jesus Christ. Who
> shall suffer eternal punishment in destruction, from the face of
> the Lord, and from the glory of his power. (1:7–9)

After all, modern Jews don't obey the Gospel! All this is also taught by the Church today. In the *Catechism of the Catholic Church* (no. 1963) we read:

> According to Christian tradition, the Law is holy (see Rom.
> 7:12), spiritual (see Rom. 7:14) and good (see Rom. 7:16), yet
> still imperfect. Like a tutor (see Gal. 3:24), it shows what must
> be done, but does not of itself give the strength, the grace of

---

[74] Second Vatican Council, Dogmatic Constitution on Divine Revelation *Dei Verbum*, 16.

the Spirit, to fulfill it. Because of sin, which it cannot remove, it remains a law of bondage. According to St. Paul, its special function is to denounce and *disclose sin*, which constitutes a "law of concupiscence" (see Rom. 7) in the human heart. However, the Law remains the first stage on the way to the kingdom. It prepares and disposes the chosen people and each Christian for conversion and faith in the Savior God. It provides a teaching which endures for ever, like the Word of God.

St. Augustine also says that St. John the Baptist was an image representing the Old Covenant, which is why he was sent before Christ. He adds that the entire Old Testament was "pregnant" with Christ, with the New Testament. A beautiful metaphor, isn't it? And how aptly it captures the transitory and temporary nature of the Old Covenant. The fact that the New Covenant will replace the Old Covenant because it is more perfect, complete and eternal, is foreshadowed in the Old Testament itself. The prophet Jeremiah announces it clearly:

> Behold the days shall come, saith the Lord, and I will make a new covenant with the house of Israel, and with the house of Juda: not according to the covenant which I made with their fathers, in the day that I took them by the hand to bring them out of the land of Egypt: the covenant which they made void, and I had dominion over them, saith the Lord. But this shall be the covenant that I will make with the house of Israel, after those days, saith the Lord: I will give my law in their bowels, and I will write it in their heart: and I will be their God, and they shall be my people. (Jer. 31:31–33)

The whole of Holy Scripture, both Old and New Testaments, has only one meaning, and that is Christ. Christ is the only meaning of all of Scripture. "*Omnis Scriptura divina unus liber est, et hic unus liber est Christus, 'quia omnis Scriptura divina de Christo loquitur, et omnis Scriptura divina in Christo impletur'*" (CCC 134): "All Sacred Scripture is but one book, and this one book is Christ, 'because all divine Scripture speaks of Christ, and all divine Scripture is fulfilled in Christ.'" The Old

Testament receives its ultimate meaning in the New Testament — all
this has been taught continuously and clearly, as you can see. Not until
the present time will you find any attempts to negate or undermine
this relationship between the Old and New Covenants. It's described
everywhere.

One more example: for St. Paul, the Old Covenant is represented
by the slave Hagar, and the New by the heavenly Jerusalem. "The one
from mount Sina, engendering unto bondage; which is Hagar," writes
St. Paul. And he goes on to explain, "For Sina is a mountain in Arabia,
which hath affinity to that Jerusalem which now is, and is in bondage
with her children. But that Jerusalem, which is above, is free: which is
our mother" (Gal. 4:24–26). Hagar and Sarah are images of two testaments, two covenants. St. Thomas Aquinas, in his commentary on the
Epistle to the Galatians, writes that by the first covenant we are citizens
of the earthly kingdom, and by the second we possess eternal goods.

Let's bring it all together and say it clearly: both the Old and the
New Testaments contradict the claim that there are two parallel covenants with God. It's an absurdity, a complete negation of God's explicit
words. One of the clearest signs indicating that the Old Covenant was
ended — or, it's better to say, fulfilled in the New — were the events
surrounding the death of Christ. "And behold the veil of the temple
was rent in two from the top even to the bottom" (Matt. 27:51). This
happened at the moment of the Lord's death. Therefore, fulfilling the
precepts of the Law by modern Jews has no salvific power and doesn't
bring salvation.

In a "correction" sent to the German monthly *Herder Korrespondenz* in December
2018, Pope Benedict XVI wrote that Christ gave us a mandate to preach the Word to
all peoples and cultures. Therefore "the missionary mandate is universal — with one
exception: a mission to the Jews was not foreseen and not necessary because they
alone, among all peoples, knew the 'unknown God.'"[75] In relation to Israel, then, what

[75] See Vatican News, "Pope Emeritus Benedict: Dialogue with the Jews, Not Mission" (November 27, 2018), www.vaticannews.va/en/church/news/2018-11/
pope-emeritus-benedict-dialogue-with-the-jews-not-mission.html.

matters is not mission, but dialogue. Those words of the pope emeritus are in complete contradiction with the whole teaching of the Church, and also, it seems, with all
those quotations and teachings that you have just quoted. After all, both the Acts of
the Apostles and the Epistles show unequivocally the opposite of what Pope Benedict
maintains in this letter: it was precisely the mission to the Jews that was foreseen and
necessary from the beginning, and everything started with it. The Church has always
prided herself on this mission. Already St. Peter exhorts the Jews to be baptized in his
first address, before the missions to the Gentiles had even started. How, then, are we
to understand these words of Benedict?

> They contradict the words of Christ. It's an arbitrary interpretation that
> can stem only from political correctness. It's unacceptable. It contradicts
> the entire New Testament, the whole two-thousand-year-old immutable
> teaching of the Church. You have already given some examples, and
> more could be cited endlessly. Christ came first to the lost sheep of the
> house of Israel. This is perfectly shown in the Gospel of St. Matthew.
> "These twelve Jesus sent: commanding them, saying: Go ye not into
> the way of the Gentiles, and into the city of the Samaritans enter ye
> not. But go ye rather to the lost sheep of the house of Israel" (10:5–6).
> After Christ's death and resurrection, the Gospel was first preached
> to the Jews, and only later did the apostles decide to extend this first
> mission to the Gentiles. There can be no doubt here. If Jesus is not the
> Messiah and Savior of the people of Israel, then He is not the Savior of
> man either. This is logical. Therefore, the Church has no right under
> any circumstances to abandon the preaching of the Gospel and Christ
> to the Jews, regardless of the fact that the genocide perpetrated against
> the Jews by Hitler's anti-Christian regime was terrible and deserving
> of unqualified condemnation. But the event of the Holocaust is not
> part of revelation, is not part of salvation history, and can't excuse
> the abandonment of the Church's mission to preach Jesus Christ to
> the Jews of our day as well. The Holocaust can't therefore be used, or
> rather abused, as a theological argument. God's command to preach
> Christ to the Jews must not be thereby overturned. The excerpt from
> the letter of Pope Emeritus Benedict XVI quoted here seems to negate
> precisely this command. Giving up the mission would reveal a lack of

love, a cowardice. How could we not proclaim Christ to the people of the first covenant, to the people who are His witnesses, to the people who live among us?

Unfortunately, the modern Church has fallen hostage to political correctness and is not fulfilling her apostolic duty to preach the Gospel to the Jews first, to direct the mission to them first and before others. I will say it clearly: if the modern Church abandons the preaching of Christ to the Jews, if she abandons her mission to the Jews, she is thereby abandoning the path set by the apostles and succumbing to the demands of political correctness. She is allowing others to tell her what to do, yielding to the spirit of this world. It also amounts to questioning the truth about Jesus Christ as the only Savior of man, the Savior of *all* men. Is anyone suggesting that Jews are some other species of people? That would be completely ridiculous. They, too, have been saved by Christ, they, too, have been redeemed by Him, and they, too, can benefit from the fruits of redemption, obtaining justification, as can every human being while yet in this life. The words of Jesus have a universal character, they apply to everyone. Christ didn't say: go and make disciples of all nations, go and baptize all nations — except the Jews. That would be absolutely nonsensical. Even more, it would be a form of discrimination against the Jews, denying them access to God's universal truth. When Jesus addressed them, He said clearly, "Therefore I said to you, that you shall die in your sins. For if you believe not that I am he, you shall die in your sin" (John 8:24). These words are still valid, they have lost nothing of their relevance. They still apply.

You are quoting these words as if they were the words of Jesus. However, many contemporary theologians believe that these were not the words of Christ, but a later account. That it's a description of the experience of disputes between the later Christian community and the synagogue at the end of the first century after Christ. That Jesus, as it were, had these words put in His mouth, a Christian polemic against the synagogue that He never expressed. Besides, it's not only an opinion of individual theologians, but the claim of the official document of the Commission for Religious Relations with the Jews from June 24, 1985. In it, we read, "The Gospels are the outcome of long and complicated editorial work.... Hence, it cannot be ruled out that some references

hostile or less than favorable to the Jews have their historical context in conflicts between the nascent Church and the Jewish community. Certain controversies reflect Christian-Jewish relations long after the time of Jesus."[76] This is essentially the position of most Catholic biblical scholars today.

No, we can't accept these arguments. We believe that Holy Scripture was inspired by God. The New Testament was written by God's inspiration regardless of which author wrote the passage. This is the Word of God. It is a binding dogma of faith for Catholics. It can't be ignored.

On the very first day of Pentecost, Peter baptized three thousand Jews. These were the first Christians, members of the Church. Peter told the Sanhedrin, as we have already said, that there is no other name whereby we can be saved but the name of Jesus. There were Jews from all parts of the world in Jerusalem at that time. They were clearly told that the forgiveness of sins was possible only through faith in Christ. All this remains true until the end of time. In the Gospel of St. Mark, Jesus says, "And he said to them: Go ye into the whole world, and preach the gospel to *every* creature" (16:15). Are the Jews excluded from this? Do they come from another planet? St. Paul writes about preaching the gospel first to the Jews, and only then also to the Gentiles. "For I am not ashamed of the gospel. For it is the power of God unto salvation to every one that believeth, *to the Jew first*, and to the Greek" (Rom. 1:16). The apostles never abandoned the work of preaching the gospel to the Jews. "And every day they ceased not in the temple, and from house to house, to teach and preach Christ Jesus" (Acts 5:42).

The Church cannot cease proclaiming Christ to the Jewish people. I think the most important contribution that the Jewish people could make today would be to listen to the voice of God, who made a covenant first with Abraham and then with Moses, so that the Jews could become living members of the Mystical Body of Christ in the new and everlasting Covenant. After all, they are not members. They don't belong to the Church, even though God keeps summoning and exhorting them

[76] Vatican Commission for Religious Relations with the Jews, *Notes on the Correct Way to Present the Jews and Judaism in Preaching and Catechesis in the Roman Catholic Church* (June 24, 1985).

to do so. He keeps summoning them to believe in His only begotten Son, so that they may have eternal life. If the Church says today that it's forbidden to evangelize the Jews, to convert them, to preach Christ to them — this is a betrayal of the gospel. It's defiance of God's design. It's a completely arbitrary interpretation, alien to the constant Tradition of the Church. Even in the declaration *Nostra Aetate* we find the assertion that "the Church of Christ acknowledges that, according to God's saving design, the beginnings of her faith and her election are found already among the Patriarchs, Moses and the prophets."[77] Thus, the faith and calling of the Church were present from the beginning, still implicitly, in the faith of the patriarchs. The Church also confesses that all who believe in Christ are children of Abraham, as the Epistle to the Galatians teaches: "Know ye therefore, that they who are of faith, the same are the children of Abraham" (3:7).

You said that what Benedict XVI wrote can only be explained by referring to political correctness. But after all, in the Church today there are around five thousand bishops, over two hundred cardinals, probably tens of thousands of professors of theology, hundreds or thousands of theology departments, and countless biblical scholars and experts with academic degrees. And yet, when Benedict writes that "a mission to the Jews was not foreseen," and these words are certainly widely known — we are having this conversation over a year after their publication — no one, literally, not a single one of these thousands of people speaks up, or raises an objection. I haven't read or encountered a single clear critical voice. How is that possible? What does this tell us about the modern world? Why hasn't a single person of the thousands of university lecturers and experts on this subject written a rebuttal?

I prepared a short article on Christian-Jewish relations, in which I did not refer to this letter directly, but I did indirectly.

I don't mean your silence — nobody reacts to various strange propositions more often than you do. I am talking about the ratio, about the phenomenon of common silence

---

[77] Second Vatican Council, Declaration on the Relation of the Church with Non-Christian Religions *Nostra Aetate*, 4.

in a situation when we encounter claims that contradict the whole teaching of the Church. I am also wondering about the effects of such silence, the effects on the faith of all the faithful. Another manifestation of such silence is the fact that today the term "New Israel" is mentioned with great reluctance in reference to the Church.

> The reasons behind this phenomenon are false theology and doctrinal relativism. False theology speaks of two still existing covenants. We have already explained this. There is no doubt that the Catholic Church is the New Israel, the new People of God. We are all one in Christ, says the apostle Paul. "For as the body is one, and hath many members; and all the members of the body, whereas they are many, yet are one body, so also is Christ. For in one Spirit were we all baptized into one body, whether Jews or Gentiles..." (1 Cor. 12:12–13). For its part, the *Catechism of the Catholic Church* mentions the Church as the New Israel: "In fact, from the beginning of his ministry, the Lord Jesus instituted the Twelve as 'the beginning of the New Israel and the beginning of the sacred hierarchy'" (CCC 877). Many criticize the term, claiming that it promotes anti-Semitism because it introduces another entity, the Church, in place of Israel, or that it implies that God rejected Israel. This accusation is false. Those who believe are the New Israel. Jews who have embraced the Faith are the New Israel together with us.
>
> At the time of Jesus, unfortunately, the majority of the Jews rejected Him, and because of this, they themselves lost their membership in Israel according to the spirit, they themselves didn't accept the Son of God. Already the prophets had said to the people of Israel that if they didn't keep obedience to God, they were no longer His people. These words are quoted again by the apostle Paul in his Epistle to the Romans, "As in Osee he saith: I will call that which was not my people, my people; and her that was not beloved, beloved.... And it shall be, in the place where it was said unto them, You are not my people; there they shall be called the sons of the living God. And Isaias crieth out concerning Israel: If the number of the children of Israel be as the sand of the sea, a remnant shall be saved" (9:25–27). It would also follow that the prophets of Israel, who judged so harshly the unfaithfulness of their people to God, were anti-Semitic. Yes, let me repeat, the Church

is the Israel of God, as indeed St. Paul says clearly again in his Epistle to the Galatians, "And whosoever shall follow this rule, peace on them, and mercy, and upon the Israel of God" (6:16). All those who believe in Jesus Christ are the true Israel of God.

Is it true, then, that every man, whether a Jew, or a Muslim, or a Buddhist, or a follower of any other religion, but also an agnostic and an atheist, has a moral obligation to obediently accept faith in Christ? If, then, anyone rejects this faith, if he does so deliberately, with knowledge, he shows disobedience to God and is subject to punishment?

Obviously. All these words we have already quoted many times apply to such people. The wrath of God forever remains over everyone who has not accepted faith in Christ. It remains! These are the words of God Himself, and that is how they must be understood. Everyone must show obedience to Jesus Christ, God incarnate and the only Savior of mankind. There are no exceptions here. God's Word applies to everyone equally.

10

The Rupture of Continuity

In your foreword to Taylor Marshall's book, you are asking how it was possible that the doctrine, the liturgy, and the customs of the Church have been distorted to such a considerable degree. This is a problem facing not just the historian of the Church, but also every Catholic. It's enough to quote the most important texts of some popes, for example, Gregory XVI's *Mirari Vos*, Pius IX's *Syllabus of Errors*, or Pius X's encyclical *Pascendi Dominici Gregis* and its accompanying decree *Lamentabili*, as well as Pius XII's *Humani Generis*, to see that everything that these popes unequivocally condemned and criticized — the separation of Church and State, the equality of religions, full freedom of conscience understood as the freedom to choose different beliefs, indifference to religious truth — is perceived as obviously true and acceptable in today's Church. Does the contemporary Catholic still belong to the same Church as his ancestors?

> The contemporary Catholic certainly belongs to the same Church as his ancestors. For the Church is indestructible. And this is true regardless of how many Christians truly profess the Faith and how many fall into heresy. Jesus clearly said that the gates of Hell shall not prevail against the Church (see Matt. 16:18). Even if today many bishops reject or disfigure some truths of the Catholic faith, even if the pope seems to be complicit in this process, the Church remains the same. The Church is the Body of Christ, not a human organization or a party. Of course, human institutions may change, and political parties may come into

237

existence and fall apart. Sometimes a political party even keeps its name but may eventually have a completely different platform. The Church, however, is always the same: one, holy, catholic, and apostolic. The Catholic truth is also immutable, even though it may happen that it's actually being obscured or distorted by many churchmen. The holiness of the Church will never be destroyed, even if it seems that sinners and sin are dominating it on earth. The beauty of the liturgy will never be completely destroyed. The number of Catholics, priests, and seminarians may also drastically decrease, as it did after the Second Vatican Council. But the identity of the Church doesn't depend on the number of believers. The first Church comprised a small group formed around the twelve apostles and our Lady.

You said that, unlike a political party changing its platform at will, the Church remains faithful to the truth. However, many contemporary theologians believe that the Church's teaching can also evolve. What was binding for earlier Catholics doesn't have to be relevant for contemporary Catholics. In their opinion, the Church must understand and read the signs of the times and adapt to the mentality of modern man or else she loses credibility.

Certainly dogmas can never be changed in any way. They are, after all, the definitive pronouncements of the Magisterium, issued with the assistance of the Holy Spirit, whom Christ Himself gave to the Church. The dogmas of the Church are immutable, always true, and have the same unchanging meaning. They may be dogmas promulgated by councils, they may be *ex cathedra* pronouncements of the pope. By the way, the papal *ex cathedra* pronouncements are few. After 1950, when the last *ex cathedra* pronouncement occurred (it was the dogma of the Assumption of our Lady into Heaven), there have been none at all.

An infallible teaching can also be that which the Church has universally and always invariably proclaimed, even if it has not been solemnly defined. If the whole body of bishops — I mean the whole body not arithmetically, but morally — has always and in the same way taught something, then it's infallible. An example of such an infallible teaching — confirmed by Pope John Paul II — was that women cannot be ordained priests. It's therefore an infallible teaching whose truthfulness has been guaranteed by God. In the case of an infallible teaching, the Church can't mislead us. If it did, it would not be God's Church, but a merely human institution.

The only thing that can happen is that over the centuries the Church can explain dogmas more accurately and understand them more clearly. Jesus said, "the Paraclete, the Holy Ghost, whom the Father will send in my name, he will teach you all things, and bring all things to your mind, whatsoever I shall have said to you" (John 14:26). Jesus entrusted to the apostles the whole deposit of faith, the treasury of divine truths. This treasure is so great that not everything could be clearly understood at once. Time and the assistance of the Holy Spirit were therefore needed to see more clearly, to explain more precisely, to grasp more lucidly the contents of this unchanging deposit of faith. I have already spoken of this, citing the words of St. Vincent of Lérins. The development of understanding always presupposes the same sense, the same meaning. Allow me to quote the saint:

> But some one will say, perhaps, Shall there, then, be no progress in Christ's Church? Certainly; all possible progress. For what being is there, so envious of men, so full of hatred to God, who would seek to forbid it? Yet on condition that it be real progress, not alteration of the Faith. For progress requires that the subject be enlarged in itself, alteration, that it be transformed into something else. The intelligence, then, the knowledge, the wisdom, as well of individuals as of all, as well of one man as of the whole Church, ought, in the course of ages and centuries, to increase and make much and vigorous progress; yet only in its own kind; that is to say, in the same doctrine, in the same sense, and in the same meaning.[78]

---

[78] *Commonitorium* 23, 28; *Commonitory for the Antiquity and Universality of the Catholic Faith against the Profane Novelties of All Heresies*, in *Nicene and Post-Nicene Fathers*, second series, ed. by Philip Schaff, vol. 11: Sulpitius Severus, Vincent of Lerins, John Cassian; https://ccel.org/ccel/schaff/npnf211/npnf211.

This is a very important statement of St. Vincent of Lérins. He wrote further:

> The growth of religion in the soul must be analogous to the growth of the body, which, though in process of years it is developed and attains its full size, yet remains still the same. There is a wide difference between the flower of youth and the maturity of age; yet they who were once young are still the same now that they have become old, insomuch that though the stature and outward form of the individual are changed, yet his nature is one and the same, his person is one and the same.[79]

That's exactly how it is. We are born with two legs and remain with two, we don't end up with three. We are born with one nose and don't become persons with three noses. Organic growth doesn't lead to a transition into another nature. Old men are the same persons they were as young men. Here is another quote:

> This, then, is undoubtedly the true and legitimate rule of progress, this the established and most beautiful order of growth, that mature age ever develops in the man those parts and forms which the wisdom of the Creator had already framed beforehand in the infant.[80]

Here we see how St. Vincent relates this understanding of growth to the essence of the Church:

> In like manner, it behooves Christian doctrine to follow the same laws of progress, so as to be consolidated by years, enlarged by time, refined by age, and yet, withal, to continue uncorrupt and unadulterate, complete and perfect in all the measurement of its parts, and, so to speak, in all its proper members and senses, admitting no change, no waste of its distinctive property, no variation in its limits.[81]

---

[79] *Commonitorium* 23, 29.
[80] *Commonitorium* 23, 29.
[81] *Commonitorium* 23, 29.

The beginning of the Faith, he proceeds, can't conflict with the end.

> Therefore, whatever has been sown by the fidelity of the Fa-
> thers in this husbandry of God's Church, the same ought to be
> cultivated and taken care of by the industry of their children,
> the same ought to flourish and ripen, the same ought to ad-
> vance and go forward to perfection.[82]

Finally, he writes:

> But the Church of Christ, the careful and watchful guardian of
> the doctrines deposited in her charge, never changes anything
> in them, never diminishes, never adds, does not cut off what
> is necessary, does not add what is superfluous, does not lose
> her own, does not appropriate what is another's, but while
> dealing faithfully and judiciously with ancient doctrine, keeps
> this one object carefully in view — if there be anything which
> antiquity has left shapeless and rudimentary, to fashion and
> polish it, if anything already reduced to shape and developed,
> to consolidate and strengthen it, if any already ratified and
> defined, to keep and guard it.[83]

And one more passage. Here St. Vincent is quoting the First Epistle of
St. Paul to Timothy, which says, "Guard the deposit, shunning profane
novelties of words" (6:20):

> Profane novelties of words, that is, of doctrines, subjects,
> opinions, such as are contrary to antiquity and the Faith of the
> olden time. Which if they be received, it follows necessarily
> that the Faith of the blessed fathers is violated either in whole,
> or at all events in great part; it follows necessarily that all the
> faithful of all ages, all the saints ... have been ignorant for so
> long a tract of time, have been mistaken, have blasphemed,
> have not known what to believe, what to confess.[84]

[82] *Commonitorium* 23, 30.
[83] *Commonitorium* 23, 32.
[84] *Commonitorium* 24, 33.

So let me sum up: if we make changes in statements, in words, in the
meaning of words of a dogma, it may signify that all our ancestors from
centuries ago until our present time didn't know what they believed,
or that they were wrong.

I would like to give examples of statements by contemporary teachers of the Faith who
speak directly about the evolution of dogma. In his encyclical *Humani Generis*, Pius
XII wrote, "Some say they are not bound by the doctrine, explained in Our Encyclical
Letter of a few years ago, and based on the Sources of Revelation, which teaches that
the Mystical Body of Christ and the Roman Catholic Church are one and the same
thing."[85] As we know, this encyclical was written in 1950. Fifteen years later, in the
Dogmatic Constitution *Lumen Gentium*, this truth enunciated by Pius XII evolved.
In 1965, the Church no longer taught that the Church of Christ, that is, the Church
founded by Christ, and the Roman Catholic Church, governed by the pope, are one
and the same, but that "this Church [of Christ], constituted and organized in the world
as a society, subsists in the Catholic Church."[86] The word *est* (is) has been replaced by
subsistit (subsists). This is a change. How would you explain it, referring to the standard
presented in the words of St. Vincent?

Well, there is certainly a change. It's not literally and directly a contradiction, but a weakening of a truth that the Church has always professed:
there is one Church founded by Christ, one holy and apostolic Church,
and she is the Catholic Church. This assertion in the eighth chapter of
Lumen Gentium is a weakening of this truth. Just to repeat, it's not an
outright rejection of the truth; that the Church of Christ subsists in
the Catholic Church is not simply incorrect, but it can lead to erroneous, ambiguous deductions. This sentence could mean that there are
two realities: the Church of Christ, the Church that God wanted, and
the Catholic Church. It would have been surer to say: the Church of
Christ is the Catholic Church and subsists in it. The mere term *subsistit*
is insufficient.

---

[85] Pius XII, Encyclical *Humani Generis*, Concerning Some False Opinions Threaten-
ing to Undermine the Foundations of Catholic Doctrine, 27.

[86] Second Vatican Council, Dogmatic Constitution on the Church *Lumen Gentium*, 8.

But you have just quoted St. Vincent of Lérins, who maintained that the only true growth consists in a transition from the vague and unclear to the clear and distinct. Yet here there is a transition in the opposite direction. That is, in the conciliar text we are dealing not with development, but with the opposite of development.

> Exactly. Instead of declaring the truth in a clearer and more sure and precise way, we have received a statement that is imprecise.

In the same encyclical *Humani Generis*, Pius XII concluded, "Some reduce to a meaningless formula the necessity of belonging to the true Church in order to gain eternal salvation" (no. 27). Meanwhile, in a 2016 conversation with Benedict XVI published by Jacques Servais, the retired pope states that when it comes to the belief that salvation can be achieved only by belonging to the true Church, "there is no doubt that on this point we are faced with a profound evolution of dogma." He went on to say that, since the 1950s, "the understanding that God cannot let go to perdition all the unbaptized . . . has been fully affirmed."[87] In other words: that which Pius XII warned against, seeing it as a departure from the Faith, Benedict considered a natural "evolution."

> A minor disclaimer. I don't want to use the term "pope emeritus," because it's unknown to the entire Church tradition. I prefer to say "former pope," or "earlier pope."
>
> Well, this statement is not correct. It must be clearly stated that the absence of Baptism is an extremely serious threat to a person's salvation. Of course, the baptized can also be condemned if they oppose the will of God. We must say it clearly: unbaptized people, if they knowingly reject Christ, will be condemned. Jesus Himself spoke about this with clarity: "If you believe not . . . you shall die in your sin" (John 8:24). This phrase, "God cannot let go to perdition all the unbaptized" and declaring it "fully affirmed" is simply false. If someone deliberately rejects Baptism, he is subject to punishment and condemnation.

---

[87] Pope Benedict XVI and Jacques Servais, "Cos'è la fede? Ecco le parole di Benedetto XVI," in *Avvenire* (March 16, 2016), www.avvenire.it/agora/pagine/facciamoci-plasmare-da-cristo-.

We have already mentioned Karl Rahner and his theology of anonymous Christianity. Very similar to it is the theory of Henri de Lubac. According to it, the Church is, as it were, the soul of humanity, from which it is supposed to follow that unbelievers are saved by the very fact of belonging to humanity. "Since a necessary function in the history of our salvation was fulfilled by so great a mass of 'unbelievers' ... so these unbelievers have an inevitable place in our humanity.... As 'unbelievers' are, in the design of Providence, indispensable for building the Body of Christ, they must in their own way profit from this vital connection with this same Body. By an extension of the dogma of the communion of saints, it seems right to think that though they themselves are not in the normal way of salvation, they will be able nevertheless to obtain this salvation by virtue of those mysterious bonds which unite them to the faithful. In short, they can be saved because they are an integral part of that humanity which is to be saved."[88] For Rahner, on the other hand, every man is saved whether he knows it or not, as long as he accepts himself. Acceptance of one's own existence turns out to be tantamount to Christian faith. What do you think about these theories? Why are they so popular? According to a survey conducted among theology students at one of the oldest and most influential Catholic universities in Europe, 90 percent of students considered Karl Rahner the most important theologian in the history of the Church. In this respect he far surpassed both St. Thomas Aquinas and St. Augustine. Why is this happening?

> Well, it's just the easiest solution. I should actually say: the cheapest, the most convenient solution. If, in any case, I am already a child of God by my very nature, by birth, if I am saved by nature, then I don't have to make an effort, to fight, to struggle, to strive. I don't have to be concerned about the Faith, about truth. I don't have to worry about keeping the Faith. I can peacefully persist with my religion or lack thereof. Everything is easy and pleasant.
>
> These theories, however, are heretical. Although *objectively* we have all been saved — even those who don't know it are redeemed by the Blood of Christ, which is the cause of salvation — not all are *subjectively* saved. Each one must freely cooperate with God's grace. God does not

---

[88] Henri de Lubac, *Catholicism: Christ and the Common Destiny of Man* (San Francisco: Ignatius Press, 1988), 232–233.

force salvation upon anyone, nor does He impose salvation or love upon them. Man must accept it voluntarily. Rahner's theory does not correspond with human dignity. It also degrades the true meaning of God's love. There is no automatism in salvation. Salvation, life with God, love — all these are personal relationships that presuppose freedom. Modern theories that provide automatism in salvation are cheap and convenient. And the masses like that which is convenient and cheap. This is why so many superficial people regard Rahner as the greatest theologian of the twentieth century.

However, the judgment of these people has no authority. It doesn't matter. More relevant is God's judgment over Rahner and the judgment of Tradition over him, the judgment of two thousand years of Tradition. And according to it, the affirmations of this man are heretical. Yes, I am convinced that in one or two hundred years, the Church will recognize that Rahner was one of the greatest and most dangerous heretics of the twentieth century. Unlike the others, he did not preach heresies directly, but spread them in an extremely clever, cunning, indirect way. He injected poison into the veins of the life of the Church discreetly and surreptitiously.

Had he openly preached his theories, he would immediately have been condemned. If someone tries to poison another person directly, he can be spotted easily. You can immediately apprehend such a person and punish him. A large dose of poison causes a person to die immediately. However, if the poison is administered in small doses, drop by drop, if it's properly diluted, the body is debilitated gradually. The disease develops almost imperceptibly and paralysis slowly takes over the body. This is what Rahner did, using his devious method. He constantly played with words, he was toying with them. Ultimately, Rahner is a representative of the new gnosis. He can even be called the greatest Gnostic thinker in the Church in modern times. When you read his books, you can see that Christ is no longer God to him. Rahner believed in universal salvation, he preached pure naturalism. One has the impression that by the end of his life, based on what he wrote in his books, he no longer had faith in Jesus Christ as true God.

The theory of anonymous Christianity has also gained favor in the Church. Some simply call it that; others refer to it in a modified form.

> Many priests, who after the Second Vatican Council became bishops and cardinals, were imbued with the theories of Karl Rahner. That's when they were infected, and they started spreading errors after they assumed positions of power.

Pope Francis clearly supports Muslim immigration to Europe. However, can we even talk about immigration here? Is it not a form of conquest of our continent? How should we view the massive influx of Muslims into Europe? Is it an invasion, a conquest, or perhaps an opportunity?

> We are clearly dealing with a conquest. Online you can find numerous statements by Muslims who are saying it themselves. There are interviews, written statements, and videos. They claim that they are coming here to conquer Europe. It's not a military conquest, but a demographic one. From a purely arithmetical standpoint we can see that after a certain time Muslims will be the majority in Europe. Then as European citizens, they will begin to exert more and more influence on politics, on parliaments, and on public opinion. Not only are more and more Muslims coming to the West, but in the countries with large Muslim minorities there are many more children born into Muslim families than into native European families. Moreover, many radicals and fundamentalists are infiltrating the West. There are already cities in Europe where Sharia law is taking effect, completely Islamic urban districts.
>
> I will share with you a story I heard in Germany. A Muslim woman lived there, perhaps not particularly zealous in her practice of the Faith, who was repeatedly beaten by her husband. Finally, she lost patience with him, hired a lawyer, and took him to court for domestic violence. Normally the law in Germany is strict and prompt in such cases, always defending the woman. So-called domestic violence is prosecuted. The trial began. During the trial, the woman's husband didn't deny the facts, but quoted the Quran, specific Quranic verses that state, "It is lawful for you to beat your wives" or "Beat them when they disobey you."

The man was citing these and other similar verses in court to justify his actions. The judge in the end decided that he was right and released him without punishment!

Thus in Germany, and indeed throughout Western Europe, a society has developed that includes two classes of citizens. It has gotten to the point where in some regions the State turns a blind eye to the marriages of adult men to underage girls, even to nine- or ten-year-olds, as permitted by the Quran. After all, they are children. So far these have been only isolated cases in Europe, but the pressure to allow such a law is growing. Interestingly, in connection with Muslims it's not referred to as pedophilia.

There is no doubt that a kind of invasion is taking place before our very eyes. This is not a spontaneous influx of people, but an organized, premeditated operation. Careful observation is enough to see that the influx of Muslims is deliberately supported by anti-Christian governments and, above all, by anti-Christian politicians in the headquarters of the European Union. All these are forces that aim at eradicating Christianity from Europe. Well, for these politicians, many of whom follow an anti-Christian ideology, the aim is to get rid of Christianity, and the means to achieving it is the mass influx of Muslims. They believe that in this way Christianity, already weakened and paralyzed, will soon be completely peripheral. These politicians are saying: we don't even have to make a special effort. Things will work themselves out. In the long run, Muslims will cause an effective de-Christianization of Europe — not only de-Christianization in the political and legal sense, as it is now. The de-Christianization of Europe has also been the aim of Freemasonry since the French Revolution.

However, God knows how to use such a situation of necessity and affliction to bring good out of it. Ultimately, God's Providence presides over everything. This situation contains also the opportunity for evangelizing the Muslims who live among us. We can lead them to Christ. Thank God, there is a movement among Muslim immigrants — perhaps still not very large in terms of numbers — of conversions to Christianity. There are also courageous priests who lead evangelization efforts among them. This is the opportunity: that the Muslims living among us will recognize Christ and receive the happiness of a life of grace in Christ. Unfortunately, the Catholic Church in Europe is too politically correct, too saturated with the false theory that says that the diversity of religions is something positive and willed by God. I consider it a great sin, a great omission, that so many bishops, so many priests in general don't want to preach the Faith to the Muslims, to show them Christ, to teach them the true religion. Of course, this must be done with respect for each person, with respect for his freedom. The lack of missionary zeal in our day toward non-Christians will go down in history as a great sin of omission. Neither the pope, nor the cardinals, nor most of the hierarchy are doing it, nor is the Vatican. The majority of high-ranking churchmen are not only not preaching Christ to non-Christians, they are often doing something even worse: they are confirming them in their false religion.

The massive influx of Muslims is also supported by numerous Arab banks and states. The Islamic states allocate enormous sums of money to build ever larger and more impressive mosques and educational centers and to propagate Islam. On the other hand, this Muslim activity is matched by the cowardice and passive inactivity of Christians. There are also those who claim that Jesus was the first immigrant refugee, that the face of Christ is visible in the face of every immigrant. The implication is that we not only need to open our borders as wide as possible to them, but also help them nurture their own religion. As a result, the Church is beginning to work with those Islamic centers, also in Arab countries, that propagate this religion.

Indeed, we are dealing with a politically motivated immigration campaign aimed at the ultimate de-Christianization of Europe. For sure, among Muslims who arrive in Europe are many honest people, simply looking for a better life. Certainly every person should be helped, regardless of his religion. According to the traditional teachings of the Church, followers of other religions must also be afforded tolerance. This means that you can allow these people to build mosques — bearing in mind, however, that they are a minority and must respect the rights of their hosts. In a majoritarian Christian country Muslims must not be granted the same rights to publicly promote their religion as the Christians have. Otherwise we will be contributing to the slow decrease and destruction of the Christian character of Europe. This would be a complete lack of responsibility toward the duty to preserve the Christian soul of Europe.

But doesn't what you are now saying contradict the teaching of the Constitution *Lumen Gentium*, which speaks in number 16 of "Muslims, who, professing to hold the faith of Abraham, along with us adore the one and merciful God?"

This sentence is ambiguous. We Catholics don't worship God together with the Muslims. The act of worship for Catholics is always supernatural. The Christian act of worship refers only to the revealed God, to the belief in the Holy Trinity. It's different for Muslims. At best, they worship God as the Creator of the natural order. Then it's an act of natural worship based on the natural knowledge of God. In principle, these are two essentially different acts of worship. Let me emphasize: *essentially different.* Yet the conciliar text speaks of them in one sentence, as if they were on one level. This is mistaken. The natural is here equated with the supernatural. This is a most dangerous virus that is wreaking havoc in our age of crisis in the Church. This virus also appears in other statements of the Council and later in the life and work of the post-conciliar Church. This is the virus that brings with it such fatal error: the equation of nature with the supernatural. The supernatural is dissolved into the natural. A blatant Pelagianism is born; we can call it neo-Pelagianism. It leads to questioning the uniqueness of Jesus Christ. The sentence you quoted from *Lumen Gentium* is extremely dangerous.

You have lived in Kazakhstan for nineteen years, currently in Nur-Sultan, and before that in Karaganda for ten years. Kazakhstan is not an Islamic country, but certainly the Muslim influence is strong here.

I would perhaps say this: it's a country where the majority of the population follows Islam.

How do Muslim Kazakhs relate to Christians? How do Muslim-Christian relations in Kazakhstan look? Are there any cases of Muslims who have converted to Christianity?

First of all, we must say that Kazakhstan is a very peculiar country. The greatest influence on its current situation is still the simple fact that for seventy years it was under Soviet rule. Communism ruled here. Secondly, Kazakhstan is the site of the greatest mass deportations, forced resettlements, and ethnic repressions. Under Stalin, the entire country served as a huge concentration camp, one big gulag. Various nationalities suffered here, subjected to constant persecution. Kazakhs themselves accounted for a significant number of the victims. This led to the development of an atmosphere of friendship, a friendship of all the oppressed and persecuted. And that happened regardless of religious and confessional differences, on the basis of simple human solidarity. Common suffering became the foundation of mutual kindness. In those days, all forms of religious life were suppressed and destroyed; mosques, churches, Orthodox churches, and synagogues were demolished. This shared experience from the Communist era continues to matter. We must remember that over a hundred different nationalities live here. Finally, I would add that the traditional Kazakh Islam has never been radical, fundamentalist, or extreme. Even in pre-Communist times and before, Kazakhs were nomads, their Islam was more a matter of custom. It was moderate in character. Moreover, they reconciled many customs from an earlier period, from shamanism and simple paganism, with Islam. While the Uzbeks, for example, are much more zealous followers of Islam, the Kazakhs maintain a greater restraint in religious matters. With that said, I wish to clarify that I am not claiming that the Uzbeks are extremists by any means, but certainly their practice of Islam is more zealous.

The Kazakhs themselves, I must say after so many years here, are very hospitable, kind, and open people. It strikes me how easily they form relationships with foreigners, how willingly they help them. This was also true during the worst years of persecution. The Kazakhs would share food and clothing, even though they themselves suffered great poverty. They helped Poles, Germans, Ukrainians, Koreans, and everyone else who had been resettled here by Stalin. Their behavior should not be forgotten; it's a great honor of the Kazakh nation.

All this provides a specific historical context. In more recent times, when Nursultan Nazarbayev became Kazakhstan's first president in

1991, he implemented a well-conceived program whose goal was to maintain and promote interreligious peace. Harmony between religions and nationalities was the constant slogan of his government. Spiritual harmony — this is the official goal of the government. This program is being systematically developed; it can be seen at all levels of the power structure, in different regions, cities, and districts. A high priority for the government is safeguarding against religious extremism, also at universities and in schools. Once a year in October, a day of harmony between nations and religions is solemnly celebrated. The government exercises a certain control over mosques and is very vigilant in preventing the arrival of religious extremists from other Islamic countries. Local religious leaders, Islamic leaders, strive to follow this official government line and make sure that harmony is maintained in their coexistence with non-Muslims. I must say that on a personal level my relationship as well as the relationships of the Catholic clergy with the imams are good.

And are there also Kazakh Catholics?

The group of Kazakh Catholics is growing slowly. I'm very happy about this. Most of them were baptized as adults, quite intentionally. They went through the catechumenate and were well prepared. Even more Kazakhs are converting to Christianity in various free Protestant churches. Separate Kazakh Protestant communities have even been established, with Kazakh pastors.

In one of his addresses in July 2016, Cardinal Robert Sarah said, "It is very important that we return as soon as possible to a common orientation, of priests and the faithful turned together in the same direction — eastwards or at least toward the apse — to the Lord who comes.... I think it is a very important step in ensuring that in our celebrations the Lord is truly at the center."[89] This is a constant thread in his speeches, interviews,

---

[89] Cardinal Robert Sarah, Address at Sacra Liturgia 2016, www.churchmilitant.com/ news/article/cardinal-sarahs-complete-address-at-sacra-liturgia-conference-in-london.

and books. As the famous liturgist Klaus Gamber and Cardinal Joseph Ratzinger have shown in detail, the current way of celebrating Mass facing the people has no roots in the transmitted, immutable Tradition. The *versus populum* orientation is something entirely new, unfamiliar to earlier generations of Catholics, and in that sense it represents a clear break with the Church's liturgical tradition. Therefore, Cardinal Sarah has been calling for some time now for a return to this ancient, authentic practice. Why has this general return to the old practice still not been successful?

The proponents of the liturgical reform, who, unfortunately, were victorious, wanted a liturgy more suited to the mentality and customs of the world. Cunningly, they made appeals to history. They would say, we must return to the ancient Church, to the Church of the first centuries, we must restore the original practice of the first Christians. But in re-establishing this "original" practice, they used an arbitrary and selective method, underpinned by certain ideological prejudices. Their approach was shaped by anthropocentrism and naturalism. They wanted to introduce prayer and liturgy that would correspond to this anthropocentric approach. Liturgy was to be stripped of what distinguished it most: theocentrism and Christocentrism. The story of a return to antiquity turned out to be mostly a ruse. True science turns to facts and forms theories based on the facts. In the case of the study of ancient liturgy, the opposite was true. Inconvenient facts were ignored or, as a last resort, interpreted to fit preconceived, anthropocentric ideas.

Let me give you an example. In some ancient basilicas, the altar was separated from the wall of the apse. Archaeological research conducted since the nineteenth century shows that this is the case. Instead of examining the various possible explanations for the altar being separated from the wall, these liturgical ideologues immediately concluded that the priest celebrated the Mass facing the faithful. This conclusion was already in their heads before they began their research, so it's not surprising that it immediately occurred to them as soon as the information about the altars being separated from the wall reached them. They didn't notice that this conclusion was impossible to accept, because it was contradicted by the unambiguous statements of the Church Fathers. It was also contradicted by more thorough archaeological research. This is clearly shown in a monograph by the German archaeologist Joseph Braun, *The Christian Altar in Its Historical Development*.[90] He proved, using all the archaeological excavations known and performed up till that point, that over 90 percent of the churches and chapels of the first millennium of Christianity were oriented toward the east, and thus the sanctuary with the main altar was directed toward the east. The direction toward the east was marked in churches by the apse. The only exceptions can be found in Rome, but those were determined by particular circumstances. For example, when it comes to St. Peter's Basilica, its original purpose was to commemorate and venerate the tomb of St. Peter. The altar was built over the tomb, and the basilica was formed in such a way as to take into account the characteristics of the terrain, that is, the fact that it was located on a hill. For this reason, the apse is on the west side, and there is a door on the east side, so the pope, when celebrating Mass, stood behind the altar and looked toward the east, where the front door was. Not toward the people, but toward the east. Moreover, the papal altar was covered during the liturgy until the early Middle Ages, more or less until the ninth century. Curtains separated the pope and the altar from the gaze of the people in the basilica. When the pope would begin to recite the Canon of the Mass, the deacons would draw the curtains so that people could not see the pope's face during the Eucharistic Prayer. Also later, when the use of curtains was abandoned, a large crucifix and candlesticks were placed on the altar, which served the same function as the curtains. This can be seen in the photographs from the pre-conciliar era: although the pope is celebrating Mass in the basilica nominally facing the people, in fact he can't actually be seen because of the crucifix and the candlesticks. The papal Masses were not about people looking at each other, but about people looking together toward the crucifix. However, let me emphasize it again, St. Peter's Basilica is an exception. You can't use a unique architectural situation, which was atypical and resulted from the topography, as an argument in favor of a celebration toward the people.

---

[90] See Joseph Braun, *Der christliche Altar in seiner geschichtlichen Entwicklung* (München: Alte Meister Guenther Koch, 1924).

These liturgical ideologues also ignored and disregarded all the testimonies of the Fathers of the Church, who as early as the second century stated that Christians always turn to the east when praying. And the Eucharist was after all the most solemn Christian prayer. From this, it follows clearly that the priest and the faithful would turn together in prayer to face the east. The priest stood on the same side of the altar, regardless of whether it was separated from the wall or not, as the faithful behind him. This is exactly the practice in all Eastern-rite churches and Orthodox churches where the altar is not adjacent to the wall. Whether we're talking about the Byzantine or other Eastern rites, the altar is located in the middle of the sanctuary, but the liturgical action is directed toward the east. St. Basil mentioned that this orientation toward the east was handed down to the Church by the apostles. That means that already in the fourth century after Christ there was a strong conviction that the orientation toward the east, the common orientation of the prayer of the priest and the faithful, has its source in the apostolic tradition.

To support their new ideology, the liturgical reformers tried to invoke later depictions without reflecting on their meaning. And so they pointed, for example, to Leonardo da Vinci's famous painting *The Last Supper*, in which Christ is seated behind a rectangular table with His disciples. However, this painting, regardless of its artistic value, historically misrepresents reality. This is caused by ignorance. Leonardo da Vinci assumed that people at the time of Christ sat at the table just as they did in his time, in the fifteenth and sixteenth centuries. However, as archaeological research has shown, the earliest reliefs and depictions of the Last Supper from the first centuries show not the rectangular table that we know, but a sigma-shaped table, like a semi-circle. People would not sit at it as we do, but would recline. Moreover, according to Jewish custom, the most important, most dignified place wasn't in the middle of the table, among the others, but at the head of the table, at its right side or right corner. There, at the right corner of the table, sat the most important, most honored guest. It was therefore the place that Jesus certainly occupied during the Last Supper. That is why John, and not Peter, was seated next to Him, and why when Peter wanted to understand who Jesus was referring to as the traitor, he addressed the question not directly to Jesus, but rather through John, since the latter reclined upon the bosom of the Lord. If Jesus had been sitting in the middle of the table, then John and Peter would have been sitting on either side of Him and Peter would not have had to ask through John. However, Holy Scripture says that John was Jesus' beloved disciple and rested on His bosom, so Peter had to relay the question through John. There was no one on the other side of Jesus — Jesus was sitting at the right side of the sigma-shaped table.

In the same way, during supper everyone was looking in the same direction — they were not looking at each other. In one of the targums (a targum is an early Aramaic translation dating back to the first century after Christ, provided along with a commentary on the words of Scripture) it's written that the Messiah will come during the Passover feast.[91] Therefore, all participants in the Passover must look in the direction from which He is to come. So it's assumed here that the participants in the Passover are looking in the same direction. This is also the case with the Holy Mass: we should all be looking in the same direction, toward the east, whence the Lord will come to us. He Himself speaks of this clearly, "For as lightning cometh out of the east, and appeareth even into the west: so shall the coming of the Son of man be" (Matt. 24:27). The lightning from the east heralds the coming of the Son of Man from the east. Similar symbolism can be found in the Canticle of Zechariah, "through the bowels of the mercy of our God, in which the Orient from on high hath visited us: to enlighten them that sit in darkness, and in the shadow of death: to direct our feet into the way of peace" (Luke 1:78–79).

Oriens ex alto: Jesus is that rising Sun (*Oriens*) coming from on high (*ex alto*). The Lord Himself is the rising of the Sun. The east, then, is the eschatological direction of prayer for Christians. From there, Christians await the coming of the Lord. This refers not only to the literal, geographical east (for a variety of reasons not all churches could be oriented in this direction, especially in later eras), but also to

[91] "The Poem of the Four Nights," in the Targum to Exodus 12:42.

the east understood symbolically. As a rule, it was the apse in churches. The name itself comes from the Greek *apsis*, axis. The apse therefore became the symbolically understood east, which was further reinforced by the fact that a cross was placed in it. In the apse there was an altar, on which the cross was also placed. Thus, regardless of the literal geographic direction, for Christians the "spiritual east" was marked out by the apse, the altar, and the cross, usually placed on the altar; prayers and liturgies were addressed in this direction.

We must remember that the direction of prayer was never neutral for the ancients. Space wasn't symbolically abstract or indifferent. This is also perfectly evident in the behavior of the Jews and in Jewish customs from that period, from the time of the Old Testament. During prayer, everyone turned toward the place where the Ark of the Covenant was kept. If the priest were to turn his back on it, it would be considered a sacrilege. And yet we in the Church have something greater than the Ark of the Covenant. The Ark of the Covenant was only a symbol, while Jesus clearly said that His Body is the temple, the living temple (see John 2:21). And His Body is the Eucharist, the sacrifice of the Mass. Also, when Jews later prayed at home, they would turn to Jerusalem, just as Muslims today turn to Mecca. We can suspect that in Nazareth when Mary, Joseph, and Jesus prayed together, reciting the psalter, they were turning toward Jerusalem. They weren't looking at each other, but toward Jerusalem. Even today in synagogues there are niches where the scrolls of the Torah are kept, and this is the direction the Jews face during prayer. It is unthinkable to pray with your back to the Torah. Jesus and the apostles, when they went to the synagogue, faced the same direction together when they prayed.

Now if we gather all these accounts: the common customs of antiquity, the manner of sitting at the table during a banquet, accounts of early Fathers of the Church — it's undeniable that from the beginning Christians prayed together with the priest, always facing the same direction, toward the Lord. For me, the current form of celebration, in which the priest continuously faces the people, is nothing other than a manifestation of anthropocentrism. It's a confirmation of those assertions found in the conciliar texts we have already mentioned, such as the assertion in *Gaudium et Spes* that man is the center and crown of all things. Admittedly, *Sacrosanctum Concilium*, the constitution on the liturgy, teaches beautifully that "the human is directed and subordinated to the divine, the visible likewise to the invisible, action to contemplation, and this present world to that city yet to come, which we seek."[92] It's obvious that the celebration *versus populum* contravenes the principles outlined in the Council's constitution on the liturgy.

A recent book *Altar und Kirche* [*Altar and Church*], a major monograph by Stefan Heid (one of the foremost experts on Christian antiquity) describing in detail the earliest Christian places of worship, makes it abundantly clear that Paul VI's reforms of the Mass and liturgy were based on faulty premises. Heid described this erroneous approach as follows: "Today's scholars almost unanimously and ecumenically claim that the earliest Christians knew neither altars nor sacred places; moreover, that these early Christians rejected both altars and sacred places."[93] But this claim, which led to the introduction of tables instead of altars in Catholic churches, has no historical foundation. On the contrary, Heid proves that all early Christian testimonies point to the reverence shown to the altar on which Christ's sacrifice was celebrated. The Eucharist was sacrificial from the beginning and was celebrated on an altar, not on a plain secular table. You just spoke about the direction of prayer. From all this it follows that the changes made to the liturgy under Paul VI are a complete novelty; they have no basis in Tradition, but rather amount to a rupture with it.

> With regard to the direction of the celebration, it's obvious. So it is also with the tables. Some might say: but what does it really matter? For sure, God is present everywhere. However, we Christians are not Gnostics; we profess the religion of the God who became man. We believe in the Incarnation. God revealed Himself concretely, in history. That is why concrete, palpable, tangible signs are so important. The Ark of the Covenant was such a sign, a symbol for the Jews. Similarly, we turn to Christ, who is present in the Eucharist, we worship His Cross,

---

92 Second Vatican Council, Constitution on the Sacred Liturgy *Sacrosanctum Concilium*, 2.

93 Stefan Heid, *Altar und Kirche. Prinzipien christlicher Liturgie* (Regensburg: Schnell und Steiner, 2019), 10.

we venerate the altar on which transubstantiation takes place. Catholicism is an acceptance of the Incarnation, not a set of abstract ideas.

I think it would be wonderful if, as a sign of our return to the Faith, all priests in the whole Catholic Church would return to authentic liturgical practice and begin to celebrate the Masses in the new rite also toward the east, toward the altar, toward Christ. We must turn again to God. *Conversio* signifies precisely such a turning. Although the priest is another Christ, *alter Christus*, he is not God. He is neither a monstrance nor a tabernacle. He is merely an instrument of God. Therefore, people shouldn't keep looking at his face — he must disappear and Christ should appear before the eyes of the faithful. The priest must point to Christ, refer to Him. The attention of the faithful should be directed not to the face of the priest, but to the Cross: the cross on the chasuble, the crucifix on the altar, or the cross in the apse.

I have also sometimes heard this argument: the altar is a symbol of Christ, so the faithful together with the priest, looking at each other, gather around the altar. But this is not serious. It goes against everything we know about human psychology. After all, such a closed circle doesn't communicate this message. The altar is not a real point of reference for those standing around it. It doesn't serve as an object of contemplation for them — no, their attention is directed to themselves, to their faces, and to the face of the priest. Only when the priest turns toward the altar does the attention of the faithful turn, as does his, toward the altar, the cross, and the apse. From a purely visual point of view, the closed circle suggests anthropocentrism. It has nothing dynamic, nothing eschatological about it.

The same is true of the tables that have replaced the altars. Even St. Paul wrote,

> Know you not, that they who work in the holy place, eat the things that are of the holy place; and they that serve the altar, partake with the altar? So also the Lord ordained that they who preach the gospel, should live by the gospel. (1 Cor. 9:13–14)

For him, the gospel is the same as serving at the altar. He clarifies it even further:

> Behold Israel according to the flesh: are not they, that eat of
> the sacrifices, partakers of the altar? What then? Do I say, that
> what is offered in sacrifice to idols, is any thing? Or, that the
> idol is any thing? But the things which the heathens sacrifice,
> they sacrifice to devils, and not to God. And I would not that
> you should be made partakers with devils. You cannot drink
> the chalice of the Lord, and the chalice of devils: you cannot
> be partakers of the table of the Lord, and of the table of devils.
> (1 Cor. 10:18–21)

For Paul, the table on which the Eucharist is offered to the Lord and
the altar are two interchangeable terms. In pagan temples, the table of
demons was simply the altar on which pagans offered sacrifices. Here,
then, we have indirect evidence that, in the eyes of the early Christians,
the table on which they offered the Eucharistic sacrifice was to them
what the altar was to the pagans. Except that for pagans, the altar was
a place of demon worship, whereas for Christians, the altar was a place
of true worship.

The widespread introduction of tables into Catholic churches
shows how strong the Protestant tendency was. For it is Protestants
who understand the Mass as a supper, as a meal and a banquet. While
an altar is necessary for sacrifice, a table is sufficient for the banquet.
The essence of the Mass is the sacrifice. Therefore, if altars disappear
and tables appear in their place, this essence is obviously called into
question. At the table you don't offer a sacrifice, you feast. The Mass
is a sacramental reenactment, a re-presentation of the sacrifice of the
Cross on Golgotha, not primarily a sacramental re-presentation of the
Last Supper. The memory of the supper, of the banquet, only comes
from and is subordinate to the sacramental sacrifice. The principle and
foundation of the Mass is the sacramental re-presentation of Christ's
sacrifice on Golgotha. The aspect of the banquet appears at the moment of Communion, but the Mass as such is not a meal or primarily a
banquet. The meal is an integral aspect of the Holy Mass, but it's not the
key aspect. Only at the reception of Communion is a table needed. For
this purpose the Church used altar rails, which in some languages are

called the "table of Holy Communion." These are openwork partitions separating the sanctuary from the nave. Usually they take the form of a balustrade. They are made of precious material: marble, stone, wood, or metal. They serve as kneelers for the faithful during the reception of the Eucharist. Often, they are covered with a white tablecloth. The faithful approach and receive the Body of the Lord from the hands of the priest with a devout posture, kneeling at the altar rails.

In his book *The Heresy of Formlessness*, the prominent German author Martin Mosebach wrote that Paul VI's reforms caused a real surge of barbarism in the churches. Almost overnight, rituals and liturgical forms used for hundreds of years disappeared, and the pope introduced completely new ones in their place. Cardinal Joseph Ratzinger was also very critical of them. He wrote, "the prohibition of the missal that was now decreed, a missal that had known continuous growth over the centuries, starting with the sacramentaries of the ancient Church, introduced a breach into the history of liturgy whose consequences could only be tragic.... The old building was demolished, and another was built, to be sure largely using materials from the previous one."[94] Occasionally, he would use even stronger terms: "in the place of liturgy as the fruit of development came fabricated liturgy. We abandoned the organic, living process of growth and development over centuries, and replaced it — as in a manufacturing process — with a fabrication, a banal on-the-spot product."[95] What is your opinion about that?

I think that any objective observer, if he compares the two forms of the Mass — the *Novus Ordo Missae* and the traditional Mass — will immediately see the superiority of the latter. Today, you will often hear the classical Roman Rite Mass referred to as the "Tridentine Mass." This is rather an invention of ignorant journalists and liturgical modernists. No such thing as the Tridentine Mass ever existed. The Mass that was commonly celebrated before the Second Vatican Council was well over a thousand years old, and its most important parts go back to apostolic

[94] Joseph Ratzinger, *Milestones. Memoirs: 1927–1977* (San Francisco: Ignatius Press, 1998), 147–148.
[95] Joseph Ratzinger, from Preface to the French edition of Msgr. Klaus Gamber, *The Reform of the Roman Liturgy: Its Problems and Background* (Fort Collins, CO: Roman Catholic Books, 1993).

times. The Mass was celebrated in exactly the same form prior to the Council of Trent. There exists an edition of the *Missale Romanum* from 1470, a century before the Council of Trent began. The order of the Mass — the *ordo Missae* — is no different from that of the Missal that Pius V approved for universal use. We have commentaries on the Mass from the twelfth and thirteenth centuries that show the same order was being followed. They explain different parts of the Mass one after the other: prayers at the altar steps, the offertory. Therefore, after the Council of Trent, the faithful hardly noticed the change; they felt that it was still the same Mass that they had always attended and that had been handed down to them by earlier generations. The only difference involved the missal, the readings contained therein, the reduction in the number of prefaces, the reordering of the liturgical calendar, the removal of the memories of some saints who turned out to be legendary figures. The Missal changed, but its order of the Mass, the *ordo Missae*, remained unchanged.

During the two thousand years of the Church's history, such a radical reform as Paul VI's had never been carried out. After all, the Eucharistic liturgy, the liturgy of the Mass, is the heart of the Church. I have no doubt that we are dealing with a revolution here. Objectively seen, it was a revolution. It was carried out with a radicalism never before known to the Church. So this is the first thing to know: it was a mistake from the very beginning. There isn't and shouldn't be any place for revolution in the Church. The very principle of the Church's life, the principle that speaks of organic growth, means that revolutionary methods in liturgy and doctrine must not be used, regardless of any potential good intentions and objectives. The public prayer of the Church is such an organic, natural thing that it's impossible to imagine revolutionary changes.

I will just mention in passing that for the first time a kind of liturgical revolution took place at the time of Pius X, concerning the breviary. The arrangement of psalms, the *cursus psalmorum* — the manner of reciting them during the week, which had been in force since at least the times of Pope Gregory the Great in the sixth century — was drastically changed. Besides, Pope Gregory the Great didn't invent the order of the recitation of the psalms of the breviary either; he substantially adopted and confirmed it. This form was in use until 1913, without any changes. And suddenly a change came. Suddenly a completely new division of the psalms was introduced. The traditional order of the psalms was kept only by some ancient orders, such as the Carthusians and the Benedictines. What I am saying now will probably cause sadness to the priests of the Society of St. Pius X and others, but these are the facts. Nobody can honestly deny that the abolition of the millennium-old order of the psalms, the *cursus psalmorum Romanae ecclesiae*, was a liturgical revolution.

I want to make it clear that I am in no way comparing this change in the breviary prayers with the liturgical revolution carried out by Pope Paul VI. As far as the content of the change is concerned, there is no comparison. What they did have in common, however, was a belief that the power of the pope could freely and arbitrarily shape the inherited, centuries- and millennium-old forms of the liturgy. This is precisely what must not be done: change regarding such a sensitive issue should only occur slowly and truly organically. Perhaps an inflated perception of the scope of papal authority was the cause, which in turn resulted from an excessive interpretation of the dogma of papal infallibility that was accepted at the First Vatican Council. For some theologians, the pope became an absolute ruler of sorts, who could do whatever he wanted. Why can he make a change? Because he has the power. He has the power, so he may do it. This reveals an excessive notion of papal authority. And even if someone has good intentions, as was the case with Pope Pius X, I don't think the pope has the power to make a revolution in the liturgy of the Divine Office, the breviary. Drastic change, which is what a revolution is, doesn't fall within the scope of papal authority. He can, however, combat heresies effectively. Here he has full authority. He can combat immorality and vice that have invaded the life of the Church, or introduce rules of life to help purge the clergy of transgressions. But he shouldn't drastically change the order of prayers, which is considered sacred and handed down faithfully from generation to generation.

Someone could tell me that the whole issue of Pope Pius X's reform of the breviary is a trifle compared to the huge change in the manner of Paul VI's protestantization of the Mass. Of course, I can see the difference. Yes, as far as the content is concerned, the change made in the arrangement of the breviary appears to be a mere trifle in comparison to Paul VI's revolution. But the point here is the principle, the way of acting.

Unlike the changes to the breviary made by Pope Pius X, Paul VI's reform had visible, unmistakable, and universally perceivable disastrous effects. And yet many would argue that it was a great achievement.

There can be no talk of a positive achievement. It's a break with a millennium-old liturgical tradition of the Church. The new rite also means a tangible protestantization of the Mass. That applies to both the rituals and the prayers. The tendency toward anthropocentrism and toward Protestantism is indisputable. It can be clearly seen in the entire order of the Mass of Paul VI. For example, the new prayers of the offertory as a whole emphasize the nature of the Mass as a meal, a banquet, virtually ignoring its essence as a propitiatory sacrifice. They were borrowed from the synagogue meal prayers. As for the new Eucharistic Prayers, the second of them mentions sacrifice only vaguely and in passing. Therefore, immediately after the reform, some Protestant pastors proclaimed that the new prayers in the order of the Mass, especially the Offertory Prayers and the Second Eucharistic Prayer, were no longer essentially sacrificial; they were prayers appropriate to the celebration of the Protestant supper. Some Protestant communities decided that they can recite this Second Eucharistic Prayer because it fits their understanding of the Eucharistic celebration as a meal. The Second Eucharistic Prayer, by the way, is the one most frequently chosen by priests because it's the shortest.

Let's take a closer look at the Fourth Eucharistic Prayer, at its first part, which is combined with the Preface:

It is truly right to give you thanks, truly just to give you glory, Father most holy, for you are the one God living and true, existing before all ages and abiding for all eternity, dwelling in unapproachable light; yet you, who alone are good, the source of life, have made all that is, so that you might fill your creatures with blessings and bring joy to many of them by the glory of your light. And so, in your presence are countless hosts of Angels, who serve you day and night and, gazing upon the glory of your face, glorify you without ceasing. With them we, too, confess your name in exultation, giving voice to every creature under heaven, as we acclaim ...

Throughout this Preface, God is spoken of as one God, as Creator. But to offer praise to God as Creator and confess His name, not as Trinity, without mentioning the Son and the Holy Spirit — that's what Jews can do too.

I still haven't heard an answer to the question about why Paul VI introduced such great and harmful changes.

I think that he was guided by the conviction at the time that the Mass should be adapted to the mentality and sensibility of "modern man." This is clear from numerous statements of his at the time. That was his motive and he was guided by it. But what is the logic behind it? If we take it at face value, the Church would have to invent a new liturgy in every era. She has never done so. For centuries and centuries the liturgy was the same. The essence of man doesn't change with the times. Following this line of reasoning, we would have to change all the psalms. After all, they don't correspond to the modern mentality. Similarly, neither do many statements of Scripture. And so what? Should we rewrite the Scripture? That is why this argument can't be accepted.

We can say even more. Today's modern man is exposed to the threat of anthropocentrism to a degree unknown in previous ages. This has been happening since the French Revolution. That's why, I think, *especially* in our times we should emphasize the sacral character of liturgy and point to its theocentric character. Perhaps man's longing for the sacred, for that which is holy, is even greater today than at any time in the past. Today man has almost drowned in materialism. He is trapped in empty activism. It's all the more important to show the contemplative character of the Mass, to have silence and recollection. That is, exactly the elements present in the traditional Mass.

It has been said that through the liturgical changes man will better understand the mysteries of the Faith in the celebration of the Mass. Holy Mass, indeed, is the most sublime act of worshipping God. It often happens that in the new Mass the celebrant gives explanations over and over again. In this way, instead of contemplation we have a lesson, a religion class. This is very Protestant. Protestantism itself is not a liturgical religion, but a religion of teaching. All that matters is the word, the instruction. It has turned what used to be the heart of our faith — the worship of God through the sacramental celebration of Christ's sacrifice on the Cross — into a religion class at best, a period of instruction. This is a serious misunderstanding of the essential meaning of the liturgy of the Mass. Fifty years after the liturgical reform, it's increasingly clear that young people in particular are looking for that which has been taken away from them. Young people, even children, long for that which is more mysterious, more profound, more sacred.

On the whole, Pope Paul VI's reform of the liturgy was a failure. I don't want to condemn everything categorically; one can find necessary and useful elements in his liturgical reform. It's also worth mentioning that the Council Fathers didn't expect any serious reform, and certainly not one that was as far-reaching as the one that was implemented. Just check how much time was spent in the Council hall discussing the reform of the liturgy compared to other issues. In fact, the thing that occupied the greatest attention of the bishops at the Council was the question of the vernacular language. Yet nowhere do we find, either in the debates about it or in the final text of the liturgical Constitution *Sacrosanctum Concilium*, a call for a complete replacement of Latin with the national languages. There was only talk of a greater presence of national languages, of giving them "a certain place." It never occurred to anyone that the Council would result in the suppression of Latin. Latin was to remain, and the scope of national languages was to be broadened. That's all.

I think, as soon as we are entering the Eucharistic liturgy in the strict sense of the word — the sacrificial part — Latin should remain as the only language. This should also be the case, I think, with the new rite of the Mass. The Latin language would express more fully the universality and unity of the Faith; every Catholic, hearing the same language, would feel strongly that he belongs to one community. It would be fitting for the new Mass to use Latin from the Preface on, throughout the world. In addition, the Eucharistic Prayer should, as a rule, be recited in silence also in the new Mass. Perhaps the biblical readings should have been expanded, but not in such an exaggerated way as the reform of Pope Paul VI did it. The idea of reading a large part of the Bible over three years results in a biblical academy. We need to go back to the millennium-old one-year cycle of the Sunday biblical readings, which has been proved to be pedagogically very apt.

While listening, or rather, reading your words, many Catholics will probably ask themselves: what, then, does it mean that the pope has the special protection of the Holy Spirit? How should we understand this doctrine? What exactly is the papacy? What is the main function of the pope? Today, many Catholics believe that basically everything the pope says is right, true, and binding. What, then, does obedience to the pope consist in?

What is the essence of the papal ministry? What is its main role? This was shown by the Lord Jesus Himself when He changed Simon's name and gave him a new name. *Cephas, Petros* — the rock. "And I say to thee: That thou art Peter [i.e., the Rock]; and upon this rock I will build my church, and the gates of hell shall not prevail against it" (Matt. 16:18), says Jesus to Peter. What does the rock represent? Constancy, immutability, a point of support, permanence, strength, and endurance. The rock is always the same; you can lean on the rock. This precisely is the mission of the pope. His role is to watch over and guard with the bishops that which the Lord has entrusted to him, the treasure of the Faith. Just like a rock. To pass it on unchanged, to care for it, so that everyone in the Church could lean on it, could turn toward it, orient themselves toward it, just as a sailor orients himself toward a goal and determines his course according to its position. The pope must be as firm as a rock, and he must not yield or succumb to the pressure of the world. Let's look at the sea: the waves hit the rock and crash, the wind is blowing, but the rock stands firm. It doesn't give way, doesn't yield under the pressure.

His second role is best described by the word "vicar." It means "deputy." The pope is in this sense a steward. Let's try to think about what a steward is: someone who is not a master. He manages the treasures, the house, the property. He still has a master over him to whom he must give an account of his management of the things that are not his. The pope must be constantly mindful of the fact that the Faith is not his property, and neither is the liturgy. His role is merely to manage it and watch over it so that heresies and other evils don't infiltrate his master's house. And if they do, his task is to get rid of the evil and cleanse the house with which he has been entrusted. Of course, he performs this task with the help of his brother bishops. The pope should repeat this to himself over and over again: I am only a steward of an estate that is not my own.

In recent centuries, this role and importance of the steward have been obfuscated. This is due to various factors, such as the fact that for centuries the pope was also the ruler of a State, the Papal States. He therefore had the power that any great secular monarch had. Perhaps because of that, his essential role as a steward was forgotten. It was beautifully expressed by Pope Gregory the Great when he said that the pope is a "servant of the servants of God," *servus servorum Dei*. The danger is that in spiritual matters the pope has sometimes, especially in recent times, started to behave as if he were the master, the owner. Fortunately, up to the Second Vatican Council the popes were very careful, even scrupulous, in matters of faith. They invariably guarded the deposit of faith. But they sometimes behaved like rulers toward the bishops, like bosses dealing with their employees. In this sense, the intention of the Second Vatican Council to think more in terms of collegiality was correct. Naturally, by declaring the dogma of papal infallibility and affirming his full authority, the First Vatican Council further reinforced this idea that the pope can do anything. Many Catholics came to believe that the Church was the private property of the pope in a sense.

I'm not saying, of course, that this is how popes thought or behaved, but this is how various radical reformers understood their role, which became evident after the Second Vatican Council, when, appealing to papal authority, they began to introduce revolutionary changes into the life of the Church. They began to change the liturgy, the law, the discipline, and the teaching. This has peaked with the pontificate of Pope Francis: the pope speaks and behaves as if the Church were his private property, with which he can do as he pleases.

You have asked about the assistance of the Holy Spirit that Jesus promised to Peter and later to his successors. The pope receives this assistance because he is to lead Christ's Church, not his own. Assistance means help. Over the centuries, the Church has recognized and defined when we can have absolute certainty that the Holy Spirit has rendered this assistance, concerning words and deeds. However, there are also cases when such assistance may or may not be sent. The Church declared at the First Vatican Council that, under certain precisely and clearly defined conditions, papal pronouncements are free from error. These are called *ex cathedra* pronouncements, which are of infallible character, in which the pope defines a truth regarding faith or morals. But to be certain that it's specifically an infallible pronouncement, the pope himself must make it absolutely clear. He must show that his pronouncement has just such an extraordinary, binding character, and he must formally oblige all members of the Church to show full obedience under threat of excommunication. He must also say that his pronouncement transmits an immutable truth contained in divine revelation. These are necessary conditions. Failure to fulfill even one of them means that the papal statement isn't formally infallible.

As for other statements of the pope in his ordinary teaching, the Church doesn't guarantee their infallibility. Theoretically, there may be errors in such statements. Fortunately, the history of the Church shows that, as a rule, popes have not preached error. Popes have defended Catholic truth beyond the cases of declarations *ex cathedra*, because they prayed, because the Holy Spirit helped them, because Providence was watching over them. However, this always depends on the papal milieu, on his advisers, and on whether the pope is faithful to Tradition.

There have also been instances in the history of the Church — very rare, we must note — when popes have preached false teachings concerning the Faith. These were not, however, *ex cathedra* statements. Pope Honorius I, for example, who lived in the seventh century, was condemned as a heretic by three ecumenical councils. However, his successors did not condemn him as a heretic but only declared him culpable for promoting heresy. This pope taught something extremely ambiguous regarding the two wills of Christ. Earlier, during the Arian crisis, Pope Liberius, under political pressure, had signed an ambiguous formula of faith that lacked the statement that the Son was consubstantial with the Father. In doing so, he reached an agreement with the semi-Arian bishops of the East and the Arian emperor. This confession wasn't heretical in itself, but in the context in which it was pronounced, it meant a great weakening of the Catholic faith. Sometimes the omission of truth can be a very grave error.

In the ninth century, Pope St. Nicholas I wrote to the Bulgarians that Baptism may be administered simply in the name of Jesus. This is not true. Baptism is always administered in the name of the Father, the Son, and the Holy Spirit. Centuries later, the Council of Florence unequivocally stated that only Baptism in the name of the Father, the Son, and the Holy Spirit is valid. These are just a few historical examples; there are not many. The measure for judging whether a pope is preaching the right doctrine is, of course, the constant Tradition of the Church, that which has been taught unanimously by his predecessors, beginning with Peter.

In the course of our conversation, you mentioned that we are living in the time of the greatest crisis in the history of the Church. You spoke of the protestantization of the Mass, of the propagation of an erroneous anthropocentric theology, of the endorsement of moral errors. At the same time, all the conciliar and post-conciliar popes, beginning with John XXIII, have been declared saints. The only exception is John Paul I, who ruled merely for thirty days. How can we reconcile these things? On the one hand, we are saying that a terrible disease has been ravaging the Church since the 1960s; on the other hand, those responsible for it — John XXIII, Paul VI, and John Paul II — have been declared saints at an unprecedented speed.

You have touched on a very important issue, that of canonization and the theological significance of it. First of all, there is no formal teaching of the Church's Magisterium that the act of a canonization is infallible, an *ex cathedra* act. In other words, the Church hasn't infallibly proclaimed that canonizations of saints are infallible acts. That being the case, we are free to debate the issue. So far there is only the common view of theologians. Other theologians claim that this is not the case. This discussion hasn't been settled conclusively.

I personally believe that canonization in itself doesn't fulfill the conditions of an *ex cathedra* declaration and is therefore not an infallible act. With *ex cathedra* pronouncements the pope refers to the deposit of faith; there must be a connection between what he is saying and the content of divine revelation. But in the content of revelation, in the deposit of faith, we can't find any basis for the fact that a historically determined, concrete person lived a holy life and is now in Heaven. And this is the essence of the act of canonization: the announcement that a given person is a model of a holy life and is now in Heaven, interceding before God for us, the living. This hasn't been revealed by God with respect to specific persons. Otherwise, God would have had to reveal each time to the popes that the concrete soul was already in Heaven. Public divine revelation ended with the death of the last apostle.

Strictly speaking, God promised the Church complete freedom from error regarding the content of revelation.

> All power is given to me in heaven and in earth. Going therefore, teach ye all nations; baptizing them in the name of the Father, and of the Son, and of the Holy Ghost. Teaching them to observe all things whatsoever I have commanded you: and behold I am with you all days, even to the consummation of the world. (Matt. 28:18–20)

So Jesus commanded us to "observe all things whatsoever I have commanded you," and infallibility applies to that. Similarly, in the text of the Gospel of St. John Jesus said, "But the Paraclete, the Holy Ghost, whom the Father will send in my name, he will teach you all things, and bring all things to your mind, whatsoever I shall have said to you"

(14:26). After all, Jesus didn't reveal that Giovanni Battista Montini or Karol Wojtyła were saints.

Of course, the Holy Spirit can also protect the pope from error in those pronouncements that aren't taught *ex cathedra*. As a rule, therefore, we can assume that if the pope performs an act of canonization after thorough preparation, after prayer, after consulting good advisers, after pious reflection, after proper and careful examination, we may trust that the canonized person is in Heaven. But this isn't an *ex cathedra* act, we can't have an absolute certainty in this case. Nor can the Church oblige us to believe with divine faith that that concrete soul is in Heaven. If the pope dogmatically defines, as Pius XII did, that the Mother of God is in Heaven with body and soul, we can have absolute certainty as to the truth of that claim. The Church guarantees it to us in an absolute way. However, we don't have equal certainty in believing, for example, that Giovanni Battista Montini is in Heaven, as we believe that our Lady is with body and soul in Heaven.

As a rule, therefore, we may assume that the pope is not wrong in acts of canonization. Jesus said, "And I will give to thee the keys of the kingdom of heaven. And whatsoever thou shalt bind upon earth, it shall be bound also in heaven: and whatsoever thou shalt loose upon earth, it shall be loosed also in heaven" (Matt. 16:19). Christ's words indicate that, under the right conditions, we can have confidence that those who are proclaimed saints by the pope are actually in Heaven. This means that we can pray to them and ask them to intercede for us. Certainly such a person can't be in Hell, since it's forbidden to pray to the damned in Hell. So I see no problem with the Church guaranteeing that I can ask such a person for intercession. The Church teaches that even the poor souls in Purgatory can pray for us.

The claim, however, that a person lived a holy life is relative. Even in the lives of great saints there were weaknesses, mistakes, and failings. Recognizing holiness doesn't mean that everything this person did, every single thing he did, every single word he said, was holy and right. It's about a holistic assessment of conduct, about whether this individual can be held up as a role model. And here we can debate whether in a particular case we were shown the right model, whether it was prudent. Therefore, I think that we also have the right to discuss the canonizations that have already taken place and whether in fact we were given the right model. We can have legitimate doubts about them, and we have the right to express these doubts.

This is the case, for example, with Pope Paul VI, who conducted a liturgical revolution, thereby doing great damage to the Church by striking at the very heart of the Church: the celebration of the sacrifice of the Mass. It has been shown that the Mass of Paul VI has protestantizing and anthropocentric characteristics. Pope Paul VI was not a simple priest. He was the pope. Therefore, he shouldered an incomparably greater responsibility. Even if we look at the big picture and don't dismiss his right and wise acts — for example, that he issued an excellent encyclical on the Eucharist, *Mysterium Fidei*; an encyclical on celibacy, *Sacerdotalis Caelibatus*; an encyclical on openness to life, *Humanae Vitae* (in my opinion a truly heroic, great act); and a wonderful profession of faith known as the Creed of the People of God in 1968 — all of these important and good acts combined are insufficient to offset the serious damage done by the revolution in the liturgy. In my opinion, Paul VI shouldn't have been elevated to the altars and declared a saint. For in this way he was shown to be a role model, and therefore his revolutionary reform of the rite of the Holy Mass would also enjoy a seeming endorsement.

Now let me present my own private opinion. I think that God takes His Church and the authority of the pope so seriously that the moment the Church declared Paul VI a saint, He freed Paul VI from further suffering in Purgatory. Therefore, I think that we can safely pray to him for his intercession. I think that his soul is in Heaven and that he has already expiated that which was necessary.

In the discussion about canonization and its possible infallibility, there is also one important argument, the historical argument. Namely, there have been cases of removing from the list of saints the names of people who, as historical research has shown, never existed. Their lives were recounted in legends, and after a thorough verification, it turned out that these people were not real. Cardinal Cesare Baronio, for example, who prepared the edition of the *Roman Martyrology* in the sixteenth century, introduced names of saints into it even though there were insufficient grounds for doing so. Even the canonical process was lacking. They were persons venerated locally, but their introduction into the list of the saints, done by Cardinal Baronio, and approved by the pope, was not preceded by any thorough investigation. I mention this because it's a serious historical argument against the claim that canonization is in itself an infallible act of the Church.

There is also a counter-argument against this approach. It has been argued that true saints are those who have been elevated to the altars only after a formal process of canonization. In my opinion, however, this argument is weak. Either you are a saint or you are not. Saints are not divided into classes — there are no first-, second-, or third-rate saints. In the *Martyrology* they are all described as saints. It doesn't say, "St. Francis, canonized after process" or "St. Hilary, canonized without process." That would be absurd. Therefore, I disagree with those theologians who claim that if the canonization process has been properly conducted, the act of canonization must be held to be infallible. There are theologians now maintaining that some of the canonizations done by Pope Francis are flawed and questionable because of their hurried process, their lack of thorough investigation, and the defects of the proceedings. In their opinion, the current canonization process lacks seriousness and therefore these acts of canonization are not infallible — unlike the canonization processes conducted during the pontificates of the pre-conciliar popes, which led to infallible declarations of elevation to the altars. However, there were cases even before the Council where canonizations were performed without a process.

In his book *The Day Is Now Far Spent*, Cardinal Robert Sarah asserts, "It is time to reject the hermeneutics of rupture, which breaks the transmission of the heritage but also the unity of the ecclesial body, as Joseph Ratzinger puts it clearly in *The Ratzinger Report*: 'To defend the true tradition of the Church today means to defend the Council.'"[96] The cardinal is thus calling for an unconditional defense of the last Council.

---

[96] Robert Cardinal Sarah and Nicolas Diat, *The Day Is Now Far Spent* (San Francisco: Ignatius Press, 2019), 95.

Is that literally what the cardinal said? I don't think he used the term "unconditional."

The cardinal is drawing on and quoting the words of Cardinal Ratzinger, who wrote, "and this today of the Church is the documents of Vatican II, without reservations that amputate them and without arbitrariness that distorts them."[97] Then Cardinal Sarah himself adds, "The council must not be retracted. Instead, it is necessary to rediscover it by carefully reading the official documents that were issued by it. It is necessary to read the council without a guilty conscience but with a spirit of filial gratitude toward our mother the Church."[98] So it clearly says that we should accept the conciliar texts without reservation, that is, unconditionally.

> For me, the term "unconditional" is unacceptable. It was a pastoral council, and that very term implies provisionality. I can only accept unconditionally or without reservation that which the Church has pronounced as dogma or that which is part of the Church's unchanging, constant doctrinal Tradition. Certainly the pastoral documents of the Second Vatican Council don't have this status.

But how am I to understand this call to returning to the Council, to rediscovering it?

> I would say that the return to the Council can be understood in this way: it's about those texts, those passages of the documents that clearly express the traditional faith of the Church. In that sense, we should definitely return to the Council. But with the stipulation that this return wouldn't include those few passages that are questionable, ambiguous, or even false. We should return to those texts of the Second Vatican Council that clearly and beautifully express the constant teaching of the Church. For example, a text worth revisiting is the passage on the universal call to holiness of all members of the Church, in the second chapter of *Lumen Gentium*. In the same way, the beautiful eighth chapter of the same Constitution, which treats the Mother of God, is worth

---

[97] Cardinal Ratzinger and Vittorio Messori, *The Ratzinger Report* (San Francisco: Ignatius Press, 1985), 31.
[98] Sarah and Diat, *The Day Is Now Far Spent*, 96.

another look. We can also revisit the first part of *Sacrosanctum Concilium*, which speaks of the principles of the liturgy — not the second part, where various practical instructions are vague and sometimes radical. We could also quote some statements from *Dei Verbum*, which talk about the Magisterium represented by the pope or the bishops as not being superior to the Word of God or Tradition, but as being at the service of them. We must always distinguish and remember that the Council is not the Gospel. It promulgated texts written in the historical context of the time. The course and the shape of some of the Council's affirmations were influenced by theological positions of that time.

Already during the pontificate of Pope Pius XII, a sharp theological dispute arose in the Church over the so-called new theology, *nouvelle théologie*. In September 1946, Pius XII publicly harshly criticized the Jesuit order during a congregation in Rome, accusing them of seeking novelty and departing from the traditional theology of the Church. In 1950, the pope published the encyclical *Humani Generis*, in which he condemned these new tendencies. From the 1940s onward, the Holy Office indexed the works of theologians such as Yves Congar and Marie-Dominique Chenu. Similar sanctions were imposed on others, for example Henri de Lubac and Karl Rahner. As a result of Rome's intervention, Fr. de Lubac, along with several other professors, had to leave the Lyon seminary and his books were subject to censorship. These theologians weren't allowed to publish, or were banned from teaching, or had to submit their works for special approval before publication. However, as Ralph Wiltgen, for example, demonstrated so well, precisely these theologians, whose orthodoxy aroused such serious doubts throughout the pontificate of Pius XII, played key roles in the drafting of the conciliar documents and in the work of the commissions. Many of them were later created cardinals under John Paul II — for example, Henri de Lubac and Yves Congar. The implication is that either the Church's Magisterium made serious errors in judging these men throughout the pre-conciliar period or, on the contrary, their errors were accepted by the later Church.

> Pope Pius XII condemned some of the claims made by these theologians, deeming them dangerous to the doctrine of the Church and to the Faith of the faithful, and thinking that they could introduce confusion. That is why he imposed various ecclesiastical sanctions on

these theologians. Pope John XXIII and his advisers decided to go in the opposite direction. Although Pius XII had removed them from teaching on specific charges and after careful scrutiny from the Holy Office, later John XXIII gave them, we could say, a completely free hand. I find this problematic. The Church has always been primarily concerned about the purity of the Faith of the faithful and has always tried to protect it at all costs. Because of Pope John XXIII and Pope Paul VI, those very theologians were allowed to operate and exercise great influence on the Church at the Second Vatican Council. Let's consider what effects this must have had: by allowing theologians whose errors had been condemned for years by the Magisterium to work freely, they were sending the message that they wanted a council at which their way of thinking would be present and prominent.

In your book *Christus Vincit*, you compared the errors contained in the texts of Vatican II with an error that appeared in one of the documents of the Council of Florence. It was about the manner of the transmission of priestly faculties. The document of the Council of Florence mentions that this is done by the handing over of the liturgical vessels, while according to the teaching of the Church, clearly expressed by Pius XII, this is done by the imposition of hands. But is this comparison appropriate? The error that you mentioned was insignificant and practically didn't enter the consciousness of the faithful at all. If anyone would have noticed it, it may have been just the experts. Nor did it have any effect on the life and faith of the faithful. But when it comes to the errors contained in the texts of Vatican II — we have spoken about several of them — the case is quite different. All the post-conciliar popes have confirmed and recognized as the Council's greatest achievements precisely such points as freedom of conscience, interreligious dialogue, separation of Church and State, and ecumenism.

What I wanted to show by referring to this comparison was not the equivalence of errors. Rather, I was debating those conservative theologians who claim that the entire Second Vatican Council is infallible. And even if they didn't use the term "infallible," they stated that all of its documents should be accepted unconditionally and without reservation — you quoted one such statement yourself. They claimed that there were no errors in these documents because the Council couldn't have made any — this is how they reasoned about it. I have met many theologians who, when we talked, were horrified and would say to me, "The Council cannot be wrong in any respect. You misunderstand it. All that is needed is a good interpretation and everything will be fine." And that's why I used that comparison. I wanted to refute the claim that even a pastoral council or disciplinary texts of a council were a priori immune from any mistakes. That's why I pointed to a specific affirmation of the Council of Florence. In no way am I comparing here the content and gravity of some ambiguous affirmations of Vatican II to those of the Council of Florence.

Since the Ecumenical Council of Florence did make a specific error that was corrected by the subsequent Magisterium, it's possible that the texts of the Second Vatican Council may also contain erroneous statements, and that they will have to be corrected in the future by the Magisterium. That is my argument, and that is why I made the comparison. We should not be scandalized at the thought of a possible future correction of present errors. This is possible because, as Pius XII mentioned in his time, the text of the Council of Florence was not an *ex cathedra* pronouncement. It was not a final, binding judgment. Even more so, such final, binding, *ex cathedra* pronouncements were not intended by the Second Vatican Council. Therefore, some of its affirmations can be corrected.

Shortly after his election as pope, in December 2005, Benedict XVI gave a speech to the college of cardinals in which he said that the best remedy for the Church's current crisis is the remedy of "continuity." According to Benedict XVI, Vatican II should be read in light of the Church's earlier teaching. But is it possible? Benedict himself, when he was still a cardinal, wrote in 1982 that the Pastoral Constitution on the Modern World *Gaudium et Spes* is a countersyllabus. "If it is desirable to offer a diagnosis of the text as a whole, we might say that (in conjunction with the texts on religious liberty and world religions) it is a revision of the *Syllabus* of Pius IX, a kind of countersyllabus ... [A]s such it represents, on the part of the Church, an attempt at an official reconciliation with the new era inaugurated in 1789."[99] According to Cardinal Christoph Schönborn,

---

[99] Roberto De Mattei, *The Second Vatican Council: An Unwritten Story* (Fitzwilliam, NH: Loreto Press, 2012), 490.

Vatican II "in a certain sense brought about a real revolution." And Cardinal Yves Congar claimed that Vatican II was the October Revolution in the Church. It seems that we can't speak of both continuity and revolution at the same time. A revolution is, in principle, a break in continuity, a violent upheaval.

> Defenders of the continuity theory will argue that 80 or more percent of the conciliar texts contain traditional Church teaching. These texts are self-evident and need no further interpretation. In this sense, we can agree with Cardinal Ratzinger that these texts must be read in the light of Tradition. However, this method applies only to those texts that are clear, which don't require any additional interpretation, any mental balancing acts or attempts at squaring the circle to demonstrate perfect continuity with the previous constant teaching of the Church.

In the course of our conversation, you have mentioned several times the mental gymnastics that anyone who tries to reconcile the classical, immutable doctrine of the Church with the new conciliar and post-conciliar developments must perform. Some third way between "yes" and "no" must constantly be sought, dialectics must constantly be used, the phrase "yes, but" is always necessary. What effect does such a mentality have on the character of new priests? Are they not constantly in the midst of a spiritual identity crisis as a result of the ceaseless mental gymnastics required of them? Aren't they forced to constantly ignore contradictions?

> Unfortunately, some texts of the Second Vatican Council and later papal documents include statements that are imprecise and ambiguous. Thus they've given rise to various mutually exclusive interpretations. The experience of the past fifty years has proven this to be the case, and as a result we have seen confusion in the presentation and proclamation of the truths of the Catholic faith. Some theologically inaccurate and ambiguous statements of the Council can be explained in continuity with the sense of Tradition. I tried to show this in my conversation with you, but the desire to properly explain one statement from *Gaudium et Spes* (no. 12) — how to understand the statement that man is the center and crown of all that exists on earth — made it necessary to write almost a theological treatise. Ordinary believers and even priests of average education who read this statement are unable to find a Thomistic

interpretation of it. The statements of the Magisterium should not be essays for theological reflection, they are not *quaestiones disputandae*. During the deliberations at the Second Vatican Council, when many Council Fathers expressed concern about imprecise wording that could later give rise to ambiguous interpretations, Cardinal Antonio Bacci — who in 1969, together with Cardinal Alfredo Ottaviani, conveyed his concerns to Paul VI about the theological deficiencies of the *Novus Ordo Missae* — admonished the Council Fathers to avoid any imprecision or ambiguity in the language, especially such that could create confusion, damage, or danger to the Magisterium. Unfortunately, neither the warnings of Cardinal Bacci nor those of other Council Fathers were heeded. As a result, there are statements in the conciliar texts that are open to misinterpretation. The most famous example is the teaching on the collegiality of bishops in *Lumen Gentium* (no. 22), expressed in such a way that Pope Paul VI felt compelled to add his own explanatory note (inserted at the end) to this conciliar text to guarantee the correct interpretation of the document. This is the well-known "preliminary explanatory note" (*nota praevia explicativa*). Various statements of the Council and of Pope John Paul II — for example, from *Redemptor Hominis*, as we have already discussed — require such explanatory notes. But the task of the Magisterium is precisely to speak in such a clear and universally understandable way that long and intricate explanatory notes are unnecessary.

11

In an Orderly Formation

Haven't traditional Catholics found themselves in a vicious circle? To find a cure, they must name the disease. To name the disease, they must show the errors. To show the errors, they must quote documents and speeches regardless of who is pronouncing them. An error doesn't cease to be an error because of who pronounced it. But it turns out that the errors are supported by the highest ecclesiastical authority. And so they fall into a trap. They want to be faithful to Tradition and the Church. But all the time they have to choose and look for ways out: either they follow their conscience, which tells them to call the errors by their name, or they listen to the authority in which the Faith is ultimately rooted.

> Yes, for me this is one of the most difficult issues, one of the greatest challenges. On the other hand, I would like to remind you that some questionable statements of the Second Vatican Council are not infallible, they are not *ex cathedra* pronouncements or dogmatic definitions or anathemas. Besides, they were not intended as such. Thus, in assessing them, we can go back to the constant and immutable doctrine of the Church. We are not Protestants who make decisions according to their own private understanding, their personal judgments, and who set themselves above the teaching office of the Church, but we adhere to the constant objective Magisterium of the Church.

This is exactly the charge raised by many conservative Catholics: they say that those who criticize either the texts of the Council or certain statements of the pope are behaving like Protestants, like Luther. They say that Tradition is living and we should simply obey those entrusted with its interpretation rather than assume the role of judges.

> I am familiar with this charge. It's incorrect. Let's ask ourselves, what is the basic difference between the approach of Protestants and that of traditional Catholics? The former believe that they can subjectively decide what the meaning of Scripture is. They reject the Magisterium of the Church altogether; they are the teaching office unto themselves. They don't appeal to Tradition, to what has been objectively, constantly, and unchangingly passed down by the Magisterium of the Church. Catholics who reject certain statements, whether from the Council or from the post-conciliar popes, behave very differently. They appeal not to their subjective opinions, but to that which is objective in the constant doctrinal teaching of the Church. They appeal to the teaching of the Church of all times, to the teaching of the Church that has always been the same. So they are not appealing to a private, subjective understanding but to how the Church has always understood a concrete truth of faith. The criterion is not themselves, but the constant voice of the Church over centuries. I have already quoted St. Vincent of Lérins, who showed this perfectly. The criterion of catholicity is antiquity, for what has always been taught is Catholic; universality, that is, whether it has been taught by all; and contemporary assent. The saint asks: What if there is a novelty in the Church's teaching, a new doctrine espoused by the majority of contemporaries? Well, he answers, if there is a difference between what the majority of contemporaries agree on and what was taught before, the conclusive criterion for certainty about what is Catholic remains the unity of teaching in the past.

However, such an attitude may provoke another accusation. Namely, that you are assuming a position similar or even identical to that of the Eastern Orthodox. For them, too, only the past matters. And yet, say the critics, the Magisterium is living and can develop. The world is changing. New problems arise; the past can't be the only point of reference.

> I expected such a charge. The argument that simply appeals to Tradition appears frequently among Orthodox theologians. However, in using it, they fall into a contradiction. For example, they reject papal primacy,

which is an unchangeable part of Tradition. Theologians of the first centuries, among them St. John Chrysostom, so highly respected and important for the Orthodox, clearly teach it. The Orthodox, therefore, while appealing to the argument from antiquity, use it arbitrarily, rejecting the clear witnesses of the Church Fathers about the papal primacy. The argument appealing to Tradition would be valid only if it could be shown that there was a time in the Church when the primacy of Peter wasn't recognized, if it was a novelty that contradicts the previous teaching. The existence of papal primacy and its acceptance belong to apostolic tradition. In the same way, it's impossible to defend the claim that only the first seven ecumenical councils are valid for all of Christianity, that everything which came later has no authoritative power. This is not an appeal to Tradition, but only to a portion of it. Luther at least seemed to recognize the first four councils and the dogmas issued by them. Why four? For the Orthodox, seven councils are authoritative. This understanding of the Faith is based on arbitrary choice and goes against the very principle of Tradition that says that the Magisterium is living. This life is also manifested on a universal level. Are we to imagine that the Magisterium died in the eighth century?

Now someone could accuse traditional Catholics of similar reasoning. They might be accused of believing that the Magisterium was at work until 1962, but not after that. That isn't true. We don't think so. As far as the Council is concerned, Archbishop Lefebvre himself argued that there are things in it that can be accepted in their entirety; some statements that are ambiguous, which must undoubtedly be interpreted in the light of Tradition; and finally, some statements that are in themselves false and must be corrected. This correction must be done by appealing to the teaching of the Church of all times. The charge of those who say that traditional Catholics behave like the Orthodox is therefore incorrect. While the Orthodox stopped at the seventh council, traditional Catholics didn't stop at the death of Pius XII. They recognize the Second Vatican Council, but they claim that it wasn't a dogmatic council — which is what Pope Paul VI also claimed. And besides, they accept those of the Council's teachings that agree with the Tradition of the Church.

One more thing should be mentioned. Some people accuse us of not recognizing a "living Magisterium." My response is, "What do we mean when we are talking about a living Magisterium?" It's simple. Those who carry it and hold the office are alive and not dead. Likewise, a living Tradition means that it's growing, but always in the same sense. This is what St. Vincent taught and what the First Vatican Council affirmed after him.

A serious deficiency of the Orthodox churches is the absence of universality. They lack an understanding of what the full, universal visibility of the Church is at all levels of the hierarchy. They are saying: yes, the Church must be visible in the person of the bishop. We Catholics agree with this and point it out to Protestants. The Church by its very nature is universal, catholic. Well, at this level, when we are talking not only about the local Church but about the universal Church, there must be a concrete, visible, personal sign of this unity. Just as Christ is the head of the Mystical Body, so the visible Church must have such a visible head on earth, and it is the bishop of Rome, the successor of Peter, the pope. The Orthodox churches beyond the local level lack this single point of reference of unity, one and the same for all, that the Lord Himself instituted in the ministry of the apostle Peter. Practically, there are local churches without a universal level, since they are lacking a visible head on that universal level. They constitute a community of bishops that lack a true visible head.

I sometimes have the impression that those who are talking about the new work of the Holy Spirit, about Him working outside the Church, who attribute to Him the introduction of changes, are confusing the Spirit of Truth with Hegel's world spirit.

Many modern radical theologians are actually Hegelians. What Hegel calls spirit has nothing to do with the Holy Spirit; rather, it's a collective mentality or consciousness that changes with time. Although these theologians are talking about the Holy Spirit, they mean the spirit of the world. They use the name "Holy Spirit" to justify their own theories. That was the case with using the term "new Pentecost" both during and after the deliberations of the Second Vatican Council. This isn't the right term. One could get the impression that in their minds, the Council represented a new stage in salvation history, the beginning of some new Church.

However, as all the Fathers of the Church said, the era of the Holy Spirit began with His descent on Pentecost and continues until Christ's return. The existence of the Church is a continuous Pentecost because the Holy Spirit is at work in the Church. There hasn't been and there won't be any new descent of the Holy Spirit until Christ's return — to claim otherwise is to preach heresy. Such a heresy already happened once in the history of the Church, in the second century after Christ. It was Montanism, a heretical movement in Asia Minor, which influenced even Tertullian. Its followers believed that the Holy Spirit descended again in their community, and the leaders of the community were considered prophets acting directly under His influence. The Church rejected and condemned this heresy. It may happen that in some individual cases the Holy Spirit bestows His gifts on certain persons — that was the case with some great saints. Such individual cases of special gifts of the Spirit have happened throughout history. However, this doesn't apply to the Church as such.

Another example of heresy were the teachings of Joachim of Fiore in the twelfth century. He founded his own community and also spoke of a new descent of the Holy Spirit, a new era of the Holy Spirit that would come after the era of the Father and the Son. His theory that the present Church would be replaced by a new, more spiritual and perfect Church was rejected by the Church.

Why, then, do John XXIII and John Paul II, as well as many other theologians, suggest that the Council was a new outpouring of the Spirit and that we are now living in the age of a new, spiritual Church?

Indeed, as soon as the news of the Council was announced, it became a symbol of the "new Pentecost." This became almost a cliché. But the Tradition of the Church has never permitted anything like this. There is a kind of arrogance inherent in that claim. For the message here is: we are so good, so wise, that what we are now doing in the Church is the work of the Holy Spirit. What a claim! A sober analysis of the effects shows exactly the opposite. There is no outpouring of the Spirit, no new Pentecost, no springtime. Pope Paul VI himself said of it: "Instead of the expected springtime, winter has come." The same pope said even more forcefully in 1972:

> We are under the impression that from some fissure the smoke of Satan has entered the temple of God. It is doubt, uncertainty, questioning, restlessness, dissatisfaction and dissipation. Lack of trust in the Church. Instead, trust is placed in the first secular "prophet" who speaks in the press or in any social movement and is asked to give formulas for real life! Without thinking that we already have these formulas![100]

In that situation, how can we speak of an outpouring of the Holy Spirit and of a "new Pentecost"?

It is enough to compare what the Church looked like before and after the Council. Before the Council the seminaries were full, the monasteries attracted more and more religious, the missionaries preached the Word of God all over the world with great zeal, they tried at all costs to bring pagans and non-believers to Christ and into the Church. And after the Council? In the whole Western world, with Poland as the notable exception for a long time, seminaries became empty and monasteries closed down. The number of vocations is a fraction of what it used to be. In Germany alone about two hundred thousand believers leave the Church every year. Never before has the Church experienced such a sudden catastrophe. Thousands and thousands of priests have abandoned the priesthood. Attempts were made to explain this. It has been said that this is a childhood disease, that these are phenomena preceding a great growth. No one is convinced by this. The numbers are clear. Let's take France: the number of priests there (diocesan and religious) has dropped by almost half over the past twenty years, from twenty-nine thousand to about fifteen thousand, and the decline is getting worse every year. Those disastrous rates are

---

[100] Paul VI, Homily for the Feast of Saints Peter and Paul (June 29, 1972).

the result of many factors, including the deepening secularization of French society. While in 1952, 27 percent of Catholics attended Sunday Mass, in 2010, 4.5 percent of the faithful did. Last year, 120 priests were ordained in the whole of France. This is one-tenth of what it was before the Council! I don't even want to talk about Holland, Belgium, or Ireland.

Jesus said that we will know the tree by its fruit.

Fifty years later there can no longer be any doubts about the fruit, about the fact that we must give new soil to the tree. We must take care that new plants grow from the root, bearing healthy and good fruit. The true renewal of the Church can be achieved only by returning to the Tradition. That which was proposed didn't work. The liturgy has been distorted. Instead of the worship of God, a form of self-adoration of man emerged. The Holy Mass has become in many places a show. Even if it's celebrated according to the rubrics, it doesn't express the essentially sacrificial character of the Mass clearly enough. With the pontificate of Pope Francis, we have reached the heights of the crisis, the greatest conformity to the world. Paganism has already invaded the life of the Church. Bishops and cardinals talk and act as if they were pagans. Recently, an American bishop said that the greatest danger to life is not abortion but climate change. Pure paganism and absurdity. Not only do these bishops not lose their offices, but they are still, apparently, supported by those who have authority in the Vatican. All these are facts that speak for themselves. Therefore, stories about the springtime of the Church or about a new outpouring of the Spirit as a "new Pentecost" reveal a complete loss of contact with reality.

According to the supporters of the current pontificate, there is no crisis. The whole period of the earlier history of Christianity was marked by the influence of political Catholicism. Only now, only with Francis, has the legacy of Constantine finally been overcome. That is the position of those supporting the current pontificate. According to Fr. Spadaro, the editor-in-chief of *La Civiltà Cattolica*, one of Pope Francis's closest collaborators, we are finally living in the age of true Christianity. In the December 2019

issue, he wrote that the contradiction between Christianity and secularism is only apparent. For the spirit is universal, and Christian thinking opposes secular thought only when the former has turned into an ideology. Except that in this sense such Christian thinking has nothing to do with Christ.[101] For it's a Christian ideology.

> Ultimately, this is a confession of apostasy. This can only be said by someone who has no faith in Christ and is himself speaking from an ideological position. What we see here is a Gnostic ideology. A vision of the world based on one's own understanding of religion, without any connection to the historical experience of the Church or to divine revelation, is being constructed here.

He believes that he represents true Christianity, free from accretions and from Tradition.

> The Gnostics also believed that they represented true Christianity. They said: this Christ that the Church teaches about — the historical Christ, born in Bethlehem, who was crucified and died on the Cross, the teacher of truth — He is not the true Christ. Nor is the Christ the one of whom Tradition speaks and who is preserved in the memory of the Church. No, *we* Gnostics are the ones with access to the true Christ who is Spirit. This is a Christ of their own ideas, not the Christ of history or tradition. Fr. Spadaro represents a form of this new Gnostic Christianity.

In his address to the Roman Curia on December 21, 2019, Pope Francis said, "what we are experiencing is not simply an epoch of changes, but an epochal change. We find ourselves living at a time when change is no longer linear, but epochal. It entails decisions that rapidly transform our ways of living, of relating to one another, of communicating and thinking, of how different generations relate to one another and how we understand and experience faith and science.... There is, finally, the dimension of time and there is human error, which must rightly be taken into consideration. These are part of the history of each one of us. Not to take account of them is to go about

---

[101] Antonio Spadaro, S.J., "Defy the Apocalypse," *La Civiltà Cattolica* (January 20, 2020), www.laciviltacattolica.com/defy-the-apocalypse/.

doing things in abstraction from human history. Linked to this difficult historical process there is always the temptation to fall back on the past (also by employing new formulations), because it is more reassuring, familiar, and, to be sure, less conflictual. This too is part of the process and risk of setting in motion significant changes. Here, there is a need to be wary of the temptation to rigidity. A rigidity born of the fear of change, which ends up erecting fences and obstacles on the terrain of the common good, turning it into a minefield of incomprehension and hatred. Let us always remember that behind every form of rigidity lies some kind of imbalance. Rigidity and imbalance feed one another in a vicious circle. And today this temptation to rigidity has become very real."[102] At the end, the pope recalled the words of Cardinal Martini, "Cardinal Martini, in his last interview, a few days before his death, said something that should make us think: 'The Church is two hundred years behind the times. Why is she not shaken up? Are we afraid? Fear, instead of courage? Yet faith is the Church's foundation. Faith, confidence, courage … Only love conquers weariness.'"[103] What is this about? In what sense is the Church two hundred years behind? This whole speech appears to herald another revolution.

> If the authors of these words, both the late Cardinal Martini and the current pope, wished to be entirely sincere and honest, instead of saying that the Church is two hundred years behind, they should say that it's two thousand years behind. That is what they would have to say. Two thousand years ago the Church was essentially what it is today. Two hundred years most probably refers to the French Revolution. But what did the French Revolution strive for? Developing a completely secular society with no place for the supernatural. During the French Revolution, the idea was to build a society that excluded God, divine revelation, and the supernatural. A society in which everything revolves around man and is centered on him. These projects are well illustrated by the writings of the philosophers of the so-called Enlightenment. Man is the only creator and constructor of values, life, society, he is the only goal and measure.

---

[102] Pope Francis, Christmas Greetings to the Roman Curia (December 21, 2019), www.vatican.va/content/francesco/en/speeches/2019/december/documents/papa-francesco_20191221_curia-romana.html.

[103] Ibid.

So when I hear that the Church is two hundred years behind, it is clearly about the present Church accepting and embracing this message of the French Revolution and conforming fully to the demands of the unbelieving world. Absolute equality must be accepted, and therefore the distinction of the two biological sexes should be abolished, so that the most radical consequence of the egalitarian thinking of the French Revolution would be achieved. *Egalité* to a perfect degree. Then fraternity. Unfortunately, the idea of universal fraternity is very strongly supported by Pope Francis, but it's based solely on the natural. It's not a brotherhood based on grace and on Christ, but a brotherhood understood in a naturalistic way. Is this not a betrayal of the Gospel? Finally, liberty. Liberty understood as complete freedom from the revelation of God. Man is bound only by the truth that he himself has invented.

I don't know what all these words about an epoch of changes or epochal change mean. The only important epochal change is our conversion — our radical conversion in the Church toward Christ, holiness, repentance, contrition, the commandments of God, and His revelation. What follows from it is also a call for the conversion of all people to the one, true, living God, the Holy Trinity. A call for turning away from the idols that people have created.

What changes does Pope Francis have in mind? A change in moral teaching? A change in divine revelation? Allowing Holy Communion for divorced persons who entered new unions, for example, was such a change. In practice, this means the approval of adultery. The sixth commandment is no longer to be regarded as binding. By approving the norms adopted by the Argentine bishops, Pope Francis has effectively permitted adultery. Similarly, the worship of the Pachamama statue in the Vatican and the signing of the Abu Dhabi declaration are violations of God's first commandment. All this is happening right before our eyes.

Taylor Marshall, author of the book *Infiltration*, to which you wrote the foreword, describes the story of Mélanie Calvat, to whom our Lady appeared at La Salette in 1846. Calvat wrote, conveying the words of our Lady, that in the future a great apostasy would take place in Rome and the Antichrist would sit on the throne of Peter. How should such prophecies be understood? This is not the only prediction of a widespread apostasy from the Faith. How can we reconcile the predictions of the coming of the Antichrist and the promises of Christ, who said that the gates of Hell shall not prevail against the Church?

> All private revelations have only a relative merit. We can never be absolutely certain that there has been no error. It can also happen that even if the totality of a private revelation is true, some details of it can be false. They may not be of a supernatural nature, but may be the record of a self-reflection of the person who received the revelation. It isn't, therefore, and certainly doesn't have to be, about a desire to mislead others or about deception, but about the insertion of a personal reflection. It can happen that what the visionary takes as the words of our Lady or Jesus are his or her own thoughts and reflections. This is the principle for understanding private revelations. I'm not sure what the situation is with this particular statement by Mélanie Calvat.

Taylor Marshall describes exactly the state of our knowledge. He points out that there are two different records of the same revelation. The first one, written earlier, doesn't mention the Antichrist. This appears in the later version, written by Mélanie in the 1870s. Marshall maintains that this version may be authentic because in the first account, which was written with the participation of Church leaders, either the passage may have been censored so as not to arouse scandal, or Mélanie herself may not have wanted to relay it.

> So the situation is not clear and straightforward.

Fine, perhaps I should rephrase the question. In the Second Epistle to the Thessalonians, St. Paul writes about the Antichrist. "Let no man deceive you by any means, for unless there come a revolt first, and the man of sin be revealed, the son of perdition, who opposeth, and is lifted up above all that is called God, or that is worshipped, so that he sitteth in the temple of God, shewing himself as if he were God. Remember you not, that when I was yet with you, I told you these things? And now you know what withholdeth, that he may be revealed in his time. For the mystery of iniquity already worketh; only that he who now holdeth, do hold, until he be taken out of the way. And then that wicked one shall be revealed whom the Lord Jesus shall kill with the spirit of his mouth; and shall destroy with the brightness of his coming" (2:3–8). At the same time we have the promise that the gates of Hell shall not prevail against the Church until the end of time. It looks as if the coming of the Antichrist were connected with the fall of the Church.

I don't think the Antichrist can assume the papal throne. It would mean that Christ's words aren't true. He can get close to the throne of Peter, be very close to it indeed, and perhaps his tools will be the people surrounding the pope. Are we not seeing this even now? But I believe that the Lord won't allow the Antichrist himself to sit upon the throne of St. Peter. Christ's promise clearly applies to the Church. Of course, the Church is more than the Vatican. The Church lives also in the souls of Catholics. The Catholic Faith is indestructible. It lives in the souls of pious people. It lives in committed priests and bishops.

Allow me to share a famous anecdote here. When Napoleon imprisoned Pius VII and confined him in Fontainebleau, near Paris, he wanted to force the pope to sign a certain document. Pius VII refused and wouldn't give in. At that time Napoleon was at the height of his power and influence. Pius VII would not give in despite various forms of coercion, so at one point the enraged Napoleon threatened to destroy the Church. Cardinal Consalvi was standing next to the pope. Upon hearing the shouting and threats of the emperor, he said, "But Your Majesty, we, priests and bishops, have been trying to do this for a thousand and eight hundred years, and we have not succeeded. So you will not succeed either."

We must believe that Christ will always be victorious in the fight against Antichrist and Satan. Even if at times Providence allows a deep crisis, we must remember that the Church won't perish. We must remember that God is looking at the world from a perspective entirely different from ours. God is not in a rush. He can wait. St. Augustine wrote beautifully that God prefers to allow evil out of which He can later derive good, rather than not allow evil at all. Let's take the example of a pope who, if we look at his actions, was probably not far from our notion of the Antichrist. This happened in the tenth century, during the so-called *saeculum obscurum*, a dark age when Rome was in complete chaos. The throne of Peter was being passed from person to person by powerful Roman clans, remarkably reminiscent of today's mafia families. At one point, Pope John XII assumed the papal throne. He ruled for over ten years. He became pope at the age of eighteen, put on the throne by his family. He was an utterly savage and dissolute man. He had no interest at all in spiritual matters or religion. The *Liber Pontificalis*, an official chronicle of that time, sums up his reign by saying that his pontificate was all about fornication and vanity. In fact, John XII turned the Lateran into an actual brothel. He died before age thirty — it seems he had a stroke while indulging in debauchery. He is also rumored to have toasted to Jupiter and Venus while intoxicated, like pagans. The attitude of such a pope is not unlike what we would expect from the Antichrist. Fortunately, he didn't attempt to change anything in Church doctrine. Even the greatest personal sins of Pope John XII or other later bad popes didn't involve an effort to change the doctrinal or liturgical tradition of the Church.

This is an important lesson for us. We need to know the history of the Church because it helps us better understand the power of the Faith, which is greater than human weaknesses and betrayals — even of popes.

St. Paul writes in his Epistle to the Ephesians, "For our wrestling is not against flesh and blood; but against principalities and powers, against the rulers of the world of this darkness, against the spirits of wickedness in the high places" (6:12). During our conversation, you often mentioned various threats to the Church from progressive theologians, Gnostics, radicals, and feminists. Is it not the case that all these are just different forms of another danger? Is it not the case that the actual, real battle is, as the apostle Paul wrote, between the powers of good and evil? Or is it just a metaphor? What role does the Archangel Michael play in this war? To what extent can we see good and evil spirits clashing in the current dispute over the Church?

Already from the first pages of Genesis we are told about an evil spirit, symbolically called the serpent, who is at war with God. The name is a metaphor, but it's referring to a real person endowed with intelligence, for only such a person can have a conversation with Eve. Similarly, hostility and persecution can only come from intelligent beings.

Likewise, the last book of Scripture, the Book of Revelation, contains many references and descriptions of the war that Satan, represented by the dragon, wages against the angels. The twelfth chapter recounts the battle of the Archangel Michael against Satan.

> And there was a great battle in Heaven, Michael and his angels fought with the dragon, and the dragon fought and his angels: and they prevailed not, neither was their place found any more in Heaven. And that great dragon was cast out, that old serpent, who is called the devil and Satan, who seduceth the whole world; and he was cast unto the earth, and his angels were thrown down with him. (12:7–9)

Or in another passage, "And he laid hold on the dragon, the old serpent, which is the devil and Satan, and bound him for a thousand years" (20:2). Satan is the one who "seduces the nations" (20:3).

This is exactly the story that St. Paul is talking about in the passage you quoted. I would include here the First Epistle of St. Peter, "Be sober and watch: because your adversary the devil, as a roaring lion, goeth about seeking whom he may devour" (5:8). Also, Jesus Himself says in the Gospel of St. John, "You are of your father the devil, and the desires of your father you will do. He was a murderer from the beginning, and he stood not in the truth; because truth is not in him. When he speaketh a lie, he speaketh of his own: for he is a liar, and the father thereof" (8:44). This is a clear indication of a person. The *Catechism of the Catholic Church* describes man's situation in the same way:

> By our first parents' sin, the devil has acquired a certain domination over man, even though man remains free. Original sin entails "captivity under the power of him who thenceforth had the power of death, that is, the devil." (*CCC* 407)

We should also mention a passage from the constitution *Gaudium et Spes* of the Second Vatican Council:

> For a monumental struggle against the powers of darkness pervades the whole history of man. The battle was joined from

the very origins of the world and will continue until the last day, as the Lord has attested. (*GS* 37)

We can say that the casting out of evil spirits and the war against Satan is — should be — the permanent mission of the Church. From the very beginning, the Church also performed exorcisms at Baptism. We must regret that in the new rite of the sacrament of Baptism actual exorcisms were eliminated and replaced with a prayer recalling that Jesus has already cast out the demons. St. Paul wrote:

> For the creature was made subject to vanity, not willingly, but by reason of him that made it subject, in hope: because the creature also itself shall be delivered from the servitude of corruption, into the liberty of the glory of the children of God. For we know that every creature groaneth and travaileth in pain, even till now. (Rom. 8:20–22)

That is why the Church, in order to free creation from the power of the devil, used both blessings and exorcisms. Since at least the third century, the Church had the minor order of exorcist as a visible sign that she has to fight the evil spirits. Pope Paul VI seemed to suppress the minor orders and the subdiaconate in 1972, but these orders have never ceased to be given within the Church among those who adhere to Tradition.

If the fight against Satan and evil spirits is such an important part of the mission of the Church, then why was the separate prayer after Mass introduced by Leo XIII that called upon Michael the Archangel for help against the devil suppressed after the Council?

It's precisely in our time, when the world is permeated with evil, when real structures of evil are at work, that the pope should have made a special effort to promote the prayer to St. Michael the Archangel! Fortunately, Pope John Paul II, when he visited Monte Gargano in 1987, called for prayers to St. Michael the Archangel, admittedly not after Mass, but in general. He said there, "I have come here to venerate and invoke the protection of the Archangel Michael, at a time when it is difficult to offer an authentic Christian witness without falling into

compromises or easy accommodations."[104] Many bishops encourage the
faithful to pray to St. Michael the Archangel and some bishops ordered
that the prayer to him be recited after Holy Mass. For example, here at
the Cathedral in Nur-Sultan we have been saying these prayers after
Mass for years. We must also remember why Pope Leo XIII introduced
these prayers. Allegedly he had received a private revelation that Satan
would gain some limited power over the Church in the future. This
was such a great shock to him that he wrote the text of the prayer to
St. Michael the Archangel and ordered that it should be recited by all
priests after Holy Mass.

As you yourself have repeatedly emphasized, we are living at a time of a radical, deep
crisis. There have been various responses to this situation. Let me list them one by
one, asking you to comment. The most despairing and disillusioned groups believe
that there is no true pope in Rome today. In their opinion, the post-conciliar popes
have succumbed to heresy and thereby lost their power and office. This attitude is
represented by various sedevacantists. According to them, since the times of Pius XII,
the Apostolic See has been vacant and the popes are, in fact, usurpers. They point to
particular statements of post-conciliar popes, proving that these are heretical claims.
They are particularly numerous in the United States, but can also be found in Europe.

This is not a Catholic attitude. Never in the earlier history of the Church
did it happen that, on the basis of accusing a pope of heresy, a group of
the faithful could claim the right to declare that the Holy See is vacant.
At the root of this attitude is the theory that the pope loses his office
automatically if he professes heresy. But this does not correspond to the
constant teaching of the Church; it is an opinion of some theologians.
Other theologians claim that the pope cannot be judged by anyone
unless he falls away from the Faith. However, even the proponents of
this approach, which can be found in old collections of laws dating
back to the late Middle Ages, as is the case in the *Corpus Iuris Canonici*,
could not point out what exactly should happen in such a situation.

---

[104] John Paul II, Address to the Population of Monte Sant'Angelo (May 24, 1987),
www.vatican.va/content/john-paul-ii/it/speeches/1987/may/documents/
hf_jp-ii_spe_19870524_monte-sant-angelo.html.

This theory, however, was never taught formally by the Magisterium. There is a document from Pope Paul IV that points in this direction. But one document, before and after which there were no others like it, doesn't constitute a sure tradition of the Church. It's insufficient to be considered part of Tradition. It is Paul IV's bull of 1559 *Cum Ex Apostolatus Officio*, which states that only a Catholic may be elected to the office of the pope and that a Catholic who was previously a heretic may not be validly elected. The reason for issuing this bull was that the pope suspected one of the cardinals of heresy, of secretly being a Protestant. This bull, however, doesn't claim that a pope accused of heresy automatically loses his office. It's one thing to forbid the election of a heretic as pope, and another to say that a validly elected pope who later becomes a heretic automatically loses his office. Besides, the bull of Paul IV was not universally recognized by subsequent popes. Later rules of conclave stipulated that even an excommunicated cardinal had the right to be elected pope.

Doesn't the imposition of excommunication on anyone, even a cardinal, mean that he is excluded from the Church?

Excommunication is a punishment that has a medicinal aim: it is intended to bring the excommunicated person to amendment. A person who is excommunicated cannot receive Communion and has no rights in the Church, but as a result of Baptism he bears an indelible mark. He has been incorporated into the Body of Christ. After doing penance, he can return to his full rights in the Church. Although he is a dead member, in virtue of the indelible mark of Baptism he belongs to the Body of Christ. Ultimately, a baptized person ceases to belong to the Church only when he is condemned to Hell.

To sum up, what the sedevacantists are preaching is not any certain or constant teaching of the Church. They want to be great traditionalists, but they cannot point to instances, not even one, when an incumbent pope has been removed in a true canonical form from office because of charges of heresy. There is no legitimate authority in the Church that can canonically depose a pope. It's true that we can invoke cases of the removal of popes by local synods in the ninth and tenth centuries, but this was more of a political nature and resulted from the interference of the secular power. God writes straight with crooked lines, and so the interferences of the Emperor in such cases occasionally would have a corrective effect, as for example during the *saeculum obscurum* of the tenth and eleventh centuries or in the case of the end of the Great Western Schism in the fifteenth century. However, in those cases the direct reason for the removal of the pope was never a formal charge of heresy. We must also be mindful of the heresy of conciliarism, especially prominent in the fifteenth century during the Councils of Constance and Basel, according to which the council was to have supreme authority, superior also to that of the popes. No ecclesiastical body — be it a synod, a council, or an assembly of cardinals — has the right to judge and depose a pope. So I notice in sedevacantism a certain closeness to this heresy of conciliarism. For the simple question arises: who would pass judgment and who would depose the pope?

There is also the famous theory of Cardinal Robert Bellarmine. This theory states that a pope who falls into heresy *ipso facto* ceases to be pope. However, the same problem arises again: who should determine that what we are dealing with is not error but formal heresy, that is, an obstinate denial of Catholic truth? From what point in time would this apply? There is simply no such superior authority to the pope in the Church — unless we fall into conciliarism, or accept the orthodox teaching on *sobornost*, granting supreme authority to a body of bishops. In my opinion, although St. Robert Bellarmine is a Doctor of the Church, his teaching on the heretical pope is not infallible.

But let's leave theology aside and appeal to common human sense. Let's assume, purely hypothetically, that Pope Francis declares that Christ didn't rise bodily from the grave. This is a heresy. In that case . . .

Then Eugenio Scalfari will quote it, and the Vatican will deny it.

Suppose, hypothetically, that he does so by making a public address to the faithful. What would happen then? This is heresy. Suppose some group of cardinals — in today's circumstances, it would be a minority — got together and demanded that the pope retract those words. But he would not retract anything. In response, this group would announce that if the pope doesn't retract his words, he will be considered an obstinate, formal heretic. Then, assuming a lack of papal response, the group would, according to the theory propounded by St. Robert Bellarmine, declare that from that very moment Francis ceases to be pope. A certain amount of time passes and this group of cardinals or bishops declares that the pope is self-deposed and then calls on the college of cardinals to elect a new pope, claiming that the Holy See is vacant. They then have to establish new conclave rules for themselves. We are in a vicious circle. How many supporters of such a solution can there be? Perhaps a few. Certainly an extreme minority. The majority will immediately issue a statement that they recognize the current pope, even if he said what he did. Then the minority will elect their own pope — an exact replay of the pattern from the time of the Great Schism after the return of the popes from Avignon. The sole outcome will be more chaos. Ultimately, proponents of such a theory fall into conciliarism. Thus, from a purely rational point of view, this theory leads to a deadlock.

I would also say that ultimately I detect in this attitude of sedevacantism a lack of faith in the Providence of God, in the fact that God governs the world, that He is the Lord of the Church. Another error is concealed here: identifying the pope with the Church. The pope is not the Church. The pope is a member of the Church. He is a part of the Church. The Church as a whole is stronger than a heretical pope. And for a certain time, the Church is able to withstand the rule of a heretical pope. The Church is a work of God and has means of defense even against such a potential threat as a heretical pope. For example, the bishops can declare a universal crusade of prayer, acts of penance, and fasting for the conversion of such a pope. They can also clearly preach the Catholic teaching, especially on those points that were obfuscated by the pope's heretical words. They can plead for God's intervention. All these are means that presuppose that the Church is first of all a supernatural community. We are not a political party. If we were a party, normal secular means could be used to get rid of the leader. But

the Church is not a political party. The Church is the Mystical Body
of Christ, a supernatural community.

**Yet another response than that of the sedevacantists is offered by the priests from the
Society of St. Pius X. What is your judgment of their approach? What do you think about
the attitude and actions of the founder of the Society, Archbishop Marcel Lefebvre?
Would you say that Archbishop Lefebvre made the right decision when he ordained
four priests as bishops without consent from Rome in 1988?**

There is no doubt that Archbishop Lefebvre's response to the crisis was
far better than what the sedevacantists propose. First of all, he himself
always explicitly rejected the views of the sedevacantists. I think that
the archbishop's actions should be considered from a broader perspective, in the context of the entire situation of unprecedented crisis in the
Church. Almost fifty years have passed since he first started his work,
and that's enough time for a detached and reasoned assessment. We
can also see how the crisis in the Church has developed.

Taking all this into account, I can say that Archbishop Lefebvre
was a great man, and I appreciate his great contribution to the defense
of the Catholic Faith. He passed on the Faith, the liturgy, and formed
new priests. He did all this in exactly the way in which it was handed
down to him, exactly as the Church passed on the Faith from generation
to generation over the centuries. He introduced no novelties. That is
why he had an inscription engraved on his tomb, a quote from St. Paul,
Tradidi quod et accepi — "I handed on what I have received." This is what
the Church should always do. It's the task of every bishop as well as of
the pope. His opposition was not directed against the pope. He always
prayed for the pope until the end and mentioned him in the Holy Mass.
In the same way, he ordered all the priests of his Society to pray for the
pope. Similarly, the priests of the Society of St. Pius X mention in the
Canon of the Mass the name of the current Roman Pontiff and of the
diocesan bishop of the diocese where they are celebrating Holy Mass.
They do not mention in the Canon of the Mass one of the bishops
ordained by Archbishop Lefebvre. He clearly affirmed the validity
of the entire hierarchical structure in the Church and expressed this

during the celebration of the liturgy. Under no circumstances should he be accused of being schismatic.

The problem was only the practical, concrete question of obedience. He objectively showed disobedience to the pope: he disobeyed a concrete papal order of not ordaining bishops. But opposition to certain concrete papal orders doesn't amount to a rejection of papal authority per se. Nor does it mean necessarily breaking sacramental communion with the pope. It was Pope Paul VI who tried to force Archbishop Lefebvre to celebrate the Novus Ordo, and this was an abuse of papal authority. The archbishop said that he could not obey such an order. In my opinion Archbishop Lefebvre did truly great things: in a time of darkness and chaos, he was one of the few clergy who saved and preserved for us the treasure of traditional rite of the Mass. It was mainly because of his resistance that the Holy See gradually gave way and dropped the ban on its celebration.

There can be doubts about some of Archbishop Lefebvre's harsh statements. I would probably use different language. Besides, we must remember that he was involved in a battle, which entails polemics and, consequently, occasional overstatements. If you consider the historical context, this becomes understandable. At times, he criticized the Council too heavily and spoke harshly of Rome. On other occasions he was more careful and subdued. But, let me say it again, it was understandable in his situation, in a situation of battle. Another of his great achievements was the creation of traditional seminaries, training priests in the spirit of fidelity to the great tradition of the Church. Look at how beautifully this work of Archbishop Lefebvre is developing around the world! I have visited the chapels run by the Society of St. Pius X. I have seen their schools, how communities are formed around them, how religious life is reborn, what positive impact they have on families. Thanks to such a work, a young generation educated in the Catholic spirit is now emerging. Of course, as in any human community, there are also problematic personalities. After my visit, I told the priests from the Society of St. Pius X that I saw a certain danger there: if they remain under their own jurisdiction for too long, they are in danger of becoming too attached to this autonomy of sorts — ecclesiastical autonomy. This is dangerous, because it's a tendency characteristic of the Orthodox churches. I'm not talking about the *theory*, but the *practice*. Self-sufficiency can be dangerous. It would be appropriate for the Society of St. Pius X to be officially recognized by the Holy See and to be fully integrated into the life of the Church with all canonical rights. I think this will happen one day.

You asked about my view of the ordaining of four bishops in 1988. This is a difficult matter. Now we can look at it from a distance. I think this was an act that Archbishop Lefebvre was commanded to do by his conscience. He said that he would have had an unclean conscience if he had not done it. He was not a superficial man. He took the dictates of conscience very seriously and his conscience had been formed in the Catholic spirit. He was also a man who lived a saintly life. He was someone who prayed and wanted to fulfill the will of God in his life. "If I don't ordain bishops, I will commit a sin against God," he thought. That's why I believe that ordaining bishops didn't render him guilty. I also think that objectively, the Church in the future will not consider this act either as a sin or a schism. We must remember that in the earlier *Code of Canon Law*, unlawful ordination to the episcopate wasn't punished by excommunication, but by suspension. The Church didn't regard this act as so grave in itself that it entailed separation from her.

Therefore, the intention of Archbishop Lefebvre must be carefully examined. Until the very end, he wished to obtain the pope's permission for the ordinations. His letters, which I have read, are very moving. With great devotion he begged the pope; like a child begging a father, truly with great fear and reverence, he pleaded, "I would like to ordain these bishops with the pope's approval." This is a clear sign that the archbishop had no schismatic intentions. If he had been a schismatic, it would have been all the same to him whether the pope gave his consent or not. He would not have worried about it at all. This is exactly what many schismatic or sedevacantist bishops did: they didn't bother at all about obtaining the consent of the Holy See. He fought until the very end to obtain the consent of the pope, until the very last moment. He begged, "Holy Father, give me your permission!" In evaluating this act, we must not overlook this circumstance. Of course, purely formally, literally, according to the 1983 *Code of Canon Law,* he was declared a schismatic. But this is only positive human law.

Let's examine the crisis that is facing the Church, the extent of the threats to the integrity of the Faith. Let's look at how much the Holy See was weakened, also during the pontificate of Pope John Paul II, and how it's still being weakened. Likewise, the Holy See insisted that Archbishop Lefebvre accept and embrace the entire Council. We have already discussed it in detail; it is difficult to accept some of the affirmations of the Council in the light of the constant doctrinal tradition of the Church. Archbishop Lefebvre was also a seasoned diplomat, having served eleven years as an apostolic delegate (a kind of apostolic nuncio), and he was well aware of the process of negotiations with Rome. He could foresee that Rome would propose to him a candidate who would sooner or later demand that the priests of the Society would have the right to celebrate also the new Mass or accept some of the ambiguous affirmations of the Second Vatican Council. The Vatican demanded at the time, as it unfortunately still does now, that the Council's teachings be accepted unconditionally and without reservation. They made only one concession, by agreeing to the formula "understood in accordance with Tradition." But this formula is unclear and can't be applied to every statement of the Council.

I would add that that we must not assign greater value to legalism, legal positivism, than to fidelity to the principles of the Faith. I don't agree with those bishops and cardinals who claim that obedience to the letter of the law, obedience to regulations, is more important than obedience to the precepts of the Faith, which demands a fight to preserve the traditional Mass, a fight to preserve unambiguous orthodoxy. In the first centuries of the Church, in the first millennium, many episcopal nominations were not confirmed by Rome. Among them were many holy bishops. Ordaining a bishop with the approval of Rome is not a mandate that belongs to the essence of Catholicism. One joins the college of bishops with the consent of its head, the pope. But the exact format in which this consent is given is another matter. It doesn't always have to involve formal consent. For over a thousand years, such consent was not a condition for the legitimacy of an episcopal ordination.

Once someone became a bishop, on the other hand, it was imperative that he demonstrate clearly his unity with the pope, with the bishop of Rome. This could have been done through a letter, or by mentioning the pope's name during the sacrifice of the Mass. Back then, that was sufficient. This is exactly what Archbishop Lefebvre and the bishops ordained by him did, by consistently mentioning the names of successive popes in the Canon of the Holy Mass. At least in this way they have been fulfilling the condition of unity that the Church had recognized for over a thousand years.

Given the depth of the current crisis, we must always keep one thing in mind: the primacy of faith. It's more important than the letter of the law.

A new phenomenon has been the appearance of a lay movement of Catholics who speak out in defense of Tradition and also oppose some Church leaders. What is your opinion of the *Acies Ordinata* movement? In January 2020, *Acies Ordinata* protested in Munich against the bishops introducing the so-called synodal way in Germany, criticizing especially the actions of the then chairman of the German Bishops' Conference, Reinhard Marx. Participants in the demonstration also called on German Catholics to stop paying the church tax in order to stop the actions of the German episcopate.

Before Munich, *Acies Ordinata* also demonstrated in Rome. I think it will be a cause of great honor in the future. Lay Catholics will be very, very proud of it. This movement is implementing what the Second Vatican Council conveyed in a positive sense, namely, that the lay faithful should endeavor to work for the preservation and purity of the Catholic faith. To me, it's also proof that the laity take their faith seriously. It's not about fighting against the pope or the church hierarchy. On the contrary, it's a fight *for* the pope and *for* the hierarchy. Catholics have the right to protest against the spreading of heresy, against deviations from true doctrine. Consequently, they had the right to show what they thought about the projects of the German bishops or the Amazon Synod. This is an example of positive service to the Church. These lay people should be commended and rewarded. They are a light in the great darkness. I regard their involvement as a fulfillment of the words of St. Paul: when one member of the Body, the Church, suffers, other members suffer with it (see 1 Cor. 12:26). Since God allows the head and the hierarchy to suffer by not standing up enough for the Faith, the lay faithful are rushing to their aid. When I witness a man harming himself or others through his actions, and when I stop him from doing so, I help him as well as the others. Even if he doesn't like my behavior, it's objectively right. The name is also beautiful: *Acies Ordinata* — orderly hosts in formation. It's not about a fight against Cardinal Marx, but a fight against the powers of darkness, against the devil who is using Cardinal Marx and the German bishops to change the Catholic faith, to distort it, to adapt it to Protestantism and even to paganism. It's a spiritual battle, a battle for Christ, a battle for the whole Church. The organizers of this movement *Acies Ordinata* should be awarded the papal order *Pro ecclesia et pontifice*. If anyone deserves it, it's certainly them. Someday, when God gives us a pious, faithful pope again, and if they are still alive, it will surely happen. There are many young people in this organization; they will live another fifty years, and I believe that God will have mercy on us and at that time a truly Catholic pope will appear.

Your Excellency, in the course of our conversation we focused primarily on the different symptoms of the crisis. But at times like these, people also look for positive role models, for witnesses to the Faith. In the past, such role models were the saints who would point us in the right direction. Who is such a model for you? Whom in particular should we invoke? Who should be emulated in these difficult times for the Church? To whom should we turn for advice or guidance?

In this age of great confusion and chaos, the greatest malady is cowardice, conformity, and political correctness. This is true of the world, but above all of life within the Church. It's a malady that affects both the clergy and the laity. Cowardice and the desire to fit in. Not everyone believes in the new ideologies, but many lack the courage to call a spade a spade. There is a very famous saying by Julius Fučík, a Czech journalist who died in Prague killed by the Nazis. Admittedly, he was politically on the left, but this particular observation is correct. He said "Don't be afraid of your friends — the worst they can do is betray you. Don't be afraid your enemies — the worst case they can do is kill you. But be afraid of those who are *indifferent* — they neither kill nor betray, but it is only with their tacit consent that all the worst crimes are committed on earth."

This is a very apt description of our current situation. That is why, for me, the most important saints are those who distinguished themselves above all by the virtue of courage. Fortitude, courage, strength of character — this is what we need. The ability to go against the tide. I am thinking, for example, of St. Thomas More and St. John Fisher. The former, being the High Chancellor of King Henry VIII, kept the Faith when he was practically on his own against all. Similarly, the holy bishop Fisher was the only bishop who didn't embrace the doctrine that the king is the head of the Church in England. I'm deeply impressed by their stance. I'm equally impressed with the position of St. Athanasius, who lived centuries earlier. He was among the few bishops who, unlike so many others in those times, defended the Catholic faith. Similarly, St. Basil and St. Hilary of Poitiers showed great resolve in their fight against the Arians.

Great examples of courage can be found in the history of persecutions under the Roman emperors. Many such stories have been preserved from the time of Diocletian. According to one such account, in Abitinae, the priest Saturninus was martyred along with his entire community. His only crime, like that of the rest of the faithful, was his refusal to burn incense before the statues of the idols and the emperor. They were captured during Mass, brought before a judge, and sentenced to torture. The youngest member of this community was still a child, a boy, Hilarion, who was six years old. He was also subjected to questioning. During interrogation by the judge, he stood firm in his faith. "Why did you come [to Mass]?" "Because I am a Christian," the boy replied. What a beautiful answer. The judge tried to scare him. "We'll cut off your ears and nose," he said. "Do what you want, I am a Christian," said the child. His sister suffered a similar death. We know this not from legends and myths, but from actual court records. As these two were being led to their deaths from the place of judgment, they met Bishop

Fundanus walking in the opposite direction. He had just come out of the courthouse where he had committed an act of apostasy. He handed over the scrolls of Scripture to the authorities and burned incense before the statues of idols. Let's ruminate on this incredible contrast. On the one hand, a bishop who denied his faith, on the other hand, an entire community, together with a child, who suffered and gave their lives for Christ. The bishop's apostasy on one side and the martyrdom and heroism of the community on the other. The martyrdom of the little Hilarion prevailed over the apostasy of his bishop Fundanus. For me, this story is extremely timely right now, when we are experiencing the widespread apostasy of bishops and cardinals. Today we also have such people: on the one hand, the young Alexander Tschugguel, who threw the statues of Pachamama into the Tiber, and on the other, Church leaders who commit treason in worshiping such an idol.

A great figure closer to our times is St. Pius X, who was able to confront both the errors in the Church at the beginning of the twentieth century and the new, dangerous ideologies in the world. Pius X showed us that no compromises must be made with modernism. And he took up the fight, despite the resistance of some cardinals. A great man from even more recent times was Cardinal Mindszenty, who resisted the Communists, even in opposition to Pope Paul VI. The pope was pursuing a new Eastern policy, a policy of compromise and agreement with the Communists, so the steadfastness of Cardinal Mindszenty was a growing problem for him. The cardinal suffered greatly because of this and felt completely alone. He persevered until the end — he remained adamant that no compromises should be made with the Communists. All of these people, who showed great courage in the face of adversity, are true role models for us. These are just a few examples; there are many more. Whereas previously great courage was required mainly to face the world, now we need it more and more within the Church herself.

I'm also thinking of Archbishop Lefebvre. He showed great heroism. He was ready to lose everything in this life, all recognition and status, respect and good reputation in the Church. He even accepted the fact that he was considered a rebel, a schismatic. And he did it in order to continue to transmit the uncontaminated, complete Catholic truth, to preserve the Mass in all its Catholic richness. To that end, he resigned himself to becoming like a leper in the eyes of the world and the Church authorities. Other bishops condemned him, Rome turned away from him. I believe that in the future, he will also be raised to the honor of the altars. I don't know when this will happen, perhaps in a hundred years, perhaps even later. He gave up everything for Christ, everything, in human terms, just to transmit the Catholic faith and the liturgy of the Mass intact. This is a beautiful model for our times.

As for examples of faithfulness to the Catholic faith among the laity, I would mention Michael Davies, an English Catholic who devoted his life to the fight to preserve the traditional Mass. He was a co-founder of *Una Voce*, a movement of lay people who defended the traditional Roman rite. I also particularly admire Blessed Emperor Charles of Austria, who was proclaimed blessed in 2004, and I think that he too is a real model for our times. He was an exemplary husband and father of eight children. During the most difficult time of World War I, mindful of his deep Catholic faith, he reigned over the nations of the great empire. He did everything he could to end the senseless war, and he made numerous peace offers, but the powerful Masonic elite that had fomented the war in Europe effectively blocked all of Charles's efforts. Their goal was the destruction of the last Catholic monarchy in the world, the Habsburg Monarchy, heir to the Holy Roman Empire, founded by Charlemagne. Emperor Charles of Austria consecrated his entire empire to the Sacred Heart of Jesus. His Christian greatness and nobility are evident in these words: "As a Catholic monarch I will never make a deal with Evil, even if I should fail to regain my throne."

For me, the person who first showed me the importance of the traditional Mass and the splendor of the liturgy was Dietrich von Hildebrand.

Exactly, he was a great figure. He was among the first to caution against the danger. He authored extremely important works, *Trojan Horse in the City of God* and *The Devastated Vineyard*. He portrayed the roots of the crisis with remarkable insight. He was a man of great courage who opposed the Nazis. He had to flee Europe. And then, with equal strength of character, he fought the modern Gnostics within the Church after the Council.

A few years ago I was in the United States, where I celebrated the traditional Mass. Afterward, I came out of the church, still in my episcopal robes. A boy came up to me and asked if he could have a picture taken with me. People coming out of the church pulled out their cameras and shot photos. You could hear people commenting about the boy, "Oh, you will be a bishop!" Then the boy looked up and said in a very serious voice, "I want to be a saint." This moved me very much. Recently I met this boy again, now a young man. He had just participated in a demonstration against the LGBT ideology. I am sure that when he is older he will continue to fight for Christ. To me, this is a great sign of hope. I see the Holy Spirit increasingly stirring up young people and empowering them to defend the Faith in society and in the Church.

We must have within ourselves the joy of suffering for Christ. We must rejoice if we are attacked for the sake of Christ and Catholic truth. Rejoicing in suffering for Christ — that is a great thing. We mustn't fall into doubt or disappointment. No, just hold on to the Faith. I remember an elderly woman I met in the USA. We talked for some time. At one point she said something that stuck in my mind: "Whatever they come up with at the Vatican, I will remain Catholic." How wonderful! Whatever happens at the Vatican, she will remain Catholic. God has put us in this situation, and we should be grateful to Him for it. He knows best what is good for us. What if our fidelity to the Catholic faith means that we are marginalized and ridiculed? This is great merit, a great opportunity for us. We must always keep victory in mind. We must not give up or succumb to doubt. "Have confidence, I have overcome the world," says the Lord (John 16:33). What, then, should we fear, since our Lord has overcome? The Communists used to say, "Proletarians of all countries, unite!" And I would say, "Catholics of all countries, unite!" Defend your faith and Tradition. Remember that you are not alone — everywhere, all over the world, there is a growing generation of people who, just like those behind the *Acies Ordinata*, understand what is most important for the salvation of souls.

Sophia Institute

Sophia Institute is a nonprofit institution that seeks to nurture the spiritual, moral, and cultural life of souls and to spread the gospel of Christ in conformity with the authentic teachings of the Roman Catholic Church.

Sophia Institute Press fulfills this mission by offering translations, reprints, and new publications that afford readers a rich source of the enduring wisdom of mankind.

Sophia Institute also operates the popular online resource CatholicExchange.com. *Catholic Exchange* provides world news from a Catholic perspective as well as daily devotionals and articles that will help readers to grow in holiness and live a life consistent with the teachings of the Church.

In 2013, Sophia Institute launched Sophia Institute for Teachers to renew and rebuild Catholic culture through service to Catholic education. With the goal of nurturing the spiritual, moral, and cultural life of souls, and an abiding respect for the role and work of teachers, we strive to provide materials and programs that are at once enlightening to the mind and ennobling to the heart; faithful and complete, as well as useful and practical.

Sophia Institute gratefully recognizes the Solidarity Association for preserving and encouraging the growth of our apostolate over the course of many years. Without their generous and timely support, this book would not be in your hands.

www.SophiaInstitute.com
www.CatholicExchange.com
www.SophiaInstituteforTeachers.org

Sophia Institute Press® is a registered trademark of Sophia Institute. Sophia Institute is a tax-exempt institution as defined by the Internal Revenue Code, Section 501(c)(3). Tax ID 22-2548708.